The Dalmellington Iron Company

ITS ENGINES AND MEN

by David L. Smith

DAVID & CHARLES : NEWTON ABBOT

Printed in Great Britain
by W. J. Holman Limited Dawlish
for David & Charles (Publishers) Limited
South Devon House Newton Abbot Devon

Contents

Illustrations

A number of words which may be unfamiliar to general readers are explained in the Author's Notes on page 247.

CHAPTER 1

The Doon Valley

Loch Among the Mountains

Deep in a great cleaving of the mountains of south-west Scotland, Loch Doon stretches its seven-mile length, largest of all the lochs of the Southern Uplands. To the east, the green giants of the Kells Range stand like a wall against the sky—Coran of Portmark, Meaul, Carlin's Cairn, and the mighty Corserine, 2,668 ft in height, frowning down upon the Dungeon of Buchan. To the west another range, higher but more distant, goes towering up to the final great bulk of Merrick itself, 2,764 ft, highest of mountains in the Southern Uplands, as Loch Doon is the greatest of lochs.

From the grim wilderness to the south, savage as any within the confines of Britain, the outpourings of thirteen lochs hurry in a series of mountain streams to swell the waters of Loch Doon. At the north end is its outflow. Now a great dam controls the exit, and surplus water can be diverted through a tunnel to aid the Galloway Hydro-Electric scheme to the south. From the huge sluices in the dam the River Doon bursts forth, full-throated, an adult river from the start, to plunge tempestuously into the narrow, tree-lined gorge of Ness Glen.

Descent to the Plains

It is a marvellous place, this Ness Glen. With room only for the foaming river and the spray-drenched pathway, the rocky sides rise sheer to a height of almost 200 ft. Geographically it is remarkable, for it marks in dramatic fashion the sudden descent from the region of the Southern Uplands to that of the Midland Plain of Scotland.

This is not immediately apparent, for the river emerges from the glen to ripple briskly through the lovely woods of the Craigengillan estate. A new town of modern 'Council' houses, titled Bellsbank, is set rather incongruously upon the hill above. Then comes the true plain, the great, wide valley-floor. The speed of the river's current decreases; it spreads out into Bogton Loch. A mile to the east the houses of Dalmellington peep shyly forth from a tributary glen, for all this flat valley, until the controlling dam was built at Loch Doon in 1933, was liable to severe flooding after heavy rains, and the people of Dalmellington built prudently clear of the flood waters.

Just north of Bogton Loch two tributary burns join with the Doon, the Cummock Burn coming from the north-east, and the Muck Water from the south. The houses of Dalmellington are built mainly along the banks of the Muck Water and up the steep sides of its glen. These two streams, their current likewise slowed as they reach the plain, have built up a large alluvial deposit which the Ordnance Survey has termed Sillyhole Moss, taking the name of a near-by farm.

The flat plain, narrowing gradually, extends to the village of Patna, eight miles downstream from Loch Doon. In those miles of plain there is little perceptible fall, the river winding hither and thither through the meadows. Patna's status as a village is now debatable, for another new town of Council houses now occupies the west bank of the river for nearly a mile.

It is hard to believe that all this flat valley has been carved out by this sluggish stream, but so it is. On each side of the valley is a plateau where the land rises abruptly to the level of the original surface at about 1,000 ft. That on the east side is rather narrow and is bounded by a range of hills which progresses in height to culminate in Ben Beoch, 1,522 ft, with its imposing face of basaltic pillars gazing out to the east.

The Lower Course

At Patna the character of the river changes. The valley becomes suddenly narrow, steep-sided. The speed of the current increases rapidly and the Doon hurries down through the fine scenery of Boreland Glen, by the blanket-making mill of Skeldon, past the pretty village of Dalrymple, winding, always winding, through fine woods and farm-lands until it reaches the sea two miles south of the town of Ayr. 'Ye banks and braes o' Bonnie Doon' wrote the poet Robert Burns, born and brought up almost within sound of its waters.

From loch to sea, in a straight line and in direction roughly north-westerly, the distance is sixteen miles. By the river's course it is twenty-six and a half miles. In that distance it has descended 700 ft.

On the map the line of the River Doon would appear to afford a natural trade route from the port of Ayr to the town of Dalmellington, thence through the narrow valley of the Muck Water to the high moors beyond, and down the lovely valley of the Glenkens to the fine farm-lands of Galloway. It is at first sight surprising, therefore, that no highway or railway has ever made use of the lower Doon valley. The reason is probably that of its very devious course with, in places, a narrowing which left little room for anything but the river itself. The flat upper valley, so contrasting to the lower, was equally impracticable, with its grave liability to severe flooding.

Early Roads

The first road into the Doon valley came not from the port of Ayr but from that of Irvine, which was then the more important. It was a mere 'pack-road', sufficient for foot-passengers and for beasts of burden, narrow, steep and paved only in rudimentary fashion where marshy ground gave trouble. It kept clear of the valleys, alike for fear of floods and of possible ambush, sweeping south by Tarbolton and Littlemill and thence over the desolate plateau by Kilmein, to descend upon Dalmellington only when it was absolutely necessary that the valley be crossed. From the little town it climbed again to the hill-tops and made its way south to Galloway. By that ancient road much smuggled contraband, landed in the nooks and crannies of the Solway coast, found its way to the markets of the big towns.

In the eighteenth century came the wheeled vehicle, late in arriving in these parts, necessitating a better highway for its speedy passage. So about the year 1800 there was constructed from the town of Ayr a road which was virtually the same as that which exists and is used to-day. Even this road did not make use of the lower valley, but went leaping over hill and dale in the country east. Not till Patna did it come within sight of the Doon, the line of which it followed, but at a respectful distance above river level. Greatly daring, however, it cut in a straight line across Sillyhole Moss to reach Dalmellington. Thence it followed the course of the Muck Water in an easy four-mile climb to the watershed at 990 ft and so to the Glenkens and Galloway.

The mile across the moss was to prove a serious handicap in later years. Flooding was frequent, and any heavy vehicle was liable to break through the thin skin of road metal and to sink axle-deep in the moss beneath.

Early Settlements

Our history begins in the year 1845. At that time there were in this upper valley of the River Doon but two small centres of population. Patna comprised a street of small houses straggling up from the west bank of the Doon to the summit of the Kirkmichael road. It then contained some 250 people. Dalmellington was much larger, its inhabitants numbering some 800. It was a place of ancient origin, very likely the station of a garrison intended to guard the pass to the south against predatory tribes. For Dalmellington is essentially a frontier town. Standing just to the north of that great geographical feature, the Southern Upland Fault, it is the last outpost of the cultivated country before one enters the wild hill-lands and it came to be a place where travellers rested and refreshed before facing the perils of the wilderness ahead. So the little town had attained a certain standing, even that of a small market-town. It had its inns, its shops, its tradespeople. It had certain small industries. In 1845 there were two small factories, powered by water, wherein woollen goods were made.

Dalmellington parish had seen great changes in the previous fifty years. Those empty hillsides had been dotted with

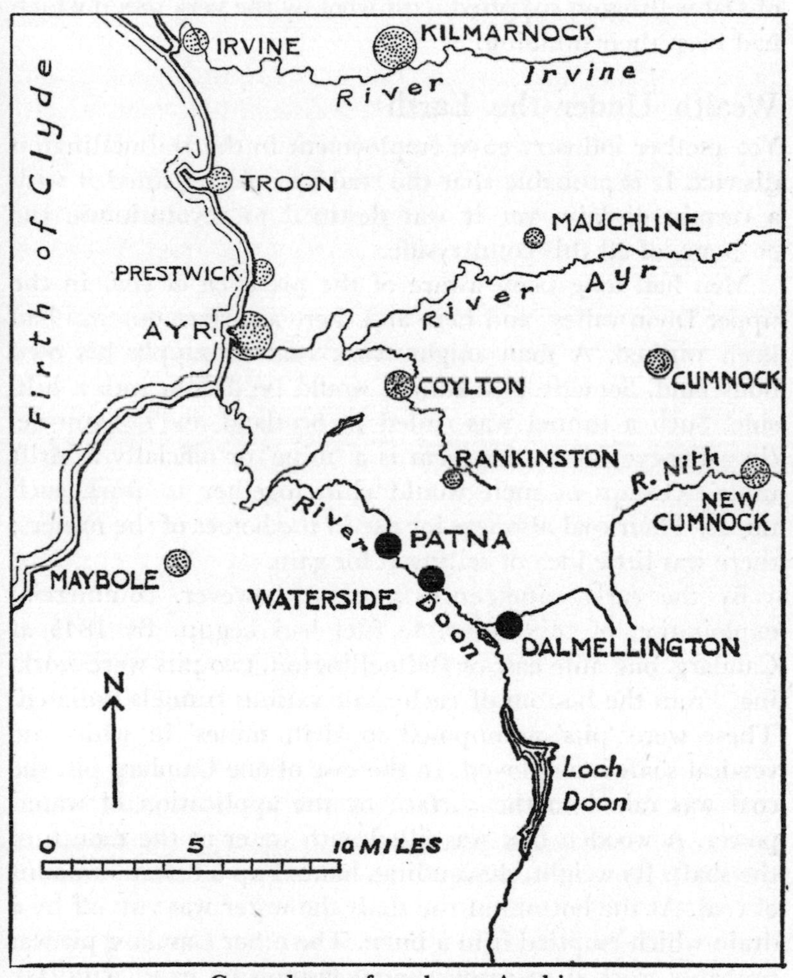

General map of south-east Ayrshire

little farms. By modern standards the tenants of those farms must have been far from prosperous, but it was the life they knew and they were content. Then, even to this quiet valley, had come the theory of quick riches by the rearing of sheep. So had ensued a small-scale version of the Highland Clearances. One man, miserably paid and living in one small house, could tend the sheep grazing on a dozen former farms. So the tenants were turned out, some going to work in the factories of Dalmellington supplied with wool by the very sheep which had been their undoing.

Wealth Under the Earth

Yet another industry gave employment in the Dalmellington district. It is probable that the tradespeople regarded it with a certain disdain, yet it was destined to revolutionise the economy of all this countryside.

Men had long been aware of the presence of coal in the upper Doon valley, and here and there a surface outcrop had been worked. A man might work coal to supply his own household. Sometimes a tunnel would be driven into a hillside. Such a tunnel was called in Scotland an 'in-gaun-e'e' (in-going-eye). Now the term is a 'mine' or officially a 'drift mine'. Groups of men would club together to work such mines. Their coal also was for use in the homes of the miners; there was little idea of selling it for gain.

By the early nineteenth century, however, commercial exploitation of this desirable fuel had begun. By 1845 at Camlarg, one mile east of Dalmellington, two pits were working. From the bottom of each shaft various tunnels radiated. These were 'pits' as opposed to 'drift mines' in which no vertical shaft is employed. In the case of one Camlarg pit, the coal was raised to the surface by the application of waterpower. A wooden box was filled with water at the mouth of the shaft. Its weight, descending, hauled up a certain amount of coal. At the bottom of the shaft the water was run off by a drain which emptied into a burn. The other Camlarg pit was probably worked in conventional fashion by hand windlass.

MANAGERS

(2a) *John Hunter, General Manager,* c.1848-1886

(2b) *J. P. Walker, General Manager,* 1886-1906

(2c) *Alex Gavin, General Manager,* 1906-1919

(2d) *William Smith, General Mining Manager,* 1901-1918

(3a) *My grandfather, David Smith*

(3b) *My father, James W. Smith*

(3c) *My grandfather, David Larmer*

(3d) *My uncle, David Larmer*

Coal-mining was also carried out at Patna. From a period in the late eighteenth century various drift mines had been tunnelled into the steep bank of the River Doon. On the hill above the village another drift mine, this time for limestone, was opened. Here, at Carnshalloch, an extensive limeworks was constructed and worked busily. Certain small pits were sunk at various times, and one in the meadow beside the Doon on the farm of Downieston must have had a considerable output of coal as the *Statistical Account of Scotland*, in a note written in 1837, records it as being worked by a *steam engine*. At Patna there had also been established a water-powered mill for the spinning of cotton thread. Unfortunately neither the cotton mill nor the limeworks was destined to prosper, but the mining of coal progressed exceedingly.

The officers of the Geological Survey, writing in 1932, said of this district: 'In the Dalmellington area there are *nineteen* coal seams of workable thickness, of which twelve have been or are being exploited'. The Coal Measures extend over a great tract of country from Smithston, north of Patna, to New Cumnock, a distance of thirteen miles, and for some eight miles from north to south. Then comes the great Southern Upland Fault, passing just south of Dalmellington. Beyond that no coal has been worked save in north-west Dumfriesshire, where the little Sanquhar coalfield forms the exception.

Dawn of the Iron Age

There was not only coal in the Doon valley; there was also iron, for in the Coal Measures seams of ironstone occur. Among these, the Dalmellington Blackband and the Craigmark Blackband were prominent. Some of the ironstone seams were at no great depth, and at a later date a small amount of open-cast work was carried on. The miners of Dalmellington and Patna must have encountered this ironstone but they made no use of it. The smelting of iron required organisation and equipment far beyond their ken or their purse. For iron-smelting, Big Business had to cater. For the Doon valley, Big Business was just around the corner.

CHAPTER 2

Industrial Invasion

The Coming of the Houldsworths

The business of exploiting the proximity of coal and iron was assuming large dimensions in the neighbouring county of Lanarkshire. Several firms were at work, none more successful than that controlled by the family of Houldsworth. Those men of enterprise, whose ancestors had been farmers in the vicinity of Nottingham, had made their way into the industrial world, first in the spinning of cotton, which they pursued in Manchester and later in Glasgow. Shrewd perception of a coming slump in the cotton trade led them to switch to the largely untried field of iron-smelting. Their Coltness Ironworks started in May of 1839, and by the year 1845 with which we are dealing had no less than six furnaces in blast. The moving spirit in this great work was Henry Houldsworth, sixty-two years of age but the essence of boldness and determination. He had the financial backing of his brother Thomas in Manchester (where cotton had weathered the storm better than in Glasgow) who had made a fortune largely on an organisation built up by Henry before he went north.

Henry Houldsworth had also the valuable assistance of three sons, Henry, William and John. Henry, the younger, was chief assistant to his uncle in the cotton business in Manchester. William was a man of great intelligence, but ill health prevented his talents from being applied in full to the family industry. John seems to have been made in his father's mould, a man of vigour and enterprise, tackling task after task with the utmost confidence and enthusiasm.

If Henry senior was the instigator of the opening up of new business in Ayrshire, it was John his son who was chiefly concerned with the execution of his father's plans. More than one of the Lanarkshire iron companies had established claims in Ayrshire, and when the Houldsworths went there in 1845 they found several promising areas already marked off in favour of their rivals. One region apparently undeveloped was in the upper valley of the River Doon. But there were grave difficulties—no rail connection, a fair but hilly road, and little labour available on the spot.

Rumours of a Railway

Plans for a railway to these parts were already afoot, on the strength of which the Houldsworths proceeded to take leases on the lands of Craigengillan and Skeldon. By the terms of the leases the holders were allowed until 1 November 1846 to make trials of the mineral field. Bores were therefore sunk at all likely spots, and soon gave most favourable findings. On 19 November 1846 the prospectus was issued detailing the objectives and routes of two railway companies, whose combined projects appeared to afford a service to the new mineral activity. The Glasgow and Belfast Union Railway had as its ultimate object the packet station of Portpatrick, from which the Northern Irish port of Donaghadee was only twenty-two miles distant. From this line a branch was authorised from Belmont, one mile south of Ayr, to Smithstone (sic), a farm some eight miles from Ayr on the Ayr-Dalmellington road. Another company calling itself The Ayrshire & Galloway Railway proposed to construct a railway from Smithstown (still another variant) to Dalmellington, after which, with an imagination which rose supreme over hard facts, the company proposed to continue through the Glenkens of Galloway and finally to a new port to be constructed at Balcary Bay on the Solway coast, the Admiralty to supervise this construction. The Belfast company had obtained its Act on 26 August 1846, but for a railway from Ayr to Girvan only.

The great project of the Ayrshire & Galloway Railway was

similarly watered down. Under examination the pipe-dreams of a trunk route through Galloway and a Solway port were eliminated. The company's Act, obtained on 8 June 1847, was for the mere seven miles from Smithston to Dalmellington. Still, with the G & BU's branch to that farm (a prospective site of operations of the Summerlee Iron Company of Coatbridge) there would be a through route to Ayr. That was all that the Houldsworths wanted. With transport assured they could go ahead. Mineral wealth had been proved, so a feu was taken on the Craigengillan estate near the small farms of Dunaskin and Waterside, three miles north of Dalmellington. Here the steep western face of the Green Hill gave favourable siting for the erection of blast furnaces. The *Ayr Observer* of 24 November 1846 notes:

> BERBETH IRON WORKS
>
> These works will speedily be commenced. We understand that on Monday an engineer was engaged in laying off the sites of several furnaces for the works. The place chosen is about two miles above Patna and near to the Dalmellington road and the line of the Ayrshire and Galloway Railway.

The name 'Berbeth' was the older name for Craigengillan, and was still used at this period. However, when the works came into being they took the name not of the estate but of the parish in which they were situated. Dalmellington parish stretches down the east bank of the River Doon to a point about a mile north of Patna. On 27 September 1848 the *Glasgow Herald* records:

> DALMELLINGTON IRON WORKS
>
> Those works, belonging to Messrs Houldsworth, Glasgow, were blown in for the first time on Monday week, and the first casting took place on Wednesday. The machinery was found to work smoothly and everything went off well. Ayrshire is now nearly girdled round with iron works.

A Changing Landscape

It is hard to visualise the terrific activity which had come to this quiet upland valley in those hectic two years. The erection of the furnaces was a mere detail in the great scheme.

Coal pits were sunk, the first in the area of Sillyhole Moss just north of Dalmellington. Ironstone seams were more easily accessible from the plateau to the east of the Doon valley and some 500 ft above it. On this plateau several pits were sunk. Railways, of standard 4 ft 8½-in gauge, were laid down to connect these ironstone pits to the furnaces, for those moors had no suitable roads. Wagons, mainly of three tons capacity, were hauled by horses to the summits of two rope-worked inclines, one to the north of the works near Drumgrange House, the other from the pits near Corbie Craigs, descending south of the works to a point level with the furnace bank, to which it was connected by a timber viaduct spanning the deep glen of the Dunaskin Burn. These inclines appear to have been self-acting, the loaded wagons, descending, hauling up a corresponding number of empties. The Drumgrange incline appears to have come down in two stages to the line of the projected Ayrshire & Galloway Railway.

Besides all this mining activity the many auxiliary buildings had to be constructed, notably the massive pile of the blast engine house, still standing and bearing the date 1847. Messrs Murdoch and Aitken of Glasgow supplied the blast engines, and it is recorded that when the great beam for these engines was brought by road from Ayr twenty-four pairs of horses were provided to haul it up the Asylum Brae at what is now called Ailsa Hospital, two-and-a-half miles south of Ayr. Workshops were erected, and various standard gauge lines were laid to connect the whole. A major problem was the housing of the workers who with their families had come to this district. Many local men previously engaged in agriculture or woollen manufacture found work in this great new industry, but many others flocked in, Irish and Scottish Highland predominating. For them an entirely new village was built in the vicinity of the iron works. In 1851 there were eighty-nine houses here, with a further ten on the plateau above Drumgrange. The iron works village had a singular confusion of names. In normal speech and on the railway nameboard it was 'Waterside', that being the name of the adjacent farm in the valley. The postal authorities for some unknown reason fixed the postal address as 'Dunaskin', the name of the farm on the hill above. To make confusion worse confounded the iron works were entitled the *Dalmellington* Iron Works, though Dalmellington was three miles away!

For Want of a Railway

The marvel is the greater when one realises how much of the material for this great construction had to be *carted* up the twelve-mile road from Ayr. For the Ayrshire & Galloway Railway was not yet. It had started well enough, with an authorised capital of £100,050 and powers to borrow £33,000. The Glasgow, Paisley, Kilmarnock & Ayr Railway had backed it. The three sons of Henry Houldsworth had subscribed liberally to it. The intentions were sound enough. There were meetings and correspondence between the railway company and Mr John Houldsworth or his staff regarding matters of detail—the course of the railway in the vicinity of the iron works, the terms upon which the iron company's mineral traffic would be conveyed upon the A & G's line. But all came down to the hard fact that insufficient shares had been purchased. There was not enough money available to justify a start with construction, even of the meagre seven miles left to them by their Act. The furnaces were there and the traffic was to be had. The A & G had no railway upon which to put it.

No, Ayr seemed as far away as the moon, but one thing had been discussed tentatively with the iron company. The section from Waterside to the coal pits at Sillyhole, near Dalmellington, entailed no heavy constructional work. The iron company were proposing that the A & G build this section and they, the iron company, would work their own traffic over it for an agreed rental. Mr Johnstone, Manager of the GPK & A Railway reported favourably on this proposal. His estimate of £24,590 was for a single line two and three-quarter miles long with rails 70 lb per yd at £8 per ton. But time went on, the first furnace commenced to turn out pig iron and still the timorous A & G made no move.

Problems of Transport

No railway! One can visualise the wrath of the vigorous John Houldsworth as he realised that this feckless railway company had failed him. But there was now no question of retreat. If the railway could not do it, then the road must. The famous Newton Carters of Newton-on-Ayr got the contract, and for eight busy years they toiled up and down the hilly road between Ayr and Waterside—limestone up and pig iron down. A man who had recently taken a lease of the toll-house at Patna made a small fortune.

Road transport was also being used to bring coal from the pits at Sillyhole to the furnaces. But soon serious trouble developed here. The road passed over a mile of the Sillyhole Moss, and its precarious foundations began to give way under the constant passage of carts. Even before the furnaces began work there had been some mild progress towards the agreed construction of the Drumgrange-Sillyhole section of the Ayrshire & Galloway and its working by the Dalmellington Iron Company. By September 1848 Messrs D. & D. McDonald, contractors, had begun operations. But by the following November there was dissatisfaction with the slow progress made. It appears that the moss was giving trouble with the railway also, and that material tipped in to give a foundation was being swallowed up overnight. Work was ordered to be stopped on the Drumgrange-Dunaskin section and all labour concentrated on the section between the furnaces and the pits, 'Messrs Houldsworth to make a deduction from their annual payment of £1,500 while the portion of the line in front of the furnaces is uncompleted'. It was not until the A & G meeting of 7 November 1849 that the Drumgrange-Sillyhole section was reported as 'now completed', and the DICo agreed to the payment of £1,500 per annum for its use, commencing on 1 October 1849. Haulage was by horses, as on the other DICo lines. The final cost of this portion of line is given as £16,433 11s 11d.

This problem was solved, but the DICo was far from being

satisfied. Still there was no communication with Ayr and the railway to Glasgow and beyond. They were obviously putting on the screw when the A & G had a report on 28 August 1850 that no payment of rent for the completed line could be obtained from the DICo. A year later there was still no payment; then came an offer from the DICo to pay £1,200 per annum, with sanction for the use of 'locomotive power'. The A & G agreed, provided the DICo maintained the line 'in proper order'. So the DICo obtained from Messrs Neilson & Mitchell of Glasgow a small 0—4—0 saddle-tank engine, which began work on the haulage of Sillyhole coal, carrying on this work single-handed for all of three years. In 1854 this engine, No. 1, was joined by another and larger Neilson, No. 2, and both were employed on this traffic.

Inclines

The Sillyhole coal and the ironstone brought down the Drumgrange incline had to be raised from the A & G line down in the valley to the furnace bank some seventy feet above. This was done by means of an incline, slanting upwards from a point just north of the Dunaskin Burn, and worked by a single-cylinder steam engine. This engine was somewhat temperamental, and its engineman not too skilful. One day he let a rake of wagons get away from him and distribute themselves about the landscape. After which, according to reports, he fled the district, and the care of the engine devolved upon one Sanny Napier, who had drifted in. He proved to be a most competent, careful engineman, both with this charge and subsequently upon the locomotives. 'An awfu' guid wee man Nap'er!' my grandfather Larmer used to say. I can just remember Sanny Napier as a very old man, landlord of the Doon Tavern in Dalmellington.

Rail Impasse

By 1852 the railway question seemed to have reached a hopeless deadlock. The five-year period allowed to the A & G to acquire land was on the point of expiring, and still they were afraid to venture further construction with the money available. Even more hopeless was the position of the Glasgow & Belfast Union Railway, which had not laid one yard of rail on even its main line, let alone its branch to Smithston. The DICo and others raised an action against the A & G for non-completion of the line and consequent damages. The railway company raised a counter action for payment of rent. It was a most unhappy situation, and the Glasgow & South Western Railway, an amalgamation of which the former Glasgow, Paisley, Kilmarnock & Ayr formed part, were disturbed and anxious. So on 2 November 1852 three directors of the G & SW had a meeting with Mr J. Houldsworth and Mr Hugh Moncrieff of the DICo to endeavour to find a way out of the difficulty. This was a fruitful meeting, which resulted in the following resolutions:

1. That the DICo guarantee dues for the piece of line completed, not less than £1,500 per annum for ten years. Traffic to be worked by the *railway company*.
2. That the DICo make no rival line to the existing one.
3. That a Bill be prepared for presentation to Parliament in order to wind up the affairs of the A & G and form a new company to make a line from Drumgrange to Ayr, and from Sillyhole to Dalmellington.
4. That the G & SW subscribe to the new company what they can realise from the winding up of the A & G plus £20,000.
5. The DICo to pay the £1,500 rent to the G & SW.
6. That the DICo do all in its power to procure the remainder of the capital for the new company.
7. That Mr Johnstone complete the necessary surveys.

This was reported to the G & SW at a meeting of that company on 22 February 1853. It was announced that the cost of completing the line as stated in clause three above was estimated at £150,000, and that the DICo had agreed to guarantee a minium dividend of four per cent on this amount, after deduction of all working charges and allowances, for a period of two years from the completion of the line.

Railway Construction

The Bill was duly submitted and on 27 May 1853 was examined by a Select Committee on Railway Bills. The principal witness was Mr John Houldsworth. He stated that he personally had subscribed £16,000 to the A & G, his brother Henry had subscribed £9,000 and his brother William £6,000. The company had three furnaces in blast at that date, their annual output amounting to 27,000 tons of pig iron, all of which had to be carried by carts to Ayr, and thence by rail or ship. The Select Committee declared themselves satisfied with the evidence given, the Bill passed through Parliament, and on 4 August 1853 this new company with the title of the Ayr & Dalmellington Railway received its Act. This authorised the construction of lines from Sillyhole to Dalmellington, and from Drumgrange to a junction with the Glasgow & South Western Railway at Newton, near Ayr Foundry, the present Falkland Junction. The length of new lines is given meticulously as 13 miles, 4 furlongs, 165 yd, and the estimated cost as £80,091 for construction and for purchase of land, £49,909.

The surveys were duly made by Mr William Johnstone, General Manager and Engineer of the Glasgow & South Western, and it is significant of the ruling interest of the DICo in the affairs of the A & D that the tenders, when submitted, were considered jointly by Mr Johnstone and Mr Houldsworth. By February 1854 the contracts had been placed. The heaviest work was involved in the section between Smithston and Ayr. There were some long and deep cuttings and high embankments, together with a stone viaduct of thirteen arches and a maximum height of 83 ft. The contract for all of this section appears to have gone to Mr Nicholas Ward; the easier section in the Doon valley was given to Mr Alexander McDonald. The terms of contract stipulated for a completion of the work by November 1855.

Mr McDonald's contract made rapid progress, and by November 1854 it was reported that the DICo had begun to work over a distance of 2,800 yd of this section, apparently to reach a point just north of Patna at which a branch line was to be laid into the coal-pits at Downieston and Carnochan. On the more difficult section to the north progress was not so satisfactory. The contractor had cut things too fine on occasion; there was no money available on pay-day, and some ugly encounters took place. The viaduct was a cause of dispute. It was made of stone from the Dunaskin quarries at Waterside, and, pugnacious to the last, the DICo fought the contractor for a price of 7d per cu. ft against his offer of 5d. The G & SW company mediated by a guarantee of an extra penny to the contractor's price and the DICo agreed. There was no chance of finishing by the agreed date. Even by March 1856 the rails were only being put in place on the upper section to Smithston, where a junction was being installed to connect with the branch of the Summerlee Iron Company of Coatbridge, Lanarkshire. This branch led after a short distance to a rope-worked incline some 50 chains in length and rising at a gradient of 1 in 11 to the owners' iron mines on the 'plateau'.

The Line is Open

All things come to him who waits, and on 15 May 1856 John Houldsworth was able to see his first load of pig iron taken down to Ayr by the new railway. The line was still single all the way, but work was proceeding on a second track from Ayr to a point some four miles to the south, from which the Ayr & Maybole Railway was under construction. The Ayr & Dalmellington Railway was worked from the start by the G & SW. On 7 August the first passenger train travelled from Ayr to Dalmellington, its advent heralded by the DICo's latest acquisition, engine No. 3, running ahead of the passenger train as an advance guard. The DICo had paid the piper, and if they could not entirely call the tune they could at least head the procession.

John Houldsworth, if he were present, must have viewed the scene with some grim satisfaction. This worry of transport had been but one of many. For the DICo each year brought a loss, until in 1853 the corner was turned and fortune began to smile upon his efforts. His father, Henry the elder, had seen the first favourable balance-sheet of the DICo just before he died three years previously. Three years later, in 1859, John himself was to die. Henry, his driving force little impaired even at the end, reached the age of seventy-nine. John was but fifty-two.

CHAPTER 3

Disaster by Land and Sea

The Collision at Dunaskin

For seven years the DICo carried on the traffic between the Sillyhole pits and the furnaces, having the exclusive use of the line. There were few safeguards and no accidents that I ever heard of. In 1856, with the introduction of passenger trains, the G & SW brought in rigid discipline and threatened penalties. Seven weeks later there was a SMASH. The two employees chiefly concerned, the driver of the passenger train and the fireman of the DICo coal train, were arrested and tried. The voluminous statement of evidence contains much that depicts the working in those days.

The line laid down in 1849 was single track. Where sidings or branches diverged there was a set of points with hand lever. This lever was weighted by a counter-balance working within an iron box which kept the points set for the main line. The balance weight was in six sections, and there was evidence that on occasion one section became misplaced and caught on the side of the iron box, thus preventing the points from returning to 'main line' position.

The Term 'Switch'

It is rather strange that throughout the evidence a set of points is referred to as a 'switch'. We regard this as an Americanism, yet such was the term used in 1856 on a line which certainly had no link with American practice. It must have changed soon after, for I never heard any railway employee, G & SW or DICo, use the term 'switch'.

It was these 'switches' which were the chief bone of contention on the introduction of the passenger service. The G & SW insisted on each switch being locked in the main line position. So bolts were duly fitted to each switch, and Robert Kirkland, Assistant Manager, G & SW, travelled to Waterside and solemnly presented to John Hunter, General Manager, DICo, eleven keys for opening the padlocks attached to the bolts. John Hunter sent for my grandfather David Larmer, then a young man of twenty-two and referred to as 'overseer', passing the keys to him for distribution to the various firemen of the DICo engines. Owing to rather frequent changes among the firemen no fewer than seven of those functionaries seem to have received keys. A lad of fifteen, one William Bell, had among his other duties that of holding switches, and he was given a key also, with strict injunctions that he be responsible for *opening* switches only. The more important *closing* must be left to the firemen concerned. Of course, in practice Bell both opened and closed switches as everyone knew, my grandfather included.

Early Signals

Besides this locking of switches an additional safeguard was provided in the shape of two signals guarding the switch which gave entrance to the south end of a loop, one for each direction of travel. This switch seems to have been situated just north of the bridge over Dunaskin Burn at a point stated to be 1,156 yd south of Waterside station. The signals were actuated by 'handles', both at some distance from their respective signals.

For these signals special orders were issued: 'The red signal is to be kept constantly shown [during the period that the DICo were using the switch] and no engine must be allowed to pass until the signal is turned off'.

This loop line was 264 yd in length and had a connection to the main line at its north end also. The anxiety shown for the protection of the south end switch is explained by the fact that it was the chief means of access to the DICo lines and was used by all coal trains coming from Sillyhole to the furnaces. G & SW trains also used this switch to leave in limestone and take out pig iron.

The DICo were now allotted definite times during which they could have the exclusive use of the railway from Dalharco Junction to the crossing of the Cummock Burn at Sillyhole. These times were: 8.30 p.m. to 7.30 a.m., 8.30 a.m. to 9.45 a.m., 11.30 a.m. to 3.30 p.m. At all other times they must clear off the main line, the fireman of the last train being responsible for the locking of the switch. Any fireman neglecting to lock the switch was liable to a fine of £5.

John Walker, Signalman

A few days before the opening of the line for passenger traffic John Walker was sent to Waterside station. His duties were to attend at the handles of the signals guarding the Dunaskin switch, to place those signals to red when the switch was being used by DICo engines, to see that those engines and trains were clear of the main line by the expiry of their allotted period of working, and then to turn the signal to green. Although Walker appears to have been the only assistant given to the stationmaster John Crawford, no written instructions appears to have sanctioned his use for any other duties than attending to these signals.

Walker had been on similar duty at Dalry Junction before his transfer to Waterside. He took a look at the new job and he did not like it. The distance to the further signal handle was 669 yd, and to traverse that and return each time to Waterside station involved quite a lot of tramping. Had Walker lived at the present day he would have characterised this business of the signals as 'a lot of hooey'. If he turned the signal to red when the DICo were using the switch it was obvious that their engines would have to pass this 'danger' signal, an undesirable manner of working. No G & SW trains would be on the line during the periods of DICo working, so to whom did the red apply? To restore the signals to green when the DICo times had expired was merely to tell G & SW drivers what they knew already, that the line was clear for them. So Walker decided that it was no use working the signals at all. He left them at green and got away with it.

His decision was not exactly induced by laziness, for Mr Crawford the stationmaster was making more and more use of Walker for the work of a porter. Walker was also accompanying guards of goods trains to the south switch and working it for them with a key which he had conveniently annexed

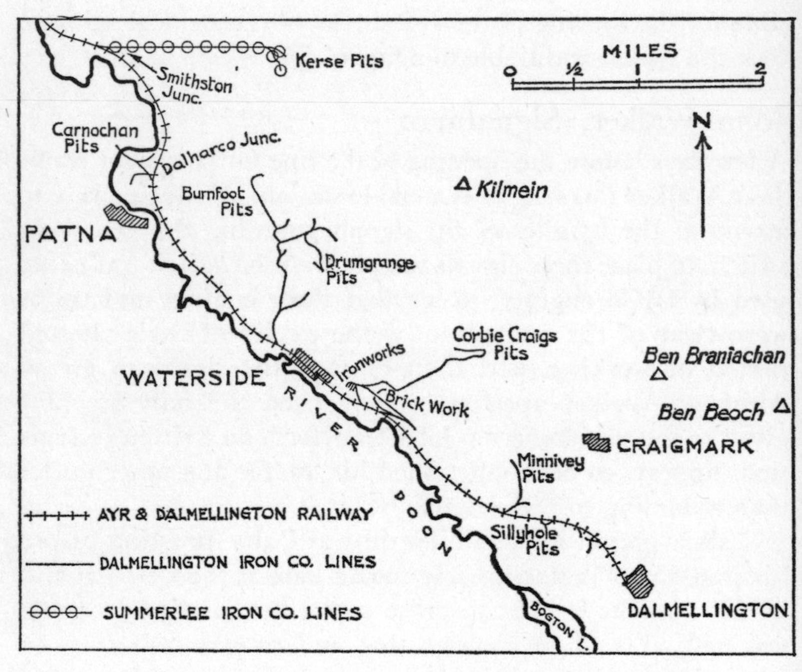

Dalmellington Iron Company's railway system, 1857

at Dalry Junction. So his contribution to safe working at the switch in question appears to have dwindled to a mere casual glance to see if the DICo were 'inside'. By a most extraordinary omission, Walker was not required to check the position and locking of the switch in question. His duties were confined to observation of the presence or absence of DICo trains upon the main line.

(4a) *Glengarnock No. 5 working at Rankinston* 1886. *Stated to be similar to DICo No. 2*

(4b) *No. 8*(1) *in yard of makers, J. & A. Taylor, Smith St, Ayr. On footplate, Mr J. Taylor. Behind engine, Archie Murdoch, boiler-maker*

(5a) *No. 6 in original condition,* c.1886. *Left to right: Matthew Poole, Guard; James McGraw, Fireman; John Yorston, Driver; John Skelly, Overseer*

(5b) *No. 6 as rebuilt* 1906. *At Lethanhill store,* c.1908. *Left to right: Harry Graham, Fireman; John Yorston, Driver; Daniel Wallace, Guard*

Appeal to Caesar

On a date in mid-September a 'book of printed instructions' was sent to Walker. Walker read it through, and in a certain paragraph he found wording which inferred that he was to be responsible for cleaning and keeping in good order and repair 'the switches under his care'. This, if true, was yet another imposition and Walker refused to 'sign for' the book. However, he was apparently persuaded to sign but on the same day, 15 September, he wrote a letter to the *general manager* of the G & SW stating that he could not undertake such responsibility as some of the switches were 'not in good working order'.

This put the cat among the pigeons with a vengeance. Mr Johnstone, General Manager, G & SW, wrote on the following day to John Hunter, General Manager, DICo, calling his attention to the complaint. During the period of their exclusive use of the line the DICo had been responsible for the maintenance of the switches, but John Hunter had been under the impression that this period of DICo responsibility had ceased at 26 June. He waited further developments until 25 September when, with his foreman surfaceman Roderick McDonald and my grandfather Larmer, he walked the line and inspected switches. All were found in order except that leading to Minnivey pits, where some keying was required. My grandfather, however, called Mr Hunter's attention to the fact that the balance weights sometimes became misplaced and that the switch did not recover to main line position.

Meanwhile Mr Johnstone, worried at receiving no reply from the DICo, wrote on 21 September to Mr Galloway 'the company's resident engineer' instructing him to have the switches repaired. On the following day he issued an order:

> Until further notice, all engine drivers must slow their speed to not more than four miles per hour while passing over the switches and crossings of all private branches and sidings belonging to the Dalmellington Iron Company. This order must be obeyed rigidly until the resident engineer gets the necessary repairs and alterations made, when due notice will be given.

On 26 September the DICo manager at last replied to Mr Johnstone's letter. On the next day the accident occurred.

Coal Train from Sillyhole

On the morning of Saturday 27 September 1856 driver James Ferguson, then a young man twenty-six years of age, was bringing a train of coal from Sillyhole to Waterside. His fireman was a year older and by name Robert Howie. About two months before, Thomas Black the previous fireman did not turn up for duty. Robert Howie, then a casual labourer, was ordered to take his place. Unfortunately the evidence, given so copiously, does not give the number of any engine involved, G & SW or DICo. Ferguson and Howie's train was the last to arrive before the expiry of the DICo's permitted period, and it was therefore Howie's duty to lock the switch when all had gone 'inside'.

It is not made clear whether Ferguson was pushing or pulling his rake. I think he was pulling, and that he slipped his coupling before reaching the switch and ran on down the main line to the water-tank being, as usual, in a parlous state for want of water. The boy William Bell held the switch and ran the rake on to the loop then he and Howie and Matthew Leggat, who had come to relieve Ferguson, ran along getting brakes down until she was brought to a stand. Certain evidence would make it appear that the rake consisted of forty-eight or forty-nine wagons. If so it was a heavy load for a little Neilson, apparently unassisted. The time was then 7.10, and the DICo had to vacate the main line by 7.30.

After getting brakes applied Howie and Leggat walked along to assist Ferguson to get water. By the time he finished it was 7.20, so Ferguson decided to go into the loop from the north end. Presumably Howie unlocked this switch. Once inside, Matthew Leggat took over from Ferguson and promptly put the engine off the rails!

That, I fear, was an everyday occurrence on the DICo lines! All hands gathered to assist—Ferguson and Howie, Leggat and his fireman John Harrison, and another crew, James

Walker and Robert Dick, who were on their engine close by.

The process of re-railing took about half-an-hour. Then Ferguson and Harrison went off to their homes. As they walked Harrison says he saw the signal operator John Walker 'in the direction of the signal handle'. Leggat sent Howie to fetch a 'tail chain' from the engine shed, as he intended to tow the wagons to the foot of the incline leading to the furnace bank. Howie was returning with the chain when he saw the passenger train coming.

Robert Dick seems to have seen it first. When he first sighted the steam the passenger train was still south of the Cutler Brig. Dick looked along the line and saw the switch lying open for the loop. The signal, of course, was at its perpetual green. Dick ran up the middle of the main line shouting and waving his cap. My grandfather saw Dick running and shouting that the upper switch was open. Grandfather ran for the signal handle—not very fast, poor man, for he was lame from childhood—but he was too late. Matthew Leggat on his engine heard the shouting, saw the passenger coming, and sounded his whistle. Just short of the switch the engine driver shut off steam, but Dick was still 60 yd away when they swerved on to the loop at a goodly pace and smashed into the rear of Ferguson's rake. Two wagons were broken to pieces; the third was badly damaged, the engine mounting upon the wreckage and coming to a standstill thus. The four vehicles of the passenger train were not derailed, but in the third class coach there was some breaking of glass and a seat was overturned. Five passengers and the guard received injuries.

My grandfather's first act after the collision was to test the fatal switch. He found it in correct working order. Some of the injured were taken into houses in the adjacent 'Brick Row' (officially 'Park Yett'). The G & SW enginemen were unhurt, the guard had gone to the DICo offices (then close to the scene of the accident) and a message had been sent to Dalmellington requesting medical assistance. There was no undue delay, however. In forty minutes one of the DICo engines (again I do not know which) had been given to the G & SW men, the coaches had been pushed by hand back to the main line, and the train was once more on its way. Dr Allan and his assistant arrived just too late but followed to Patna, whence all the injured passengers had been bound.

8 a.m. Ex Dalmellington

It was a wedding in Dalmellington the previous evening which had provided a quite large number of passengers for the 8 a.m. ex Dalmellington. One of the parties must have had Patna connections, for many of the guests belonged to that district. The festivities probably carried on until 5 or 6 a.m. —forty dances (with extras) was a very normal programme, and the young folk, still merry, were rounding off a happy evening by a journey in this exciting new means of transport. The journey was to prove just *too* exciting, as it turned out!

One train crew only was stationed at Dalmellington in those days: William Frew engine driver, William McBirnie fireman, and Robert Maxwell guard. William Frew stated that he had seen the special notice restricting speed to four miles per hour over DICo switches. He thought this restriction far too severe and in practice slowed down to the minimum at which he could still keep time. On the morning of 27 September 1856 the load of the 8 a.m. train ex Dalmellington was three coaches (first, second and third class) and van. The rails were greasy and he estimated that he had not exceeded eight miles an hour (sic) until the accident. The signal was green, which was not surprising, and Frew got no warning until, from a distance of about 40 yd, he saw the open switch. He reversed and the fireman applied the tender brake, but they could not stop. Frew jumped off before the collision and was not hurt. He did not see Robert Dick running. The engine was probably a Bury, with high, domed firebox which would obscure his view.

Fireman William McBirnie was supposed to travel with his back to the engine and his gaze directed upon his train. He was, however, singularly well informed about what was going on *ahead*. He also noted the green signal and saw Robert Dick running. Simultaneously his driver called to him that the switch was open and he began to brake. He remained on the engine until she struck and escaped injury.

Robert Maxwell the guard had the unenviable post, seated upon the roof of, I think, the first coach. He saw the green signal and then a man running and waving his cap. He could not see what was wrong, but applied his brake and whistled to the driver. The steam, however, beat down and he could see neither engineman. In the collision he was thrown down on the roof of the coach and his eye cut and blackened. He also estimated the speed at eight miles per hour. I think that Matthew Leggat's estimate of twenty-five miles an hour before the shutting off of steam is pretty accurate.

Trial by Jury

Robert Howie, the man who forgot to lock the switch, was the villain of the piece, but poor Frew was caught by that wretched 'special notice' limiting the speed over switches to four miles per hour. It was obvious to all that the collision had been caused by a speed far in excess of this figure. So Howie and Frew were both arrested. They appeared before the Ayr Sheriff Criminal Court on 4 February 1857, charged with culpable neglect of duty. Sheriff Robison presided. Mr F. L. Maitland Heriot, Advocate-Deputy, appeared for the prosecution. Mr George Morton, Writer, appeared for Frew, and Mr Lucas, Writer, appeared for Howie. With the huge mass of evidence, the hearing lasted ten hours. Both prisoners were by unanimous agreement of the jury found guilty. Howie received four months imprisonment and Frew two months. They took railway accidents seriously in those days.

Mr Johnstone, General Manager of the G & SW, had in evidence given Frew a very good character, and it is obvious that he was very pleased that the precious 'special notice' regarding speed over switches, while condemning Frew, had 'let the company out'. So all the time that Frew languished in Ayr prison, his wife was given his full pay, and on the evening of his release Frew walked up to the passenger station, the 'spare man' who had been officiating stepped off, and Frew drove his train to Dalmellington as usual. Of Robert Howie's subsequent career I know nothing. If he stuck to 'The Pugs' it may have ended fatally. It was all so new and there was so much to do; men took risks. But they got the work done. The evidence of driver James Ferguson is truly illuminating. He says '. . . I went off home and was at breakfast when I heard of the collision. I did not go to the place, as I had been working *all night and the day preceding*'. No complaint, just a statement of fact.

'The Bridge is Down'

I cannot give an exact date for this incident. It was after 1858, possibly not long after. My grandfather Larmer, 'overseer' in 1856, had risen in rank to be 'traffic manager'. His office was no sinecure. To be in two places at once would have been quite an advantage. On this particular day he was trying to do just that.

He was up on the furnace bank. From there he dispatched No. 4, with driver Matthew Leggat and fireman Robert Dick, with ten empty wagons for Carnochan pit beyond Patna. He wished to accompany them to Carnochan, but first he had to interview the stationmaster. No. 4 would take some time to go away to the Cutler Tip and back down to the main line. Grandpa cut down through the gardens and calculated he would be able to see the stationmaster and catch No. 4 as she came past.

The stationmaster must have been a bit long-winded or Leggat had been a bit too nippy, for as my grandfather emerged from the office door the rake was trundling past. Grandpa had just time to grab the last wagon and step on the buffer. In this fashion he rode the two miles down to Patna.

Carnochan Viaduct

The junction for Carnochan was just north of the main road overbridge north of Patna station. The branch swung sharply to the left and there was a short spur into which the engine lay, slipping her coupling and letting the wagons down past her. It must have been a rather steep descent to the side of the River Doon, where a timber viaduct with stone abutments conducted the line across to Carnochan pits on the further bank.

Grandpa remained on the buffer of the last wagon and they went down the hill at a good pace. Looking ahead, he saw the first wagon reach the viaduct. Then the wagon gave a violent lurch; there was a splintering of wood, another great lurch, and the wagon toppled over into the Doon. Next moment the second wagon lurched likewise and over *it* went. The third did the same. Grandpa said he thought he had stood there long enough, so he stepped off and let them run, and the whole rake went into the river. Into the bargain they broke one of the two main beams and took half the bridge down with them.

Repair and Rejoicing

Consternation—the bridge was down, the pit was shut; nothing could get out or in. Down came John Hunter, General Manager, *on a white horse*. 'Hold everything! Not a man to leave the job till the bridge is repaired!' The remaining beam was measured and a man dispatched on horseback to Ayr to get a new beam cut and sent up from Paton's. While he was gone the rest set to work to salvage the wagons from the Doon. When the beam finally arrived it was 'all hands' to get it up into position and secured. Then came the repair of the timber-work. Forty-eight hours they were at it continuously. Some had never broken bread during all that time.

At last it was finished. 'Come on boys, all up to the inns at Patna!' Up they trooped, the whole lot of them, and there were the tables, long tables, all set, the food piled up, a bottle of whisky opposite each man, and John Hunter standing at the head of the table whanging down the beef. Down they sat, ravenous, and they ate and they drank till they could hardly see.

Some got home that morning, some didn't. Leggat and

Dick managed to get No. 4 to the shed at Waterside, but Rob Dick couldn't get any further and fell asleep with his head on the rail. My grandfather *did* manage the remaining half-mile to his home at The Cutler. He got to bed and fell asleep. That was the Thursday. He slept the rest of that day and all day Friday. When he was still sleeping on into Saturday evening they got alarmed and sent for Dr Allan. The doctor came and sounded him. 'When was this man in his bed last?' he inquired. Oh, they couldn't remember. . . . It hadn't been that week anyway. 'Let him alane' said the doctor. 'The man's tired. He'll wauken when he's restit.'

Great labours, but they took their toll. I remember my grandfather in his last illness. Two years he had to sit up in bed, snatching his sleep bowed over an arm-rest. 'I never kent I had a he'rt till noo!' he said. No, they didn't worry about heart strain in those days of mighty toil. The job was there to do and they did it.

Maritime Tragedy

A Doon valley man scanning his newspaper in the first month of 1857 probably passed unheeding an all-too-familiar story of shipwreck, of a vessel lost on the rocks near Land's End, Cornwall. Then his eye might catch the name of the vessel—DUNASKIN, and its owners—*The Dalmellington Iron Company*! It is quite likely that our reader did not know that the DICo possessed a vessel! But they did, and the story of the *Dunaskin* takes us far from the little farm of that name and the valley of the Doon.

The Good Ship Dunaskin

As far as can be ascertained, the *Dunaskin* was the sole maritime possession of the DICo. She was built in the year 1854 at Port Glasgow, though most exceptionally the particulars of her registry do not give the name of her builder. She was a most unusual craft for her time, being a *screw* steamer, two-masted, schooner-rigged, and with one funnel. She was 'clencher'* built of wood, with iron framing, a square stern, and a 'scroll' bow. Her length was 115 ft, breadth 18.8 ft, and depth 10 ft. Her registered tonnage was 122.

To be strictly accurate, the *Dunaskin* was not at first recorded as owned by the DICo. Her owner is given as 'John Houldsworth, of Ayr, Merchant', owning sixty-four shares. As this owner was the managing director of the DICo we may accept the fact that the *Dunaskin* was obtained for use in the company's business. She was registered at the port of Ayr in March 1854.

On 12 August 1856 a minute of the Traffic Committee of the G & SW records with a disapproving note that the DICo are sending their pig iron from Ayr to Glasgow by their own *steamer*. (Singular.)

Some correspondence upon the subject probably ensued, after which a further minute of 23 September of that year announces that the DICo has applied for a reduction of rates for the carriage of its pig iron from Ayr to Glasgow by the G & SW. The latter company agreed that the rate be reduced to 3s per ton, on condition that *all* such pig iron be carried by the G & SW.

Further correspondence evidently took place. On 21 October 1856 it is reported that the DICo would not bind themselves to send all iron by the G & SW. They had, however, come to an agreement that their steamer should carry only such pig iron as would supply *their own foundry in Anderston*.† The DICo further agreed that *no other iron* be carried on their steamer and that she carry 'no goods to Ayr' on the return journey.

In General Trading

These were very hampering conditions, and it is not surprising to find that two months later the *Dunaskin* had been taken off the Ayr-Glasgow run and, apparently now in general trading, was loading at Lisbon a cargo of fruit (mainly oranges)

* Another form of the term 'clinker'.
† The Anderston Foundry Company, a Houldsworth enterprise.

for Bristol. She left Lisbon for Bristol on 28 December 1856.

The *Dunaskin* was in the charge of Captain John Macfarlane. A native of Troon, Captain Macfarlane had moved his home to Newton-on-Ayr, where his wife and young family were staying. The captain, in the account in the *Shipping Gazette*, is recorded as being of excellent character and highly respected. In previous perilous conditions he had displayed great courage. The mate, William McMorlan of Ayr, is described as an aged man who had had long service in coasting craft, first as seaman and finally as master. He had captained the brig *Magog* of Ayr. Two engineers were carried, John McWalter and Patrick McMahon, both residing in Ayr. There were three firemen and five seamen, twelve souls in all.

At about eight o'clock on the evening of 1 January 1857 the *Dunaskin* made the Lizard light. In view of the impending catastrophe one cannot overlook the coincidence of this date of traditional Scottish conviviality, which has led to shipwrecks before and since. A careful examination of the account, however, reveals nothing more than the normal hazards of the sea, with more bad luck than bad guiding.

The Lizard light bore about east by north, distant ten miles. The *Dunaskin's* course was then NE half N, the wind being about SW by W, fresh, the weather thick and squally. The master altered the course to NW by N half N, and very soon made Scilly light on the port beam. Shortly afterwards the weather became thick and hazy and both lights were lost sight of. Between ten and eleven o'clock another light appeared on the starboard bow. The master interpreted this as the Seven Stones light and ordered the vessel to be kept away, so as to bring the light on the port bow.

Catastrophe

This was a fatal decision. The light, seen in the clearing of the squall, was not the Seven Stones. It was the Longships. A few minutes after the change of course the unfortunate *Dunaskin* struck on the outer ledges of Guthen Brose near Tol Pedn Penwith. She forged over the rocks but it was found that the middle or engine compartment was stove in and had almost immediately filled with water.

The master ordered the boats to be got ready. The longboat was at once got out and nine of the crew got into her, the master, mate and one seaman remaining on board. They were in broken water, and the longboat, holding on alongside the *Dunaskin,* began to fill. The boat's crew had no alternative but to cut the painter and drop clear. In two or three minutes the *Dunaskin* went on shore against a very high rocky cliff, broadside on.

After the ship struck the seaman who had remained, James Foley of Dublin, got out on the bowsprit and from it dropped on to a narrow ledge of the rocks. The master, a strong, active man, could easily have followed him. Instead, he busied himself getting the frail old mate out upon this perilous path to safety. Next moment a movement of the vessel snapped the bowsprit off against the rocks, and with some difficulty the master hauled the mate back again to the ship's deck. Shortly afterwards both masts and the funnel went over the side and the *Dunaskin* broke up and sank in about three fathoms of water. The master and mate were both drowned.

The remainder of the crew, in scarcely less peril in the longboat, managed to keep the boat's head to sea abreast of the wreck for about twenty minutes, but at length were compelled to keep her away before it. They reached Penzance about three o'clock in the morning.

The seaman James Foley, left alone at the base of the cliff, made his way with some difficulty along the rocks and up the cliff. About four o'clock in the morning he reached the fishing-cove of Porthgwarra and roused the fishermen there. They treated him with great kindness and at daybreak went to the spot of the shipwreck. Nothing of the wreck was visible except the ends of two or three spars which floated but were fast to the vessel below. The body of Captain Macfarlane came ashore on 5 January 1857, and was interred in St Levan's churchyard, Penzance. A gold ring, purchased by him in Lisbon as a gift for his wife, was found upon his person.

CHAPTER 4

Nineteenth Century : Prosperity

Spade-Work of the Fifties

The opening of the Ayr & Dalmellington Railway solved several problems. It also created some. The G & SW, who operated the A & D, imposed their code of rules and regulations for its working and restricted the hours at which the DICo could use the line. This was nowhere more hampering than on the Dunaskin-Sillyhole section. There were five coal pits working on the lands of Sillyhole and three on Minnivey. There was a coal pit opening at Chalmerston on a branch to the east, and another was soon to follow. There was an ironstone pit just south of Sillyhole level crossing. There was an active tile works close by. Engines Nos. 1 and 2, in the hours permitted to them, were working to the limit of their power. The collision at Dunaskin did not encourage the G & SW to relax its restrictions to any extent. Indeed some correspondence ensued between the A & D company and the Board of Trade. The latter refused to approve the rules for working so long as persons other than the railway company were permitted to use the single line. The position was far from satisfactory. Traffic was increasing still further, and on 23 February 1858 we read that the Board of the A & D had resolved to lay down a second line of rail between the iron works and Sillyhole. 'The road has been prepared and the present low price of rails is some inducement.' Nevertheless the wheels moved slowly, and it was not until 1 October 1859 that this 'relief line' was brought into use. It was operated in somewhat unusual fashion. G & SW trains had now the uninterrupted use of the original line, while DICo trains had the use of the new one. As the new line was concerned chiefly with the Sillyhole traffic it was always known as 'The Sillyhole Road'. The second line paralleled the original as in ordinary double-track working. It extended from the sidings at the south end of Waterside to a point about ten chains south of Sillyhole crossing. Branches from it gave access to the Sillyhole pits, the Chalmerston pits, and the Minnivey pits.

Increased traffic to the furnaces gave rise to a new arrangement of sidings at the furnace bank and a line giving access to it by locomotives. The latter was achieved by means of a line, rising at 1 in 40, which had conveyed spoil to a tip south of the works and high above the Cutler Burn. From this line another, also rising steeply, was led in the opposite direction to reach the furnace bank. To achieve this, the deep glen of the Dunaskin Burn was crossed by a high embankment pierced at its base by a short tunnel. This served the double purpose of giving an outlet for the Dunaskin Burn and also, by means of a wooden staging above the waters of the burn, giving entrance to the glen for a railway serving two large quarries in freestone and a brickwork. Clay for the brickwork was procured from a small pit about half-a-mile further up the stream, an extraordinary little place, jammed in between the stream and the steeply-rising side of the glen. The clay was brought to the brickwork by a narrow-gauge hutch line with horse haulage. The clay pit worked intermittently, perhaps for a year, until a sufficient stock had accumulated, then it would close down for perhaps two years. At each re-opening, of course, much pumping was necessary to clear the workings, and I am told that there were also sent up the pit hutch-loads of frogs which had bred in its dark recesses. The tunnel which gave access to the glen was always referred to as 'The Quarry Brig', and it was a limiting factor in regard to the locomotives. From rail to crown of arch the distance was only 9 ft 2 in. Some engines could not go through it at all, others had to have the funnel hinged to fold back.

On 27 July 1858 the A & D Railway was absorbed into the

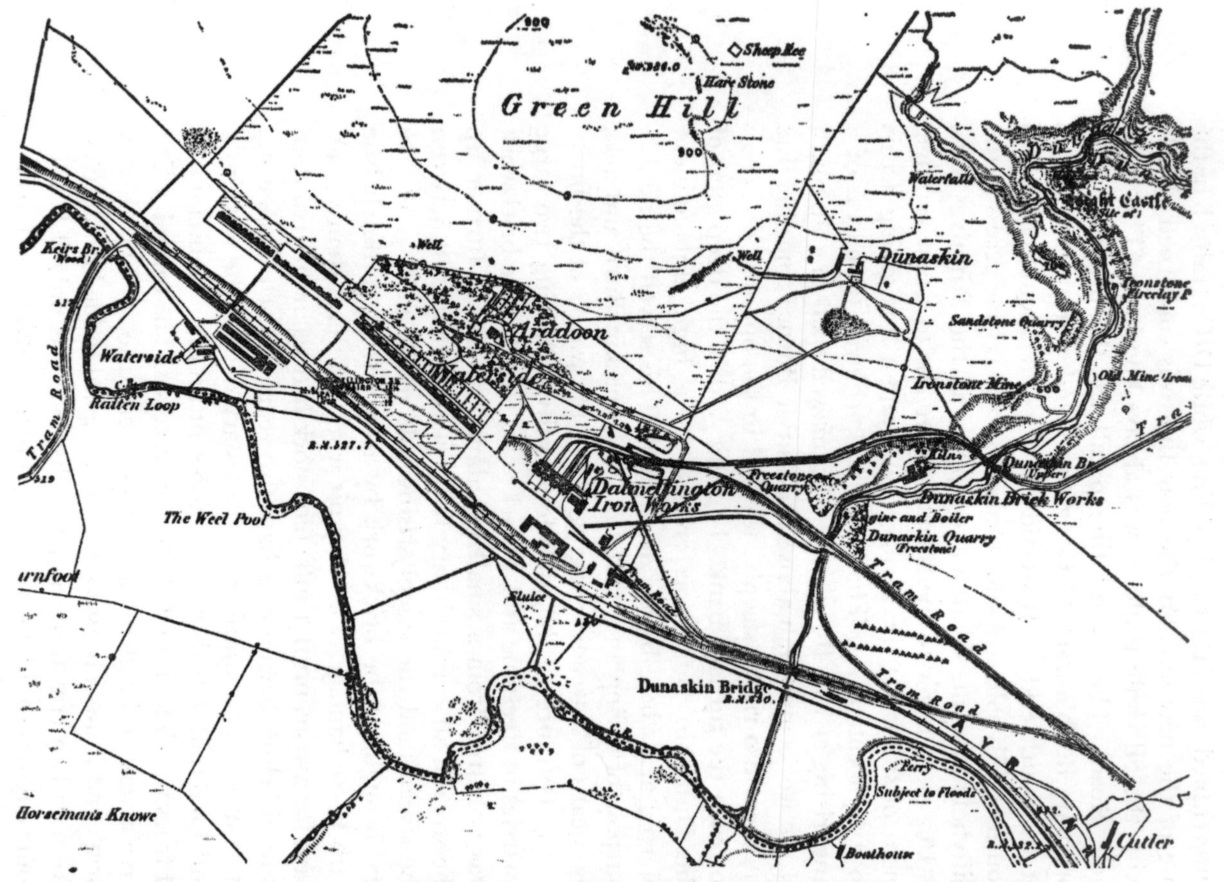

Waterside and iron works, 1857, from Ordnance Survey 6-in map, sheet Ayrshire XL.

G & SW, but the relations of the DICo with the railway company continued to be 'extensive and peculiar'. Beyond the agreed working of the DICo engines as far as Smithston, I cannot trace any agreement for their use of the line, but I am informed that at times of pressure it was no uncommon thing for Nos. 3 and 4 to go down to Ayr Harbour and bring up a train of limestone. This necessary commodity could not be produced locally in anything like the quantity required for furnace work and had to be imported, mainly from Ireland. The DICo had also some small ironstone pits at Raithhill farm near Coylton. The char from these was carted to Hollybush station, and No. 3 would collect it from time to time.

The DICo traffic was not the only mineral traffic on the Dalmellington line. Every evening at 9.45 a G & SW train would leave Shiels Road (sic) Glasgow for Smithston, bringing empty wagons, departing from Smithston again at 2 a.m. for Shiels Road with ironstone for the Summerlee Iron Works, which no doubt the Caledonian Railway would take on to Coatbridge.

Engines Nos. 3 and 4 were products of the firm of Hawthorns of Leith, with whom the DICo were to have pleasant relations over the years. No. 4 was a huge engine for her time, an 0—4—0 side-tank, 22 ft 6-in in length over buffers. She was engaged mainly on the coal traffic from Patna, which presently reached large dimensions. A branch went off the main line immediately to the north of the road bridge at Patna station, a spot designated in the working time table as Dalharco Junction. Thence it descended steeply, one branch turning westward to Downieston pit, the other continuing downhill until it crossed the Doon by a timber viaduct with stone abutments, the remains of which can be seen to-day. Just across the Doon was one of the Carnochan pits. The other was some distance up the hill towards Shankston. I do not know if both pits had standard-gauge rail connection. North of the main line junction, just beyond the overbridge leading to Dalharco farm, was Dalharco No. 1 pit with a short branch of its own from the main line.

New Villages

The fifties saw also a great progression in the number of houses provided for the workpeople, and is a fair indication of the growth of the labour force. Waterside had grown out of all knowledge, there being 237 houses by the end of the fifties. A completely new village named Craigmark had been erected about a mile north of Dalmellington. It comprised 100 houses. On the elevated plateau there were now thirty-one houses near the top of the Drumgrange incline and ten at Corbie Craigs, the summit of the southern incline. Even with the above construction there was insufficient accommodation, and for a period after 1851 large huts set up at Waterside accommodated many men and sometimes their families also.

Menace from the East

Almost simultaneously with the Doon valley venture there had commenced at New Cumnock a similar enterprise, the Nithsdale Iron Company setting up furnaces at Bank, west of New Cumnock, and opening up mines in the neighbourhood of the farm of Beoch some six miles to the west. These produced coal and iron, which was conveyed to the furnaces by a standard-gauge railway. This had in its course two rope-worked inclines, powered by stationary steam-engines, the remainder of the haul being performed by horses. The Nithsdale Company was financed from England, and the DICo, being suspicious of this approach to their territory, hastened to lease an additional area lying towards New Cumnock. Other leases were taken in the fifties, at Sundrum, Downieston, Dalharco, Kerse, and Skerrington, and the small properties of Carbieston near Coylton, and Dockra, which lay some distance east of Beith in North Ayrshire. At Dockra there was a very productive quarry yielding lime, that much-needed ingredient. The partners were subscribing to all those purchases without hope of any early return. By 1852 £46,866 had gone into the building-up of the firm, but still more capital was required, and, shortly before the death of Henry Houldsworth, James Murray, a Scot who had been very successful in the cotton spinning trade of Manchester became a partner. It was mainly due to his advent that in the year 1853 the capital subscribed had risen to £56,584. There also joined the company as a partner Henry Wickham, a Yorkshireman with extensive experience of the iron trade. He was one of the MPs for Bradford and chairman of the Lancashire & Yorkshire Railway. These gentlemen, with the brothers Henry and John Houldsworth, and their nephew Thomas, son of William, constituted the company in the middle fifties.

The Expanding Sixties

The death of John Houldsworth in 1859 left a vacancy in the partnership of the DICo which was taken by his son William T. Houldsworth, then a minor. This was not to the liking of the other four partners, three of whom resided in England, and had been deprived of their managing partner who had lived on the scene of operations. Here we begin to learn of that commanding personality John Hunter, their general manager. He was a younger brother of James, who about this time became managing partner of the Coltness Iron Company. John had not yet been admitted to a partnership in the DICo, but, especially after the death of John Houldsworth, he appears to have assumed an attitude of great power and authority.

This authority was certainly needed, for the developments of the sixties must have taken some guidance. In the valley were two very active coalfields; to augment the output in the Patna area a new and larger pit, Jellieston No. 1, was sunk to the west of the main line south of Patna station. Then, much further afield, another pit was sunk on the farm of Carbieston near Coylton, and Carbieston coal became famous. Its output, and presumably that of the small Raithhill ironstone pits if they were still working, justified the making of a branch from a point on the Ayr-Dalmellington line which was 72 chains north of Hollybush station. This branch, following a general direction of east-north-east, had three level-crossings of public roads, and for some distance skirted the south shore of Martnaham Loch. At this source of water supply an elevated tank was erected and a pulsometer, actuated by a steam connection from the locomotive, pumped up water to fill the tank.

The connection to the main line had not then attained the dignity of a block post. It was most likely a pair of locked points only, for the DICo engine which worked the branch remained on it, working three trips a day to and from the point of junction, from which the G & SW conveyed the coal to Waterside. For this job a fifth engine was obtained, another product of Neilson, and was stationed at Coylton.

Ironstone Pits

So much for the coal supply to the furnaces. The mining of ironstone had gone on with equal vigour. As has been stated, the ironstone pits were almost all situated on the plateau east of the Doon valley. Some idea of the intensity of this ironstone mining may be given by the fact that from first to last there were no less than *thirty-seven* ironstone pits or mines on the plateau. There was also some open-cast work which is probably not listed in the record of mines. Each pit or mine was named after the farm on whose land it was situated, the pits on each farm being numbered in order of opening date. There were two Bowhill pits, two Polnessan pits, two Downieston pits, eleven Burnfoot pits, nine Drumgrange pits, and eight Corbie Craigs pits. In addition there were the three Kerse pits which were worked by the Summerlee Iron Company.

Of course, those ironstone pits were by no means all worked simultaneously. Seams were thin and working lives in some cases quite short, but each pit had its full equipment and at each was situated a great, flat, open hearth upon which the ironstone, spread in thin layers interspersed with layers of coal, was slowly burned to rid it of some of its impurities. The resultant purified product was known as 'char'. It appears to have been the custom to leave this char exposed to the air for a period of six months before use in the furnaces, this having proved to give good results.

By the sixties the transport of this char had outgrown the capacity of horse haulage and the two inclines. Additional furnaces were in process of construction, and even more openings would be necessary to cater for their needs. So the line along the furnace bank was extended to the north to join up with the Drumgrange incline at a point about half-a-mile from its summit. This incline was equipped with a double line of rails throughout, the half-mile rising at a gradient of 1 in 6, with rope and gear heavy enough to handle main line eight-ton wagons. The self-acting principle remained, the loaded wagons, descending, hauling up others, mainly empty, but a few containing coal for the char hearths and pit engines. The lower part of the incline leading down to the main line was abandoned and removed, and the Corbie Craigs incline with its spectacular wooden viaduct likewise demolished. The sidings on the furnace bank were remodelled and a 'high level' line constructed on which hopper wagons could be placed for discharge to the shovelling platforms beneath.

Horse haulage on the plateau lines was discontinued. An engine was taken up—the first to go being the Old Faithful No. 1. Dispute has arisen as to the method employed in taking her up to the higher level. In after years engines were frequently taken up and down the new Drumgrange incline when necessary for repair or replacement. An appropriate number of wagons provided a counter-balance. There is, however, an intriguing story that No. 1 was taken up the *Kerse* incline of the Summerlee company and that she was partially dismantled in order that she might not be too heavy. Certainly, by whatever means, No. 1 reached the plateau lines, for the engine shed which was then erected was unfortunately made to her minute dimensions. Subsequent engines had to have their funnels shortened in order to get in.

Villages on the Hills

At this point, adjacent to the summit of the incline, a new village was speedily coming into being. By the end of the sixties, 190 houses had been erected here. Again there was confusion in the name of the village. The larger part was known officially as 'Lethanhill', but the row to the north, slightly apart from the others and ultimately comprising over ninety houses, was called 'Burnfoothill', and the whole village was more often called by this name. After a time, however, the people of the district shortened the title to the simpler one of 'The Hill'.

A mile east of Lethanhill yet another village was growing up. This had at first forty houses but was increased to a final total of eighty-four. The name selected was 'Benquhat'. In after years, the spelling 'Benwhat' was commonly used, but the registration authorities always insisted on the antique spelling. This village, situated well over the 1,000 ft contour line, ranked as one of the highest villages in Scotland. Rather strangely, though both Lethanhill and Benwhat had roads leading down to the valley, no road connected the two villages. They were, however, connected by railway which, in the case of the DICo, was equivalent to a public footpath!

The DICo erected and staffed schools at Waterside, Lethanhill, Benwhat and Craigmark. They also provided stores where a large range of the necessities of life could be purchased. Waterside Store was the central depot for the rest, and supplies were sent from there to Craigmark by road, but to Lethanhill and Benwhat in special wagons and vans which were hauled up the incline. On more than one occasion a mishap on the incline resulted in a somewhat messy pile-up. The stores were all licensed for the sale of beer, but not for spirits.

Eight Furnaces

The blast engines supplied in 1847 were now inadequate to deal with the increasing number of furnaces. By 1864 five were at work, and preparations were well advanced for a sixth. By the end of the sixties there were eight. So in 1865, the engine house was doubled in size, using the same imposing architecture. A second set of blast engines, similar in capacity to the first, were installed by the Lilleshall Engineering Co.

of Oakengates, Shropshire. This excellent company was geographically rather remote, and we may assume that directorial or managerial influence obtained for them this contract. Possibly managerial, for it is recorded that in the following year, 1866, the Lilleshall company was requested to supply a locomotive 'to the order of Mr John Hunter'. When No. 6 arrived, she was sent to Burnfoothill shed, where no doubt the tiny No. 1 was finding the work rather beyond her. No. 6 remained on the elevated section through almost the whole of her working life, but it was soon necessary to send a second engine to Burnfoothill. In summer one engine sufficed. In winter, with impediments of snow and gale-force winds, the second engine turned out and helped. No. 3 had a long spell as neighbour to No. 6.

With eight furnaces in blast the disposal of the residual slag had become a serious matter. Various small 'tips' had been run out to the south of the works but more space was required, so two bridges spanning the main line and the main road were laid with rails, and the tipping of slag was begun on the level meadows bordering the river. When the first 'bogie' of slag was tipped here few can have realised what an enormous geographical feature was being created. To-day the great 'Slag Hill' continues to tower over the valley, with no apparent diminution from the day that the last tipping took place in 1921.

The conveying of the slag to this Slag Hill was now a full-time task for an engine, and No. 7 was obtained, the first to be built for the DICo by the firm of Andrew Barclay of Kilmarnock. The engines supplied to Waterside in the present century have, with very few exceptions, come from this firm. Their first Waterside engine was a very small one and was very hard worked, being completely worn out after twenty years, when she was withdrawn and scrapped.

In 1861 a new deed of partnership had been signed. Capital was increased to £150,000 in six parts, one-third held by James Murray and one-sixth each by the other four—Henry the younger, Henry W. Wickham, Thomas Houldsworth son of William, and William T. Houldsworth son of John. A rule in the agreement laid down that no partner should take a financial interest in any mineral field within twenty miles of the company's works unless such lease had been first offered to the company and refused. This threw some light upon the fact that the very able general manager John Hunter had not been taken into the partnership. It appeared that he had several irons in the fire and that there had been considerable friction with the company on this subject. At one point John Hunter had threatened to leave the service of the DICo, but fortunately for the company at this period he did not do so. A courageous commander was still required at Waterside and John Hunter was surely that.

The Roaring Seventies

The early sixties saw the end of the Sillyhole pits. They had produced well but had always been difficult to work, as my grandfather Smith well knew. As a young man, he had them under his supervision. Water was heavy, pumping equipment primitive, and for years he could not count upon a night's sleep unbroken by a call for his services in some emergency. The Sillyhole Road, however, still functioned, for Minnivey pits were still working; a new branch from a point just north of Sillyhole farm led to two pits at Craigmark, while the Chalmerston branch was extended in 1868 to a new pit just east of Pennyvenie farm, Pennyvenie No. 1. This was the territory of the old Camlarg pits closed down some years before, but this big new pit could go down to far greater depths than they had ever attained. The extension of the railway to Pennyvenie must have entailed some very steep gradients. The track is still to be traced in the wood to the north of the Dalmellington-New Cumnock road, but its upper course has been covered by the 'bing' from the later pits of Pennyvenie Nos. 2 and 3.

The two new locomotives added to stock about the start of the seventies both worked on this line. No. 9 was a sturdy standard 14-in Barclay from Kilmarnock. No. 8 was a much greater curio, being one of only *two* locomotives which I have been able to trace as being built in the town of Ayr! She was built by the firm of Taylor in Smith Street.* They had a wide experience of mining machinery and of ships' auxiliaries but knew nothing of locomotives, and No. 8 suffered accordingly.

Big Money

The period of the early seventies, following the hold-up in trade caused by the Franco-Prussian War, was a time of great activity and prosperity in British industry, and the Dalmellington Iron Company was then probably at its zenith. The wages of miners rose to £7 and £8 per week. My grandfather, manager over some five pits, received no increase. His salary remained at 35s per week. He had to 'keep the time' of all his workers and do his own surveying!

The Coylton Line

An interesting development took place in the mid-seventies. The DICo had opened further pits in the Coylton area on the estate of Sundrum, and extension of the Coylton branch was necessary. It was planned to cross the main Ayr-Cumnock road on the level, but the Ayr County Council objected and insisted that a bridge be built to carry the road over the railway. There was a quibble over the resultant steepening of the gradient. Mr Hunter, General Manager, stated that it would now be 1 in 47. In later years the figure of 1 in 50 is quoted. The bridge was built and still stands.

With the increased traffic from the Coylton line to the iron works the DICo proposed that they now haul this coal by their own engines over the whole of the distance, this being some twelve miles including the six-and-a-half miles over the G & SW metals from the point of junction. The railway authorities, anxious to retain the haulage for themselves, objected and stated (so I was informed) that they could not permit any *four-wheeled* engine to operate traffic over their

---

* The site is now occupied by the works of John Wallace & Sons, Ltd, Engineers.

line. The contention was a ridiculous one, for not only had four-wheeled DICo engines been working over the G & SW line for years, but a large proportion of the mineral traffic of north and east Ayrshire was hauled by 0—4—0 tender engines of the G & SW! However, the DICo did not waste time in argument. They applied to their old friends Hawthorns of Leith, who produced an engine which, it was said, had lain seven years in stock, awaiting a purchaser. This was a most remarkable 2—4—0 well-tank engine, which was purchased and numbered 10 in the DICo stock. Having conformed with requirements the DICo were able to haul their Coylton coal

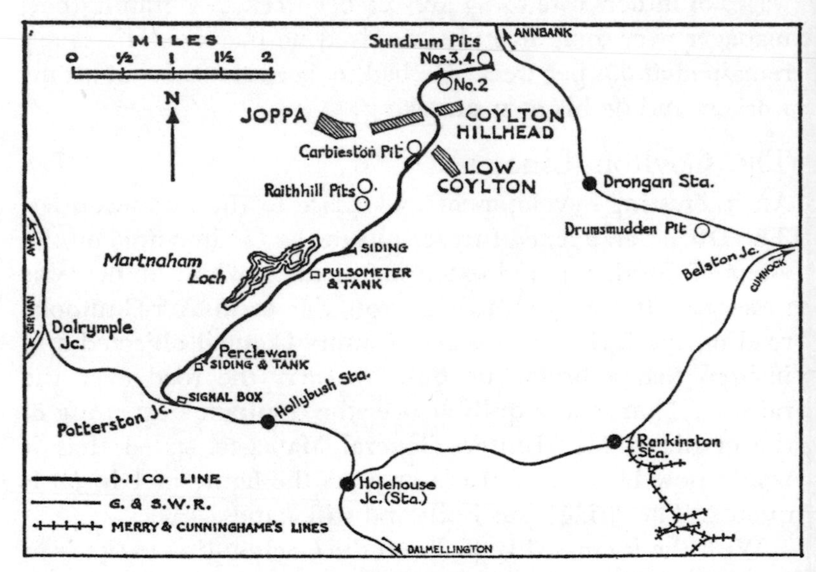

The Coylton Line

from pit to furnaces, No. 10, stationed at Waterside, making two trips a day. No. 5 returned to Waterside. The junction with the Coylton line became a block post with the name of Potterston Junction.

A somewhat strange circumstance may be here explained. Sundrum No. 2—generally referred to as Meadowhead pit from the name of the neighbouring farm—was only about a mile and a half from the Ayr and Cumnock line of the

G & SW. Why, then, was it necessary to make that long haul across country to join the Ayr & Dalmellington line? There are several reasons. When the DICo first penetrated into the Coylton area, the A & C line was not in existence. By the time the DICo arrived at Meadowhead the A & C had been built, but though this line could have been reached by a short branch the coal, destined for the Waterside furnaces, would have had a somewhat longer journey via Belston and Holehouse Junctions. This would have been on G & SW metals, and we may be certain that the G & SW would have insisted on haulage by their own engines, with corresponding charges.

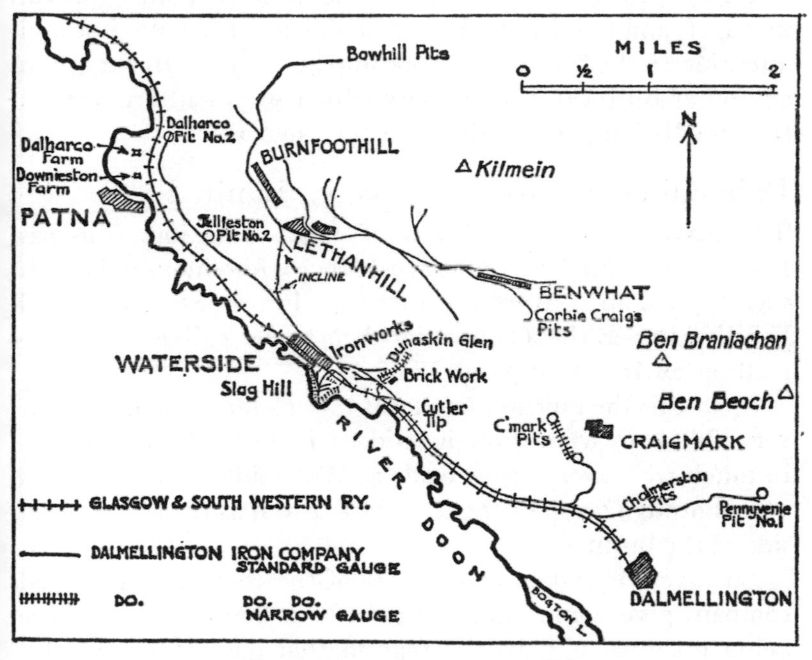

The DICo railway system, 1875

The ironstone pits on the plateau were working feverishly, but with the great demand for iron there was still anxiety that the supply would run short. A lease was taken in Cumberland, on the lands of Holebeck near Frizington, and mining commenced there in 1869.

A further reorganisation of the company took place in 1874, when the capital was increased from £150,000 to £310,000 in thirty-one shares of £10,000 each. These were allotted to the partners as follows:

James Murray	Twelve shares
Joseph H. Houldsworth	Six ,,
Thomas Houldsworth	Six ,,
William T. Houldsworth	Six ,,
John Hunter	One share

The strange mistrust of John Hunter is reflected in this meagre allotment, hedged about by the conditions that he could hold the one share only so long as he remained general manager, and that he was bound 'to devote his whole time and attention to the business of the company and not to engage in any other business in a capacity which would interfere with the due discharge of his duties as such manager'.

Dalmellington Iron Company, Limited

The above arrangement was of short duration. Thomas Houldsworth died in February 1876. A few months later it was decided to convert the company into one with limited liability under the Companies Act, to be called The Dalmellington Iron Company, Limited.

In all this the guiding hand was that of James Murray, that very able man who, though resident in England, was always in touch with every move made at Waterside, and who had a very thorough grasp of the technical as well as the commercial side of the business.

An inventory taken at the time of the change to a limited company gives some interesting statistics. Seven coal pits were being operated and in the year to that date had produced 128,181 tons of coal. Nine ironstone pits had an output of 105,221 tons. Eight furnaces were in blast. The company held eight leases, including one in Cumberland, and owned two small properties from which limestone was obtained. In the four parishes of Dalmellington, Dalrymple, Straiton and Coylton 906 houses had been built for the workers, while

Burnfoot House and five other houses were leased. Burnfoot House, between Waterside and Patna, was the residence of John Hunter. By 1876 the company had provided, staffed and maintained five schools and five stores. Four of these have been enumerated previously; the fifth was at the little hamlet of Kerse, about one-and-a-half miles north of Patna and in Dalrymple parish. There were twenty-one houses at Kerse and forty houses at Tongue Bridge Row a mile to the east. At Patna the inn was held on lease from the Duke of Portland.

It may be remarked that in all this great increase of housing in the valley and its adjacent hill-country the villages of Dalmellington and Patna remained almost unchanged. A large proportion of their men-folk were employed in DICo service, but the houses remained under private owners. No DICo houses were erected in Dalmellington until the year 1903. The DICo evidently preferred the New Town policy which we see so much to-day.

Considerable changes were taking place at the Patna end of the undertaking. The activities of the Summerlee Iron Company in the Doon valley appear to have ceased about the end of the sixties. By the early seventies the Downieston and Carnochan pits had been worked out. Two new and successful pits, Jellieston No. 2 and Dalharco No. 2 had, however, been sunk at a higher level. Rail access to these was given by an extension of the furnace bank line past the foot of the incline for a distance of some two miles. Jellieston No. 1 ceased production about the end of the seventies but was retained as a pumping station. I can just remember the siding beside the wooden post of Patna down distant signal, and the Coylton engine putting in wagons of dross for the boiler.

Competitors

Summerlee was no sooner gone from the scene than another competitor began to threaten encroachment. To the south of Littlemill Messrs Merry & Cunninghame of Glengarnock Iron Works in north Ayrshire began operations. A branch line to their pits led south from the G & SW's Holehouse

Junction-Belston Junction line and made its way by steep grades and reversing junctions to the high moor. The DICo countered by an extension of their Burnfoothill lines to new openings at Bowhill within a mile of their rival's pits. These Bowhill pits, of which there were two, were very successful, the last of them working until 1913.

Another competitor who had at one time given some anxiety had long since ceased to trouble. The Nithsdale Iron Company at Bank, New Cumnock, had given up after a life of under ten years. Their furnaces were dismantled, but some at least of their plant, after lying derelict for many years, was

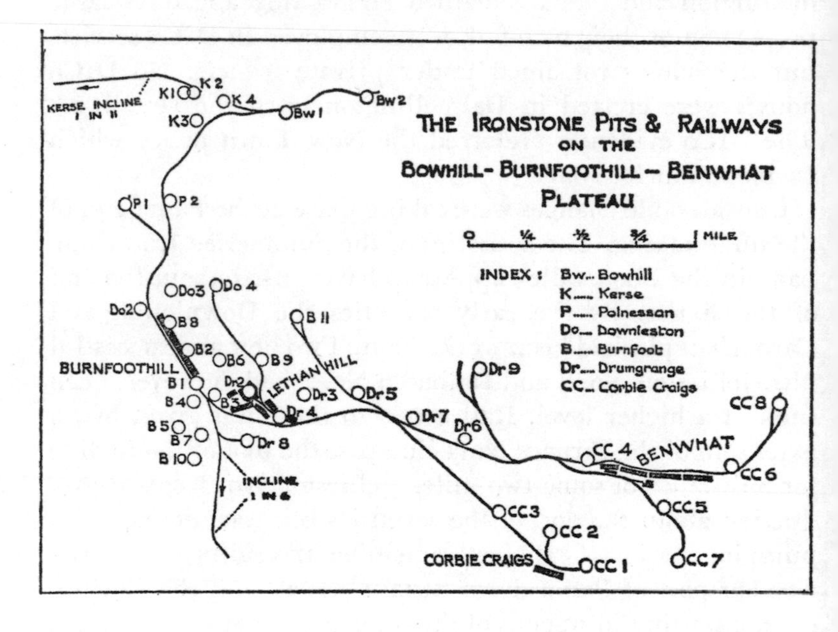

sold in the seventies. The DICo purchased some railway wagons, which were hauled on their own wheels across some eight miles of mountainous road until they could be put on rail at Pennyvenie. An even more adventurous task was the transport of a boiler. This seems likely to have been the boiler of one of the stationary engines employed on the rope-worked inclines. After purchase the DICo set a gang of men to *roll* the boiler across the moor to its new situation. All went well until they approached the houses of Beoch village when, on a down grade, the boiler got away from its escort. Downhill it thundered, making straight for the two end houses of Beoch! Then by a fortunate chance it struck a stone, was diverted from its former course and rolled safely past. It was as well, for these poor little houses of Beoch, erected by the Nithsdale company, wouldn't have stood up to much in the way of a charging boiler. They were later taken over by the DICo, who opened small coal mines in this area. They also appear to have worked the famous Auldnaw mine, which is close to Beoch village. This mine produced smithy coal, and old people in Dalmellington could remember strings of carts coming to it from all over Galloway. The farmers had an agreement that as soon as harvest-time was over each farmer would, at his own expense, fetch one cart-load of coal from Auldnaw mine to the smithy he patronized.

The Beoch mines did not warrant the extension of the standard-gauge railway; instead, a narrow-gauge hutch line was laid across the moor. It was single-line, with passing loops, and the hutches were hauled by a horse in trains of about twelve hutches. This line brought the Beoch coal to the screening-plant at Pennyvenie No. 1.

My uncle David Larmer told an amusing story of this little line. With some other engineers he was bound for Beoch one morning following a heavy snowfall. As they left Pennyvenie and got out to the open there appeared ahead of them a line of little lights, all dancing up and down upon the snow. For a few minutes they must have thought the fairies were out, but no. The line was drifted up, and when the miners arrived they were told that they must either set to work to dig the line out or there would be no work. So each man, with his open pit lamp upon his cap, was stooping and rising, stooping and rising as he shovelled snow.

I travelled on this line once, about the year 1909. There were two rather large timber viaducts on it in the crossing of two deep glens.

CHAPTER 5

Nineteenth Century : Adversity

The Hungry Eighties

'The Time o' The Big Money.' In the mid-seventies, £7 or £8 a week and an American organ in every house in Benwhat. By the mid-eighties, some men back to 25s a week and the American organs cluttering up the furniture shops of Ayr.

There were several causes for this sudden and terrible depression which came upon the iron trade of Scotland. Certainly the demand had fallen, but an additional factor was the extent to which English firms were capturing the Scottish market. All Scottish firms were suffering, but the DICo had serious handicaps far beyond its counterparts in Lanarkshire. Remote in its south Ayrshire valley, the DICo had to compete with Lanarkshire firms and sell its iron in Lanarkshire, while paying 4s to 4s 6d per ton for carriage. This was a big handicap, but it had been overcome by their customers' regard for the quality of the DICo iron, for which they were willing to pay 5s to 6s per ton more than the price offered to English producers. But of late years Middlesbrough in particular had improved the quality of its iron very greatly, and this preference no longer held good. English firms also appeared to get better terms for the transport of their pig iron to Scotland—quoted as low as 6s per ton. The chairman of the DICo notes also that the cost of producing one ton of iron at the Middlesbrough works was 10s per ton less than at the DICo.

Yes, the hard fact remained that besides the handicap of the distance from its markets the DICo had a far from up-to-date plant. Surveyors who made a report on the undertaking at the time of the formation of the limited company were somewhat sparing in their praise:

> The iron works are in good, substantial repair, and have evidently been well cared for. Judged by the standard of modern works, the blast furnaces—eight in all and open-topped—are small, with stoves which can only heat the blast to a very moderate temperature, and wanting appliances for economical working that are general in Cleveland and elsewhere. The works have been very well laid out, as have also the railways, storage-places and other necessary conveniences for moving and dealing with the large masses of raw materials used and the pig iron produced. . .

Good maintenance and good intentions could not counter entirely that dragging burden of transport charges. It was naturally affecting very adversely the company's finances. About the year 1882, the chairman, writing to the factor for Craigengillan estate, states that some time before the death of Mrs McAdam Cathcart (proprietress of that estate, who died in 1878) she 'kindly reduced the lordships on the minerals we worked on her estates, and some time after her death we received notice to revert to the terms of our lease'.

The chairman then proceeds to outline the parlous condition of the company's finances and makes the following statement: 'During the last eight consecutive years we could just have paid one-half of our present lordships and received no return whatever for the large capital we have laid out at our works, which will show you at once how serious our position is.' Later in his letter the chairman gives further grave tidings: 'We may mention that at a meeting lately held by the partners of this company the advisability of blowing out our furnaces entirely and permanently was seriously considered; in which case, we should have endeavoured to pay our fixed rents out of the coal-field as now. Of course, in that case we should have dismantled the furnaces and realised what we could out of them. . . .'

Twenty-five shillings a week. No wonder it had come to that. My grandfather Smith, still at his figure of 35s a week while the men under him made four times that figure, recorded with gratitude that when wages came tumbling down his remained at his princely 35s.

Drastic action was recommended by the ironmasters of Scotland. There were extensive proposals to put certain furnaces out of blast and to close down other furnaces for a year. These proposals hinged upon the agreement of English ironmasters to do the same. Cleveland, however, refused to comply, and the scheme was not carried out, but by stress of circumstances the DICo had closed down three out of their eight furnaces by 1879.

Depression

Grandfather Smith, who had been in charge of the pits at the Dalmellington end of the undertaking was appointed general mining manager in 1884, and so moved house to Waterside, the headquarters of the company. My father, then a boy of thirteen, told me of the dejected appearance of Waterside at this time, of the great stacks of unsold pig iron built up in front of Greenhill Row bearing the bankers' labels in token of their having advanced money to the company. Grandfather Smith was strongly critical of the management at this time. Little coal was exported in those days, but they had struck an excellent house-coal in the Pennyvenie area, for which all the company's agents were continuously clamouring. Nevertheless this precious coal was being fed into the furnaces to produce iron on which 'one shilling a ton was being lost'. (I quote his figure.)

His opinions may have carried some weight, for it is just at this apparently unpropitious time that the DICo embarked upon its largest mining project to date. This was the sinking, in the early eighties, of another and larger pit some half-a-mile north of Pennyvenie No. 1. This was Pennyvenie No. 2, which was reinforced by the sinking of No. 3. The shafts of Nos. 2 and 3 were adjacent, and they shared the same screening plant, but the workings were in different areas. There was also erected at Pennyvenie No. 2 a battery of coke ovens, the coke being for furnace use, and a small plant for the washing of coal.

(6a) *No. 3 as rebuilt* 1903 *tipping slag on spur off line from furnaces to station,* c.1909. *Left to right: James Love, Fireman; Hugh Brogan, Driver; Wm Rutherford, Guard*

(6b) *No. 12 leaving for Slag Hill,* c.1907. *Left to right: Hugh Brogan, Driver; Wm Stewart, Fireman; James 'Bangor' Brown, Guard*

(7a) *No. 9 in engineer shop,* c.1895
(7b) *James Ferguson, Driver of No. 9*

New Line to Pennyvenie

With the prospect that the tonnage from this area would be more than doubled in the near future it was necessary that some better means of transport should be found than the route of the old Sillyhole Road. All traffic thereby had to go down steep gradients to the Sillyhole Road in the valley, only to be hauled up more steep gradients, with a reversing siding, to the level of the furnace bank at Waterside. Clearly a direct line from the furnace bank to the two Pennyvenie pits was indicated, and this was constructed and opened in 1884, the year in which Pennyvenie No. 2 commenced operations. The route of the new railway seems a strange one. From the contours it would appear that an extension from the Cutler Tip following the hillside west of the farm of Laight would have given a gradual ascent to the neighbourhood of Craigmark, and so by a level length to Pennyvenie. Instead, the new line diverged from the Cutler Tip line by a sharply curved junction almost on top of The Quarry Brig, and by a series of curves and a gradient of one mile at 1 in 37 reached a summit-point *north* of Laight farm, from which it had to descend for one-and-a-half miles at 1 in 44 to reach Craigmark. This extraordinary piece of mountaineering may be explained by the fact that at the summit was a drift mine, the Laight Mine, which was producing ironstone, and which the new line was designed to tap. It was scant justification for gradients which for the next forty-three years were a sore trial to the engines engaged in the working.

Craigmark No. 1 pit closed down at this period, but its screening-plant remained to deal with coal from No. 2 pit higher up the hill. The coal was brought down from No. 2 by a hutch line, crossing the Pennyvenie line on a length of track which could be raised by poles at the four corners to clear Pennyvenie traffic. The remaining Chalmerston pits, Nos. 2 and 3, were also closed. Minnivey pits had gone some twenty years before, so no more coal came now by the Sillyhole Road. The track, however, was allowed to remain, but all branches were removed save for the stump of the Pennyvenie line which, cut short at the crossing of the road to Craigmark village, formed a short siding. I am informed that the part of the Sillyhole Road extending south of the level crossing was used to load timber from the woods devastated by the great storm of 11 December 1883. This operation extended over three years, after which the road was in use only as a storage siding from the Waterside end, except for the occasional trip of an engine carrying officials.

Haste to the Wedding

This latter practice was a prominent feature of those pre-motor days. Train services were sparse, and a DICo engine was often utilised for such purposes. Even the Dalmellington parish minister made use of this form of transport. There was for many years no other minister in the parish licensed to perform the marriage ceremony. New Year's Day was about the only holiday in the worker's year, so a great number of weddings were always arranged for 31 December. There were no church weddings in those days, so the minister had to go from house to house. On 31 December the Rev G. S. Hendrie, a forthright man of commanding presence, would set out for a round of Waterside, Lethanhill, Benwhat and Craigmark, performing perhaps a dozen or fifteen wedding ceremonies in the course of an afternoon and evening. No road connected Lethanhill with Benwhat, so on 31 December the Waterside office would receive an imperious order: *'Have an engine* waiting for me at Lethanhill at 5 p.m. to convey me to Benwhat.'

So in spite of depression life went on. Gradually the prosperity in the coal trade began to lighten the darkness. Pennyvenie No. 2 proved a great success; it is still producing today. A less happy venture was a break into new territory by sinking a pit on the farm of Drumsmudden in the parish of Ochiltree. It was situated on the west side of the Ayr and Cumnock line a little to the west of Belston Junction. The coal produced was of first-rate quality—a very old engine-driver told me that he had never experienced anything so good—but there was endless trouble with faulting. Every now and then the run of the seam would be lost, and profitless work expended on exploring up and down until it could be located again. Drumsmudden never paid for anything except its sinking. It closed down in 1904.

Two of the engines were withdrawn from service and broken up during this period, the old veteran No. 1 in 1882 and No. 7, the little Slag Hill engine, in 1888. There were two new arrivals, however. Both engines were 'stock jobs', that is, engines built during quiet spells in their firms' works and put in stock to await a customer. No. 11 was seen by John Hunter during a visit to Hawthorns of Leith in 1881 and purchased by him on behalf of the company for the sum of £1,100. No. 12 was an even better bargain, for Grant, Ritchie & Co. of Kilmarnock charged only £750 for her. Both engines proved most useful workers and amply repaid the modest sums spent upon them.

Death of John Hunter

This may be the last reference in our history to John Hunter. He died, at the age of sixty-six, on 18 January 1886. He had been a good manager for his times—loud-voiced, commanding, perhaps tyrannical, but with a quality of sympathy and fair-dealing, feared perhaps by some but respected by far more. With the Houldsworths concerned more with affairs at Coltness and further afield, John Hunter* had kept Waterside going through those trying times. His heavy but steadying hand was sadly missed in the still difficult days ahead.

His successor was James P. Walker, the son of a Dalmellington land-owner, who had been employed in the drawing-office for some years. He had a big task ahead and he was not a John Hunter.

---

*John Hunter's wife was Agnes Stirling, daughter of the Rev Robert Stirling of Galston. Two of her brothers were Patrick and James Stirling, the eminent locomotive engineers.

Recovery in the Nineties

The start of another decade saw little betterment of the situation in the Scottish iron industry. Output continued to decline to an all-time low in 1895, after which there was a definite improvement. In the case of the DICo an additional difficulty had arisen. The use of steel was now well-established. The Dalmellington iron, made from the black-band ironstone, was unsuitable for steel-making. A mixture of haematite ore from Cumberland with the native product had been tried, but was either unsuccessful or insufficient in quantity. Use had to be made of ore from Spain. This was a suitable ore and obtainable in large enough quantities, but at a price. For the ore had to be shipped to some Ayrshire port and hauled thence to Waterside, an expensive process which made it still more difficult to make ends meet, let alone to show a profit. The unhealthy dependence of the Waterside furnaces upon imported supplies was borne home forcibly by the great railway strike of 1890.

The 1890 Strike

This was still a topic of conversation among railwaymen when I was a boy. It was the first major railway strike in Scotland and its effects were widespread. Even certain DICo engines and men were involved. It is with this circumstance that I have to deal.

Trouble had been brewing for a long time. Things were really very bad. For an increasing traffic the railways were short-handed. It was against the excessive hours of work rather than the very poor remuneration that the men protested. The G & SW, the principal Ayrshire railway, had its black spots, but its general picture was far more favourable than that of its two great neighbours the Caledonian Railway and the North British. These three companies alone were involved. The strike did not spread to the Highland or the Great North of Scotland.

The final declaration of war was from a meeting held in

Glasgow and presumably attended by men from all three railways. This was on Sunday 21 December 1890, when by an overwhelming majority the decision was taken to order a strike for the next day.

Other centres were not so whole-hearted in supporting strike action. A meeting held in Ayr voted thirty-four to thirty-two *against* a strike. But when Monday morning dawned, not a man of the goods and mineral crews turned out for duty. But the older passenger men were at their posts, as were most of the platform staffs, and for that day the passenger service seems to have been conducted in an almost normal fashion. Tuesday told a different tale. Men had come down from Glasgow to 'get the Ayr men out'. The signal boxes were deserted. Block working had to be suspended and such trains as still ran 'proceeded with caution'. Porters and shunters had cleared out.

Considering those conditions, a fair service of passenger trains was maintained. But things were far otherwise with the goods and mineral side. Not a wheel was turning. One goods train reached Ayr from Glasgow on the Tuesday, but only one. Half-a-dozen ships lay idle in Ayr harbour, unable to unload or receive cargoes. And, of course, the various iron works in Ayrshire were in dire straits. All their limestone and a goodly part of their iron ore came from those ports. In a few days the furnaces might require to close down.

I think that the first proposal of the DICo was that the G & SW should lend them engines to bring their limestone and ore up from Ayr harbour. These engines would be manned by DICo crews, who did not belong to any railway union. For some reason the railway company seemed reluctant to lend engines. The matter was urgent. The DICo resolved to go it alone.

DICo Engines to Ayr

Two engines were to be used. By a sad misfortune the engine best fitted for a 'long haul' of this description, No. 10, which was already covering an equal distance in her run to Coylton, was laid up for overhaul. 10's driver, Thomas Rutherford—known to all by his nickname of 'Nanny'—had the usual substitute, the little 0—4—0 saddle tank, No. 11. However, it was the best that could be done, so Nanny with No. 11 and James Ferguson with his No. 9 were given a train of coal and the Coylton brake van, and sent off to Ayr harbour. This may have been as early at the Tuesday, 23 December.

It was not a nice job. James Ferguson's family were sorely concerned for his safety. The approach to Ayr harbour was beneath a number of bridges which were most convenient for the discharge of missiles. The little DICo engines had no protecting cabs. There had been some ugly scenes with the strikers and the inevitable hooligan element which accompanied them. Older drivers remaining at work had been followed home by jeering and threatening crowds. But Ferguson and Nanny went their way and did the job and nothing happened to them.

G & SW Engines on Loan

These were two good little engines, but they were only fourteen inches of the cylinder, and the loads they could haul were limited. The DICo apparently persisted in their demand for G & SW engines, and the railway company relented. No. 143A, a Patrick Stirling 0—4—2 tender engine built by Neilson in 1866, was sent up to Waterside. True to tradition, Ayr had given them the worst that they had. 143A was in a sorry state. Ferguson got her in exchange for No. 9, and he worked the whole of that night at Waterside packing her. They resumed the run to Ayr Harbour with No. 11 piloting 143A.

If Ferguson got anywhere near Ayr shed he probably gave them his considered opinion of 143A, for later in the week he was given in exchange a much better engine. This was No. 173, a Patrick Stirling 0—6—0 tender engine of the batch built by Neilson in 1869. 143A was returned to Ayr shed, and Ferguson drove 173. Nanny continued to drive wee No. 11 throughout, and very strange she must have looked, coupled to this big main line engine.

The strike dragged on. The strain and the threats began to tell on some of the older men, and they began to absent themselves. The small efforts of the DICo men were having an effect. In the week to Thursday 25 December, Ayr harbour shipped 6,700 tons of coal. The furnaces were kept supplied. Further afield the engines of the Eglinton and other iron companies were doing similar work.

Over the weekend a change of heart seemed to set in. By the beginning of the week the surprising news came through that at Hurlford, which had been a storm-centre, there had been a great return to work. This sparked off a riot but did not deter the men from a re-start. On Tuesday 30 December, Ayr men followed suit. 'All goods drivers and firemen offered to return to their posts and with the exception of two all were re-engaged.' A few 'pointsmen' (our signalmen were always so-called by the general public) chose to remain on strike, but the local press remarked with a note of satisfaction that 'their places had been filled'.

The 1890 Strike certainly produced some good effect in calling attention to the very bad conditions of labour. It had other and less happy results, the echoes of which had hardly died down by the time that I was getting to know the railwaymen in the early 1900s. With this, however, we are not concerned here. I wish merely to record a rather outstanding episode in the history of the DICo engines and their men.

Spanish ore was also necessary because of the approaching exhaustion of the ironstone seams in the DICo pits. A return of mines operating in the year 1894 gives ironstone mining as being carried out at five places only, Nos. 1 and 2 Bowhill, Nos. 5 and 7 Corbie Craigs, and the Laight mine. Coal was being worked at Dalharco No. 2 (abandoned in that year), Jellieston No. 2, the three Pennyvenies, Sundrum and Drumsmudden, with workings on a small scale at Beoch, Benbain and Craigmark No. 2. To balance the loss of Dalharco, there was sunk in this year No. 10 Drumgrange, close to the foot of the incline, but it did not appear to prosper greatly and was abandoned after a life of only ten years.

Changes on the Board

In the mid-nineties important changes took place in the constitution of the DICo. For many years the chief shareholder had been that very able man James Murray, a relative by marriage of the Houldsworths and now advanced in years. His keen desire was to have his son in a place on the Board, and to that end he had been buying up shares until he had now the controlling interest. Soon after, he died, leaving his son James H. Murray this legacy of shares and control. In a short time, however, the younger Murray died also. His widow married in 1895 a London solicitor, William (afterwards Sir William) B. M. Bird, who thereby inherited the shares and the controlling interest.

It was fortunate for the company that William Bird was a man of broad vision and enterprise. He had become aware, probably from dealings with the elder Murray, that the DICo was sadly lacking in modern equipment and ideas. Through his influence there were brought on to the Board two outstanding men—Charles Stoddart of Stanton, Notts., who was an expert in furnace work and Dr Robert T. Moore, a prominent Scots mining engineer. Charles Stoddart succeeded William Houldsworth as chairman.

In the department of coal-mining the influence of Dr Moore was soon seen in the embarkation, in 1899, upon a very big project, the sinking of a large and deep pit north-east of Patna. It was only some half-a-mile from the defunct Dalharco No. 2, but at a higher level. The work of sinking extended over the years to 1901, when coal was found at a depth of 203 fathoms. This sinking was my grandfather Smith's final task in his official position as manager. He had come a long way since, as a shepherd boy at Garryhorn, Carsphairn, he first studied the operations of mining at the Woodhead lead mines. Aged seventy-one and having given fifty-four years' service to the DICo he now retired, and his assistant William Smith, who had also become his son-in-law, was appointed in his stead.

The Houldsworth Pit

The new pit was very fittingly named The Houldsworth, in commemoration of the family who had brought all this great industry to the Doon valley. The Houldsworth had the distinction of being the deepest pit in Ayrshire until the sinking of the Barony pit at Auchinleck ten years later.

Locomotive Famine

The revival of prosperity in the late nineties, gradual as it was, found the transport department of the DICo in a somewhat tight corner. The enlightened minds upon the Board were not apparently expected to trouble themselves about small matters like engines. These were left to the general manager. A natural parsimony had been the only method employed in the long years of depression, and about the year 1897 the results began to pile up to a near-crisis. No. 2 had been scrapped about 1890, No. 3 had never recovered from an injudicious rebuilding in the early eighties, No. 5 was at the end of her tether. No. 11 was being kept going with difficulty. Nos. 4, 6 and 10 were in urgent need of new boilers. The disastrous fire which destroyed the engineer and pattern shops on the night of 24 July 1897 added to the difficulties. Nos. 4 and 10 were reboilered by outside firms in 1898. The rest had to make do as best they could. With the prospect of heavy traffic from the new pit a new engine was an urgent necessity. But when permission for its ordering had been finally obtained the DICo found, as did several railways of Britain at this period, that builders of locomotives were booked to capacity and could take no more orders for a long time ahead. In the emergency Barclay of Kilmarnock hired to the DICo an engine built by Dick & Stevenson of Airdrie, taken in part payment from a customer. The hired engine was returned to Barclay after a brief period full of trouble. At last a builder was found who could oblige—the relatively untried firm of Gibb & Hogg, also of Airdrie. They built an engine which was delivered to Waterside in the last weeks of 1899.

In sequence, her number should have been 13, but the general manager was superstitious and vetoed this with some force. No. 5 had been scrapped some months before, so the vacant number 5 was given to the new possession. By a coincidence she was also No. 5 in the books of Gibb & Hogg. She was allocated to the Houldsworth traffic when the new pit came into production.

'The Night the Engineer Shop was Burned'

It was the night of 24 July 1897. My father was headmaster of Waterside School. He was unmarried and lived with his parents in the flat above The Store, close to the railway station. My mother's folks were in No. 1 Greenhill, a stone's throw from the nearest furnace as befitted grandfather's occupation.

My father and mother were to be married on the 29 July. No house was available in Waterside but they had obtained a flat in Dalmellington, the top flat of 'Helenbank', next to the parish church. So on the afternoon of 24 July, my father travelled to Dalmellington. His primary object was to 'give in the cries', in other words to give particulars to the session clerk in order that the proclamation of banns could be made in church on the following day. He also wanted to lay some linoleum (waxcloth they called it in those days) in his newly-acquired flat, so two of my mother's brothers, David and William Larmer, went with him to lend a hand. They got the various tasks completed and returned to Waterside by the 7.40 p.m. train ex Dalmellington.

At Waterside the Larmers asked father to come up to their house and have some supper. He would be nothing loth, I have no doubt. So it was about ten o'clock when he left Greenhill, crossed the Slag Brig, and walked down the long sloping road to the main road and the Store.

The Blowing of the Horn

He was just in the hollow before you rise to the Store when the works horn began to blow . . . at ten o'clock on a Saturday night! Father looked but could see nothing. He went up into his house. Grannie was all alone. Grandpa Smith, with his assistant my uncle Willie, were to be away all night on a big job. They were lifting the pumps from No. 4 Corbie Craigs for transfer to another pit.

Grannie met my father as he entered. Had he heard the horn? What was the matter? He could not imagine—thought someone was playing a prank. He went through to the front window, pulled aside the blind . . . the whole sky to the south was ablaze! He ran down the stair, round the corner, and away.

Back up the sloping road to the Slag Brig. As father began to rise the brae he heard other feet running. A man, going at top speed, racing up the railway line. . . Next minute my father had topped the brae and he saw the whole fury of it. The engineer shop . . . men were running from all parts.

Just in front of the furnaces it was, the engineer shop. It occupies the same place to-day. In those days, however, the pattern-making shop was in a floor above. It was in the pattern-shop that the fire had started.

Old Andrew Smith the pattern-maker had an assistant who was a smoker and a careless one at that. Several times Andrew had reproved him for matches thrown down, cigarette ends tossed away. In that tinder-house it did not take much to start a fire. Whether the assistant was responsible for the catastrophe could never be proved.

I cannot remember who first saw smoke. Investigations were made. Nothing could be seen. Then someone opened the door of the pattern-shop. In a minute the whole place was alight.

Willie Laidlaw

It was Willie Laidlaw that father had seen running up the line. Laidlaw's family kept the post office next to the station. Willie was sitting reading the evening paper when someone put his head in at the door and called 'That's the engineer shop on fire!' 'My God, my *tools*!' cried Laidlaw. He had at his bench a great kit of tools, the gathering of a long life as an engineer. Laidlaw tore up the railway, climbed the cutting-side, got in at the back door. Above him the pattern-shop was a raging inferno. Attached to the blazing wooden ceiling were the heavy shafts and pulleys, all ready to wrench away and fall. Laidlaw ignored them all, got his tool-kit and carried it out. He was the only man who saved his tools that night.

'Water, water!' was the cry. 'Get hoses!' Father got up to find Grandpa Larmer and his furnacemen collecting all the hoses from the pig-beds. There were plenty of them, but they were poor, useless things, too short, some half-burned. But Grandpa did the best he could, got them joined, end to end; lapped the joints with old bags and string, or teased-out rope, rags of any sort. They laid them out across the railway lines. Father, like many others, tended a hose-joint. He recalled that in front of him stood the scarcely recognisable figure of Alexander Gavin, Secretary to the DICo—my grand-uncle. He was stripped to his immaculate white shirt and trousers; between his knees he was holding desperately a defective hose-joint from which a cascade of water was ascending and soaking him to the skin. Up on the roof of the adjoining smithy, one dare-devil, silhouetted against the flames, sat calmly astride and threw pails of water into the blaze.

Messenger to Dalmellington

And now in the middle of all the confusion someone remembered that the general manager must be informed. J. P. Walker was spending the weekend up at Dalmellington at his father's house, Bellsbank. Word must be got to him. No telephone. The last train gone up and the stations closed for the night. An engine must be dispatched. The only one in steam would be the 'Bogie Engine' on the Slag Hill job. She was at her post, but the difficulty was the getting of her past the fire, for the line passed close to the burning shop. All hoses were hauled clear and Bob Shaw took old No. 5 round the curve as quickly as he could with safety, then down the hill to the sidings and on to the Sillyhole Road.

The old road must have been clear of wagons—probably was on a Saturday night, and away they went as fast as they could, tail-first into the wind—no cab or shelter of any kind. They had their 'big jaickets' on, stout, double-breasted pilot jackets. Something tickled Bob Shaw's neck. He brushed it away. It tickled again. He brushed it a second time. Then again. . . The fireman gave a yell. The whole back of Shaw's jacket was on fire, the flames streaming away from him like the tail of a comet. Only when one flame eddied for a moment and tickled his neck had he felt anything. When they tore off his clothes they found his 'big jaicket' and his dungaree jacket both well-burned, and the flames starting to his shirt!

Meanwhile at Waterside the work went on. But it was a hopeless task. The pressure of water was feeble at the best—now, with such a demand and such losses from leakage the amount available for fire-fighting was pitifully inadequate. The conflagràtion simply went its ruinous way until it had burned everything combustible. It was fortunate that none other of the line of shops caught fire.

Up at Corbie Craigs, high above the valley, my grandfather and my uncle, busy with their all-night task, were sorely perplexed by the ominous glow in the sky. But there were no phones or walkie-talkies in those days. Not until they tramped down to Waterside in the light of the Sunday dawn did they see the reason for their anxiety. By then there remained nothing but a litter of smoking ruins.

It was the most disastrous fire in the history of the DICo. In the pattern-shop were patterns of every piece of machinery back to the start of the works in 1847. All were destroyed. The reorganisation of the whole engineering establishment after the fire must have been an enormous task. But it was accomplished, as was many another great work.

CHAPTER 6

The Final Thirty Years

Pre - 1914

The new century dawned with, for the DICo, a quite hopeful aspect. The furnaces had been re-arranged and the plant brought nearer to modern requirements. Two furnaces had been demolished, making room for larger and more efficient stoves for the heating of the blast. The waste gases, which had hitherto flared to high heaven in spectacular but unprofitable fashion, were now trapped and made use of, partly in the new stoves and also in a new 'ammonia works' which dealt with various by-products.

The Two Davids

My maternal grandfather David Larmer, who had been manager of these furnaces since 1873, retired in 1901. It was strange that both of my grandfathers should have retired in the same year. They were both men of strong character and great integrity, both thoroughly practical men who knew every move of the work to which they directed others. Grandfather Smith retired to Dalmellington, Grandfather Larmer to Ayr. The community of Waterside lost thus two of its number who had been pillars of strength to their village life and institutions.

Decline of Iron

So the furnaces remained the high light of the DICo picture, but at a heavy expense. The little ironstone pits up on The Hill were being extinguished one by one. By 1905 only the

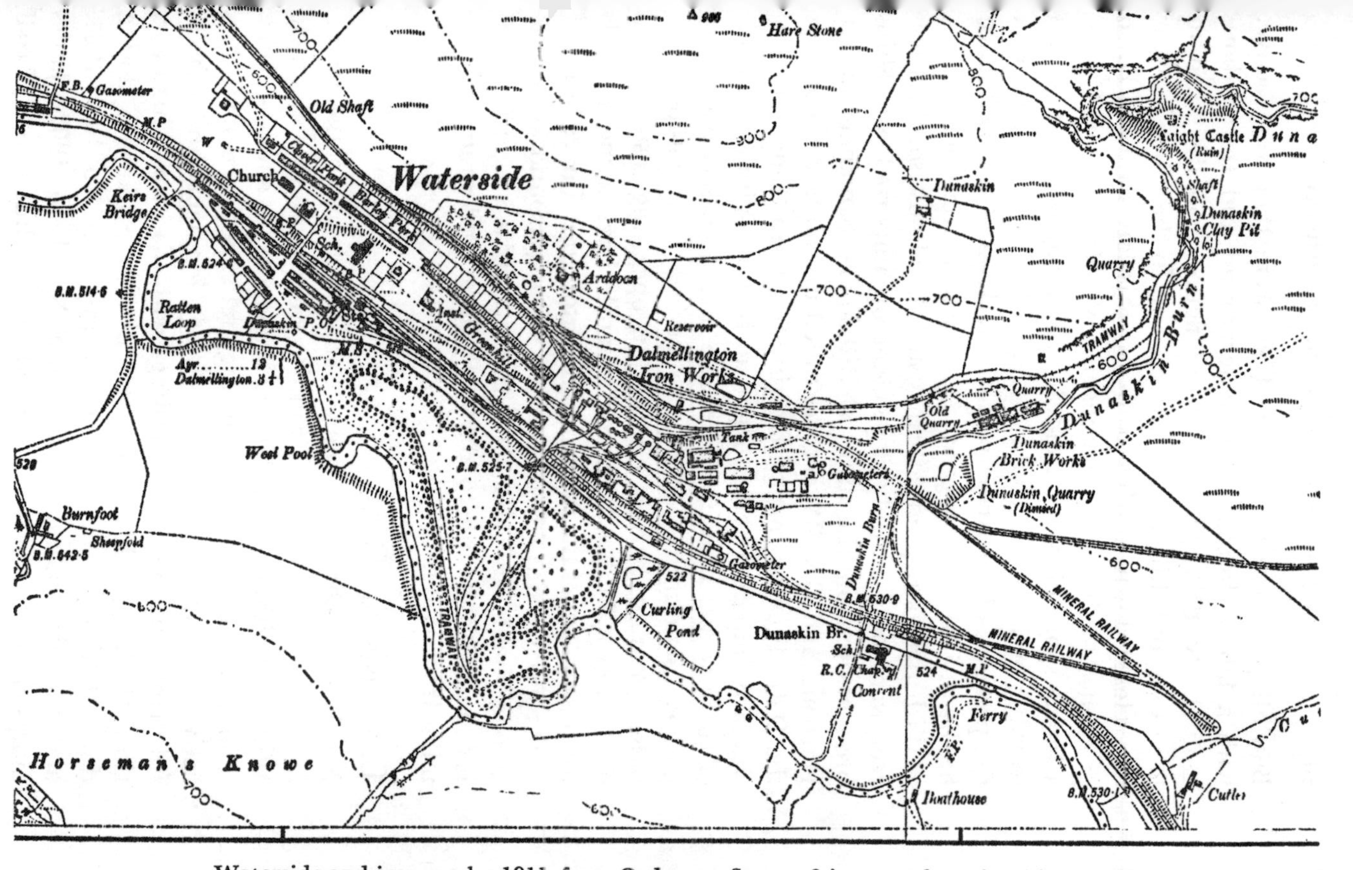

Waterside and iron works, 1911, from Ordnance Survey 6-in map, sheet Ayrshire XLVI.
(Crown Copyright reserved) Scale of above reproduction approx. 5.5-in per mile.

Bowhill pits were producing. They were then very active, with a labour force of 233 underground and thirty above ground. By 1912, however, these figures had dwindled to ninety-six and thirteen respectively and in the following year they closed down. Rather oddly, at this late date the DICo proceeded to sink another ironstone pit, No. 8 Corbie Craigs, a lonely spot north-east from the village of Benwhat. It was working by 1908 but trouble developed—it was thought from the presence of a near-by volcanic neck—and it closed down finally in 1919, having produced very little ironstone.

With the local product exhausted, or almost so, the furnaces were now entirely dependent on imported ore. Ships brought ore from the mines of Bilbao and Santander to Ayr Harbour, and G & SW engines toiled up the heavy grades of the Dalmellington line with train after train. Limestone was similarly imported and brought up by rail. With equal loads of coal and pig iron in the reverse direction, relatively prosperous communities supporting actively the not-too-lavish passenger train service, and the low operating costs of those days, even a Dr Beeching could hardly have found grounds for the closure of the Ayr-Dalmellington line. I have heard of *four* special trains with limestone milling around Waterside at one time! And this on a line which is single from its junction with the line to Maybole, Girvan and Stranraer, nine miles from Waterside.

Emphasis on Coal

No. What profits were being made were not in the manufacture of iron, but in the winning of coal. In this my uncle William Smith, General Mining Manager, was a master hand. Thoroughly equipped by learning and experience, he had an active, eager mind, alive to all new developments, and a cheerful, happy manner in his dealings with his men. This was a time of change. The older coal pits were likewise closing down, Jellieston No. 2 in 1902, Drumgrange No. 10 in 1904, and the old stalwart Pennyvenie No. 1 in 1907. James Simpson, pitheadman, had tipped the first hutch-load of coal

(8a) *No. 4 on furnace bank,* c.1894. *Driver (on footplate) Robert Frew. On front of engine (sitting) John Ireland; Robert Young (standing). On ground, left to right: John Weir, Adam Ferguson, Robert Ferguson, Wm McDonald, Wm Weir (Foreman on bank), Thos Ireland, Hugh Brogan, Wm McGraw, Robert Kirk (boy in weighhouse), James Geddes, Wm Hamilton, Alex Young*

(8b) *No.* 5 (II) *on furnace bank,* c.1900-1901. *Left to right: Joseph Hawthorn, Alex Young, Alex Campbell, Wm Boyd, Wm Rutherford, Adam Ferguson, James Bryden, James Geddes, Thos Rowan, Wm Hamilton, Thos Ireland, John Ireland, Alex Beattie, Robert Frew, John Weir (first Driver of No.* 5(II)), *Wm McGraw*

BARCLAY SIXTEEN-INCH

(9a) *No. 16* (1910). *No. 14 was similar*
(9b) *No. 19* (1918)

which came out of it in 1868. He drew the rails out of it in 1908.

Now various boring operations carried out in the fifties and sixties in the region north-east of Dalmellington had failed to locate coal in any paying quantity. This confirmed a theory held by my grandfather when he was mining manager. He was of opinion that volcanic activity during the formation of Ben Beoch had destroyed all coal measures in its vicinity. Of late years, however, it had been discovered that one of the borers had been guilty of inaccurate, if not actually dishonest work, and that this might not be the true story. Boring operations were resumed and before long a very large field of coal was discovered. So in the year 1910 there was commenced the driving of a very large drift mine at a point about one mile north-east of old Pennyvenie No. 1. This was producing by 1912 and had soon a large output. A standard-gauge railway line was constructed from railhead at No. 1 to the 'Big Mine', which received the official title of Pennyvenie No. 4.

In justice to the suspected borer it may be mentioned that in the driving of Pennyvenie No. 4 they came upon one of his bore-holes. This one at least was genuine. The unlucky man had missed the coal by a matter of inches!

When the Big Mine opened the Beoch hutch-line was switched to deliver its coal to this new screening-plant. At the same time a new haulage system was introduced, both in the Big Mine and on the 'Beoch Road'. The latter was doubled throughout, and both were worked on the endless rope system. The rope, driven by an electric motor, went out by the one road and back by the other, moving at a speed of about three miles an hour. The hutches were clipped to the moving rope individually as they came to hand. We thought it was strange to see these little dots moving slowly across the moor without any visible means of propulsion.

All these new developments were a far cry from the early days when the Houldsworths first cut the turf in the Doon valley. The last of the family left the Board of the DICo in December 1906, when Joseph Henry Houldsworth of Rozelle,

Ayr, resigned. Control was now in the hands of that capable trio, Charles Stoddart, William Bird and Dr Moore, and there was little link with the Houldsworth family. In the same year the general manager, James P. Walker, retired. He was succeeded by Alexander Gavin, who had been secretary to the company for thirty years.

Alexander Gavin was a man of fine appearance and dignity of bearing. As secretary, general manager and managing director successively he served the company faithfully and well. It is a pity that a strange stiffness of manner coupled, I think, with a certain shyness, prevented any easy friendship with his workpeople. Silent, absorbed in his thoughts, he went his way through the works, speaking to few. His wife had died in 1904. He must have had a lonely life in his house, 'Arddoon', on the hill above the iron works. He was my grand-uncle. My grandmother Larmer was his sister. I scarcely knew him until, during the First World War, I had to visit him on business of Dalmellington Parish Council, of which he was chairman. He treated me then with a quiet kindness which I like to remember.

Modern Motive Power

In those early days of the century there was need of improvement in transport. The veteran engines were still hard at work. The heavy coal-traffic from Pennyvenie was being wrestled over the Laight Brae by No. 4 of 1858 and No. 9 of 1871. Even No. 3 of 1856 received in 1903 an extensive overhaul and renewal. But much more modern power was required, so in 1906 Barclays of Kilmarnock supplied one of their 16-in 0—4—0 saddle tanks. This engine, No. 14, was very successful, and when she was joined in 1910 by No. 16, a sister engine, the Pennyvenie Road was more adequately provided for. In 1909 there had come No. 15, rather unusual in being one of the limited number of engines built by Markham & Co. of Chesterfield. No. 15, in a colourful livery of gamboge, went to The Hill to replace that other English engine, No. 6. And then at last the great step was taken. From four-coupled the DICo was to advance to six-coupled. In August 1913 Barclay delivered No. 17, a standard 0—6—0 side-tank with 18-in cylinders, weighing no less than forty-five tons in working order, twelve tons more than her Barclay colleagues Nos. 14 and 16. She was and is a most successful engine.

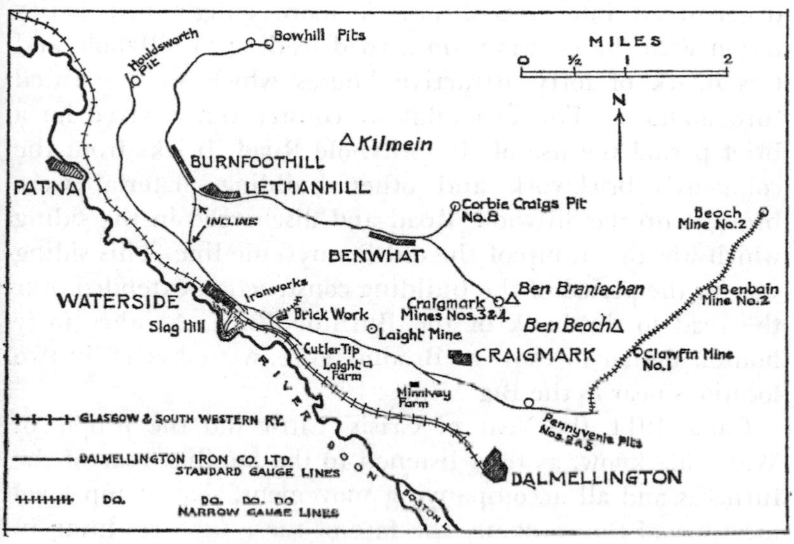

The DICo railway system, 1910

The scrapping of three old engines, No. 11 in 1906, No. 6 in 1911, and No. 8 in 1912 had left the company short of engines which could work through the Quarry Brig, so in 1913 Barclay supplied also a 14-in 0—4—0 saddle-tank with boiler mountings and cab cut down to a minimum for the negotiation of the constricted tunnel. This engine was numbered 18.

Numbering of Furnaces

The furnaces had been numbered northwards from the blast engine house, Nos. 1 to 7. No. 8 was inserted between the engine house and No. 1. Later, Nos. 2 and 3 were demolished, leaving the final arrangement 7, 6, 5, 4, stoves 1, 8.

Modern Housing

With so much work at the Dalmellington end of the parish housing problems were arising there, and in 1903 the company erected its first houses in Dalmellington. These were brick tenement buildings named 'Knoweview'—ugly raw things with the minimum of amenities. Not unnaturally they degenerated into near-slums. A more enlightened policy began with the erection, on a road leading to Sillyhole and Craigmark of forty attractive houses which were entitled 'Broomknowe'. The Broomknowe construction revived for a brief period the use of the Sillyhole Road. Bricks from the company's brickwork and other building material were brought up the Sillyhole Road and discharged in the siding which was the stump of the old Pennyvenie line. This siding was for the period of the building construction extended over the road to the bank of the Burnton Burn. Another forty houses, similar to those at Broomknowe, were erected in two locations near to the Big Mine.

Came 1914, the Year of Crisis. Little did the people of Waterside know, as they listened to the familiar roar of the furnaces and all accompanying movement, that at top level meetings of the company the fate of those furnaces hung in the balance. Not for much longer could they be kept going on a vain hope of better things. Then in August 1914 came the bolt from the blue. WAR. With its advent the company stayed its hand.

War and Strife

Truly the scene had changed for the DICo. Their products were suddenly in great demand, and at a good price. If there were wage demands they could now be met out of greater financial resources. There were few distractions for firms far inland in this First World War. The company had but to gird its loins and get on with the task in hand. The only large war operation which came to the Doon valley brought benefit to the DICo.

In the year 1916 the construction of a 'School of Aerial

Gunnery' was begun at Loch Doon. It was a scheme far exceeding the knowledge or capacity of the constantly changing personnel to whom it was entrusted. After two years of heavy expenditure no part of the project had reached completion when by another governmental whim the whole labour force was withdrawn and the enterprise abandoned. But to the DICo it had brought much engineering work, they being the only engineering firm in the neighbourhood. The scheme required also much electricity. Before the war, the DICo had contemplated the construction of an electric power station. In 1917, by a joint agreement with the government, the building of this power station was carried out. It was a large and modern installation, erected to the east of the Waterside furnaces. The power station remained and was used by the DICo and its successors until transfer to the grid system in 1956.

Another by-product of the Loch Doon scheme was an enlargement of the railway siding accommodation at Dalmellington. The terminal part of the old Sillyhole Road was relaid and incorporated in a new loop line whose northern entrance points were to be operated from the little signal-box at Sillyhole crossing. But, like the Loch Doon scheme itself, this scheme fell through; the points were never connected, and after some fifteen or twenty years they were removed and the loop lifted. In the 1930s the Sillyhole Road itself was cut back to buffer-stops at the underbridge leading to Laight farm. It is now still further curtailed to the Cutler overbridge.

In the middle of the war period an old servant went to the scrap-heap: No. 4, the wonder engine of 1858. Her old Hawthorn companion No. 10 was pretty far gone, but managed to struggle on at the diminishing Coylton job until October 1918, when two long-expected new engines arrived. No. 19 was another of Barclay's standard 16-in 0—4—0 saddle tanks. No. 20 was a nice little 14-in 0—4—0 saddle tank from Hawthorn, Leslie of Newcastle. She replaced No. 10 on the Coylton Road—strange indeed that after forty-four years a Hawthorn of Newcastle should replace a Hawthorns of Leith.

Then the war ended and troubles far greater than those of the period of conflict began to assail the DICo. The demand for iron and coal fell, and after the necessary replenishment and reconstruction had been carried out by industries at home and abroad, it fell even more alarmingly. Arrears of maintenance were equally apparent at the DICo's works, and the cost of materials had soared enormously. Wages began to recede after the war-time boom. There was much industrial unrest. In October 1920 the DICo miners joined a national strike which lasted some three weeks. The demand for iron fell still further. By March 1921, with the threat of another strike in the coal industry looming ahead, the DICo at last took the final sad decision. The furnaces were blown down, never to be lit again.

Waterside Tragedy

It came as a terrible blow to the people of Waterside. Coal and ironstone pits had closed time after time, but always the industry was continuing and there was easy transfer to another pit. But this was different. Furnacemen were a race apart. They were skilled in their own trade; they knew no other. Not only had their works gone, their whole industry was toppling. Away in their isolated valley there was no other work to which they could turn. A few got employment as common labourers here and there, but work was scarce everywhere. For the majority it was a case of unemployment benefit, and when that had run its allotted course, public assistance. The nearest places of payment were at Dalmellington, three miles away. There were no buses; they could not afford the train fare. So they walked. My father, in his school at the north end of Dalmellington, was moved to tears by the sight of the pathetic weekly procession of men whom in his Waterside days he had known in their pride of manhood and vigour, now grown old and grey, weary and hopeless. The minister of Waterside, the Rev John Cadenhead, an odd little man at whom some had mocked, left himself hardly enough to keep body and soul together, that he might help his stricken people. 'I am afraid,' he said to my mother with an apologetic smile, 'that we are getting rather shabby.'

Nor could the coal industry help. The threatened strike began on 1 April 1921, and through all those lovely months of May and June the pits stood idle. Men and employers, geared up to high wages and profits in war-time, could not bring themselves down to face the grim fact that customers would not pay the necessarily high price. A spirit of reckless militancy, probably stemming from the war, raised its ugly head. In former strikes it had been a point of honour that the safety-men, those workers who kept the pits free of water, gas, and roof-falls, should be left at work. Now these were peremptorily withdrawn, an act of suicidal sabotage which in some parts of the country ruined many pits entirely and left the miners without work indefinitely. In the case of the DICo, the managerial and office staffs kept the safety services going. There were threats and some intimidation by the hotheads, but the pits did not suffer. Work resumed in July, but the problems had not been solved and there was no lasting peace.

Changes of Management

It was a trying time for a general manager. Alexander Gavin, who in 1914 was approaching eighty years of age, intended to retire and it was anticipated that William Smith, General Mining Manager, would succeed him. The outbreak of war delayed matters, then unfortunately William Smith fell ill and died in September 1918. Alexander Gavin remained in office till the following year, when he was succeeded by William Dalrymple.

William Dalrymple, a brother of that very successful manager of Glasgow Corporation Tramways, James Dalrymple, was a modest man who did not court popularity. On his devoted head there was heaped abuse for matters which were quite outside his control. But he kept faithfully at work throughout this time of trouble and achieved gradually a reputation for fair dealing and attention to duty which was well deserved.

Despite the unrest in the mining world the company's coal workings were not allowed to languish. Craigmark Nos. 3 and 4 had worked out their modest seams but new developments were promised by the opening up of Chalmerston No. 4, a drift mine close to the Craigmarks but intended to tap the Chalmerston seam. This was followed by no fewer than three adjacent mines.

When the furnaces closed down the coke ovens at Pennyvenie Nos. 2 and 3 were likewise discontinued, as was the small coal-washing plant. Washed coal was now a necessity for the general market, and a large new plant was erected in 192[illegible] near the farm of Burnton, adjacent to the village of Craigmark.

Naturally, in this period of depression, there had been little addition to the engine stock. A rather inexplicable purchase had been that of a small engine from Grant, Ritchie of Kilmarnock. This, No. 21, was delivered in October 1920. Like No. 18 she had boiler-mountings cut down to the minimum to fit the Quarry Brig, a cab being omitted altogether. No. 21 was apparently intended to replace No. 3 on the Slag Hill workings, but the closure of the furnaces six months after her arrival left her virtually without a job. Then in April 1923 the company received from Barclay a fitting companion for the solitary No. 17 of ten years previously. The new engine, No. 22, was similar in boiler and cylinders to No. 17 but was given water-tanks of considerably larger capacity. Two old stalwarts departed at this period. No. 3, of 1856, was scrapped in 1924. No. 10, after lying derelict for some five years, was broken up in 1923.

So the work of the DICo went on while, in all the country round, wordy warfare was waged over the grievances of the miners. Gradually it became apparent that something bigger than a strike of one set of workers was threatening. The term 'General Strike' was being freely used throughout the whole of the country during the final days of April. On 3 May 1926 the storm broke, and the general strike of all unions became a reality.

The General Strike

It was truly a major crisis, yet the General Strike itself left the DICo relatively unaffected. Once more the safety men at the pits were withdrawn; once more the salaried staff undertook this unaccustomed work; once more there were threats and a few 'incidents'. Then in ten days the General Strike was over, and once more the weary business of the Coal Strike dragged on alone. Once more the miners spent those days of a glorious summer as they saw fit. Many of them went off on long tramps of exploration in the hill-country to the south. But the months passed, and autumn began to bring chill winds. No settlement had been reached in those months of negotiation in London. In twos and threes men began to drift back to the pits. In early December there was a general resumption of work. The economic situation was now worse than ever, but the company held on and no pit was closed.

End of the Dalmellington Iron Company

In the circumstances prevailing at the end of 1926 the DICo might have been forgiven for adopting a policy of 'wait and see'. Instead, they embarked upon what is probably the biggest piece of railway construction in their history. For many, many years the engines of the DICo had toiled up those exhausting gradients of the Pennyvenie line, so unnecessary now that there was no Laight mine and now that coal no longer went to the furnace bank. Conditions had changed completely since 1884. So a new line was planned, diverging from the old one near the Burnton washing-plant. Deep cutting was necessary to pass behind Minnivey farm; then by a sweeping curve the line kept westward of Laight and descended alongside the main line to a set of sidings newly installed by the London, Midland & Scottish Railway, successors to the G & SW, and known as Cutler sidings. From Craigmark to Cutler the line descended at 1 in 66, a heavy gradient but an improvement upon the 1 in 37 and 1 in 44 of the old line. On the new formation the gradient was 'with the load'; only the empties had to be brought uphill. The new line was in use by the spring of 1927.

Craigmark village was now but a memory. In 1924, the DICo erected, on a fine situation near the farm of Burnton, a new village of eighty-eight houses. This village was entitled Burnton, and to it the people of Craigmark were transferred and their old village demolished. Few can have imagined that this was the beginning of the end for all those DICo villages.

In truth it could not be said that the DICo, beset as they were with many difficulties, were sparing in the outlay of their capital. Their coalfields were being steadily developed and the output kept well up. Craigmark Nos. 3 and 4 had ended their quiet little lives but Chalmerston Nos. 4, 5 and 6 were flourishing. By 1930, these Chalmerston mines were giving work to something over 250 men. Pennyvenie No. 6, a drift mine, was rising in importance; on the hill just west of Dalmellington, a new mine, Bogton, was in process of driving. This was the only coal working which was ever within *sight* of Dalmellington town. Its coal was taken by a rather ugly overhead ropeway to the Burnton washer, where it was screened and put on rail. There was plenty of work. The difficulty was that it yielded insufficient profit. For two years at the end of the 1920s better times appeared to loom ahead, then came further disaster. The great financial collapse of 1929 seemed at first a catastrophe affecting America alone. By the next year its repercussions were felt throughout the whole world. Great firms, with resources far in excess of those which our Doon valley firm could command, were collapsing. By 1930 the Dalmellington Iron Company Limited had reached the end of the road.

Enter Bairds

It was the much larger concern of William Baird & Company Limited which came to the rescue of the coal industry of the Doon valley. Bairds had always been the ruling power in eastern Ayrshire, but that was only a part of their many and greater interests in central Ayrshire and Lanarkshire. They were a powerful and well-equipped company. Under their direction a new company was formed and titled 'Bairds & Dalmellington Limited', to purchase the assets of the DICo, to combine them with their own, and to continue the work of the DICo as part of this great new undertaking.

In October 1931 the terms of the agreement were announced. Actually three former companies were involved—the DICo, Bairds, and a subsidiary of the latter, Sanquhar & Kirkconnel Collieries Limited. The new company was to acquire as from 1 July 1931 all railways, rolling stock, lands, minerals, house properties, leases and subsidiary undertakings of the vendor companies, together with the three iron works owned by Bairds—Eglinton, Lugar and Muirkirk. Collieries and auxiliary subjects were to be taken over on a basis fixed by the profits of 1929 and 1930. Lands and minerals were to be valued to the mutual satisfaction of the parties.

The consideration for the sale of the assets to be transferred to the new company was £469,832. Of this, the DICo could contribute only £74,195. The authorised share capital of Bairds & Dalmellington Limited was £1,750,000, all in ordinary shares of £1 each. The Dalmellington Iron Company Limited were to cease operations and to go into liquidation. Shareholders would get six new shares for every existing five ordinary shares. In addition, it was estimated that the liquidator would be able to pay in cash not less than 7s in respect of each ordinary DICo share. Preference shares would be repaid in cash at par.

The directors and shareholders of the DICo had these terms presented to them at an extraordinary general meeting held in the Merchants' Hall, George Square, Glasgow, on 23 October 1931. The terms were approved. The final composition of the Board was as follows:

Sir Wm B. M. Bird, London, chairman.
Dr Robert T. Moore, Glasgow.
James A. Clarke, Annbank, Ayrshire.
Charles Ker, LL.D., C.A., Glasgow.
David Cooper, Glasgow.

Nothing remained of the iron works or its ancillaries, but in October 1931 the following were producing coal:

	Men employed	
PITS	Underground	On surface
Houldsworth	219	78
Pennyvenie Nos. 2 and 3	288	56
MINES		
Pennyvenie No. 4	180	45
Pennyvenie No. 5	16	3
Pennyvenie No. 6	80	11
Beoch Nos. 2 and 3	90	39
Clawfin No. 2	58	4
Chalmerston Nos. 4, 5 and 6*	215	59
Bogton	48	11
Sundrum No. 3	111	32

Eleven engines remained in the stock of the DICo in 1931—Nos. 5 (II), 12, 14, 15, 16, 17, 18, 19, 20, 21 and 22. The old hero No. 9 had been scrapped in 1928.

* Chalmerston No. 6 was a *pit*.

CHAPTER 7

The Sequel

Bairds and Dalmellington Limited

The new company, successfully floated, took over the business of the Dalmellington coalfield with much increased resources. Trade was brisk. In 1930 1,274,665 tons of coal were exported from Ayr harbour. Some 850,000 tons went to Northern Ireland and 170,000 tons to foreign destinations. A goodly proportion of this came from the Doon valley. There was no lack of orders. The difficulty was still the problem of making a profit.

Bairds & Dalmellington did not make any spectacular changes. The first task was to overtake certain arrears of maintenance, then to examine certain schemes for the development of the coalfield. These had been prepared by the DICo, but their financial position had made it impossible to proceed further.

The first scheme concerned the exploiting, on a profitably large scale, of the great area of coal north-east of the Pennyvenie operations. This began in a somewhat unspectacular way by the gradual expansion of the mines at Beoch. In 1933 one hundred and fifty men were employed there. In 1947 the number had risen to three hundred and thirty-five. A further mine was erected at Chalmerston—No. 7. B & D were also active in other areas, and two of their acquisitions may be mentioned as they affected the destinies of certain DICo engines. In the early 1930s Mauchline Collieries were taken over, and about the same period there came into the combine a mine at Rankinston in which anthracite had been worked at somewhat intermittent periods.

Another step in modernisation was the replacement of the coal washing plant which the DICo had installed near Craigmark. This had never been a very satisfactory installation and a new and large plant was constructed on a much more central site adjacent to Cutler Sidings at Waterside. In order to enter the washing plant sidings direct from Pennyvenie, a connection, mostly in cutting, was laid to link up with the old line to the Cutler Tip.

New Brickwork

It was necessary also to modernise the brick-making plant. The brickwork had certainly been erected no further in time than 1908, but it was small. Down in its narrow glen there was no room for expansion, and the only access was through the restricting Quarry Brig. The demand for bricks was rising rapidly. The site of the former furnaces, cleared of all but the massive pile of the blast engine-house of 1847, was chosen. On this a large and modern brickwork was erected. Many refuse 'bings', particularly of the ironstone pits, were drawn upon for supplies of brick-making material. A great deal of the output went by road.

Sub-Standard Houses

The activities of the County Council in rehousing tenants of houses declared sub-standard were responsible in great part for the demand for bricks. A much higher standard in matters of accommodation, water supply and sanitation was now in force. This yardstick found a great many of the B & D houses sadly lacking. In addition there had, through the difficult years, been much neglect of upkeep. To bring the houses up to modern requirements would have entailed very great expense. Already through County Council rating B & D were subsidising housing to a very substantial extent. It was more profitable to continue this payment and leave to the County Council the provision of new housing for the inhabitants of villages declared sub-standard.

Rehousing had begun by the transfer of Craigmark's population to Burnton in 1924. In the late thirties the poor little houses at Beoch, a legacy of the Nithsdale Iron Company, were evacuated and the inhabitants transferred to new housing schemes in Dalmellington. A new group of County Council houses was erected at Polnessan one mile north of Patna, and these took the people of Kerse and Tongue Row,

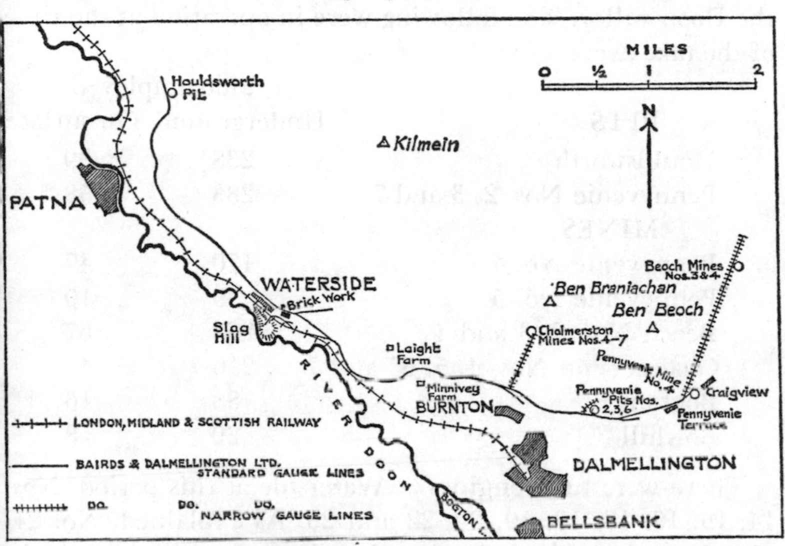

Bairds & Dalmellington railway system

which were demolished. A start had been made with the clearance of Benwhat when in 1939 came the Second World War.

War Once More

I think it would be true to say that this second great war had less effect upon the industries of the Doon valley than had the first. There was no enemy action in this area. Troops came and went upon exercises, but no camp was established. The company went on with the winning of coal and the making of bricks unchecked. There was a plentiful demand for both, so much so that 250 young men on national service who had been directed to the mining industry were brought in. A hostel was erected for them in the glebe of Dalmellington manse half-a-mile from Pennyvenie Nos. 2 and 3.

The Second World War ended in 1945. No doubt the post-war period would have brought its grave problems, but B & D were soon to be relieved of those. In 1946 there was constituted the National Coal Board, and on 1 January 1947 the new body assumed command of all coal-mining activities in the Doon valley. The following were in operation at the time of the take-over:

	Men employed	
PITS	Underground	On surface
Houldsworth	238	39
Pennyvenie Nos. 2, 3 and 7	283	58
MINES		
Pennyvenie No. 4	170	47
Pennyvenie No. 5	59	10
Beoch Nos. 2, 3 and 4	268	67
Chalmerston Nos. 4, 5, 6* and 7	216	41
Bogton	88	16
Bowhill	29	8

There were nine engines at Waterside at this period. Nos. 14, 15, 16, 17, 18, 19, 20, 22 and 23. As explained, No. 21, after her advent in 1920, found little to do and was sold in 1932 to a firm of chemical manufacturers in Leith. In 1934 No. 5 (II) was transferred to B & D's Mauchline Collieries, while No. 12 went to Rankinston in 1937 to work traffic from the anthracite mine. The decline in numbers was due in part to the closing down of two lines which had the virtue of age but scarcely that of economy. The Burnfoothill lines, together with the picturesque incline, had for some years been handling only the moderate output from the Craigmark/Chalmerston mines. Now a double-line of narrow-gauge track, with haulage by endless rope, was laid down the hillside from the mines to the screens at Burnton, scarcely a mile away, and the long round-about *via* the incline was eliminated. The far-

* Chalmerston No. 6 was a *pit*.

away Sundrum pit, with its long haul to Potterston Junction, could not now justify its existence; it was closed down in 1934 and the railway with it.

There was, however, a new-comer to the Waterside shed. B & D's Eglinton Iron Works at Kilwinning had closed down in the very early 1920s. For some years one of their engines, No. 6, a neat little product of Grant, Ritchie, had lain idle. In 1937 she was brought to Waterside, and after certain overhaul was re-numbered 23 in the Waterside stock and set to work. She is still in working order and has proved a most useful engine.

The National Coal Board

For the Doon valley coalfield the outlook had changed completely. No longer had private owners, with one eye on dividends, to scrimp and save and give up many a good scheme for lack of money. With the backing of the Treasury the new organisation could go ahead to modernise and develop in ways most desirable but hitherto beyond reach. A policy of reform was pursued with the utmost vigour; soon conditions of service were available such as the miners of the district had never known. With wage rates stepped-up to equal or better those of corresponding industries, men in their work had never known it so good.

Re-Housing

It was very soon equally good in their homes. The process of transferring Benwhat's population began again about the year 1948. By 1951 the last of its sturdy race had left their mountain cottages for the new houses of Bellsbank. Next, the much larger community of Burnfoothill-Lethanhill had to be transplanted. For them there were houses in the new district adjacent to Patna village. In April 1954 the folks of 'The Hill' had been moved down to the valley. Finally, and rather slowly, Waterside was cleared, its inhabitants going mainly to Patna. Two of the more modern sets of houses, however, were permitted to remain at Waterside.

For administrative purposes the first title adopted for the Doon valley coalfield was 'Ayr and Dumfries Area; Sub-Area Dalmellington'. By 1951 the Sub-Area is referred to as 'Dunaskin'. By 1952, the Ayr and Dumfries district had been divided in two, with titles 'West Ayr' and 'East Ayr' respectively. This arrangement continued until 1964, when the two districts were re-amalgamated with the name 'Ayrshire'.

Sweeping Changes

With the area as its unit the NCB proceeded to centralise. All engineering work, with the exception of some on-the-spot maintenance, was concentrated in two large and modern establishments. That for West Ayr was at Glenburn, Prestwick; East Ayr's centre was at Lugar.

A number of transfers of engines took place under NCB management. The first to go was the short-funnelled No. 18 (I), which went to the New Cumnock district. No. 15, the Markham engine, followed her some time after. Neither engine ever returned to Waterside, and both were withdrawn in the early 1950s. Both of the early Barclay engines, 14 and 16, were transferred. No. 14 went to the great new sinking at Killoch in 1954. No. 16 went in 1956 to Mauchline, apparently to replace No. 5 (II), which had been scrapped in the previous year. No. 20 was another migrant to Mauchline about this time.

These transfers would have left Waterside rather shorthanded, but two new 'standard Barclay sixteen-inch' were sent there in 1947 and 1951. These were numbered 1 and 21 respectively, these being numbers which presumably were not duplicated within the area. Then in 1953 came another 0—6—0 side-tank from Barclays. Except for certain details she is similar in capacity to No. 22, receiving the number 8.

In 1955 there arrived at Waterside an engine which had belonged to the Coltness Iron Company and which, I am informed, had not previously entered NCB service. She was a large and ungainly 0—6—0 side-tank with *inside* cylinders, another product of Barclays. This Coltness No. 3 had not, I gather, been very popular at Coltness, and as West Ayr No. 18 she has not improved her reputation at Waterside.

No. 14 remained at Killoch until the sinking had been completed, when she returned to Waterside and put in some three years' work before she was scrapped in 1964.

In that year the forming of East and West Ayr into one area was found to produce duplication of numbering among the engines, and two of the Waterside stock were renumbered. No. 1 became No. 10, while No. 8 was given the number 24. In 1965 this engine was fitted by Barclays with a Giesl ejector. There are therefore eight engines now stationed at Waterside, Nos. 10, 17, 18†, 19, 21, 22, 23 & 24. They are now excellently housed in a shed erected in 1964, a long-overdue replacement of a cramped little edifice which had been out-of-date in the nineteenth century.

Great and sweeping changes in mining installations marked those years of NCB operation. Costs and figures were judged without sentiment and all non-productive pits cut away. Two large schemes were put through successfully and are bearing fruit. One was for a large new shaft at Pennyvenic Nos. 2 and 3. This new shaft was numbered 7, and gradually replaced No. 3. Then on the site of the former Burnton washing plant a large new mine was driven. Its two components were numbered and named Minnivey 4 and 5. The final list of coal-producing installations shows with startling clarity the changed order:

	Men employed	
PITS	Underground	On surface
*Houldsworth	185	39
Pennyvenie Nos. 2 and 7	623	95
MINES		
Beoch Nos. 2 and 4	352	90
Minnivey Nos. 4 and 5	405	59

* Closed 10 December 1965.
† Scrapped 1966.

CHAPTER 8

Dalmellington Iron Company Transport

Railways

As soon as the DICo was established in the Doon valley, railways were laid down to link up the various works. These were partly standard gauge (4 ft 8½-in), and partly of a narrower gauge. The narrow-gauge at present employed is one of 2 ft 10-in, and as far as I can trace this dimension has not been altered since I knew these lines. The exception was Houldsworth pit where, above and below ground, a gauge of 2 ft was in use.

Standard Gauge Lines

In the vicinity of the furnaces at Waterside there was an extensive network of these lines. From them lines radiated to the various pits. Connection was made at Waterside with the Ayr-Dalmellington line of the G & SW Railway.

The lines at Waterside may be summarised as follows:

(1) *The furnace bank.* These lines were on a space cut out from the hillside and on a level with the tops of the furnaces. Coal, ironstone and limestone were brought to the bank and unloaded on to flat iron plates. From these, large iron barrows conveyed the materials to the furnace mouth.

(2) *The pig iron beds.* At the foot of the furnaces. A line adjacent to these conveyed the pig iron to the main line.

(3) *The slag bays.* Here the slag from each furnace was collected and taken to the Slag Hill. These lines crossed the pig-iron line at right angles.

(4) *The brickwork.*

(5) *The connections to the main line.* One line ran direct from the pig-iron line to Waterside station. Here, until Cutler Sidings were laid down about 1927, all out-going traffic was assembled and marshalled. There was a further connection to the main line some 52 chains south of Waterside station. At this point a four-lever ground frame, its hut bearing the name *Dunaskin,* controlled a connecting cross-over. This ground frame was unlocked by the Waterside-Dalmellington tablet.

The principal lines connecting the ironworks to the pits were:

(1) *The Sillyhole Road.* In use 1849-86. 2.2 miles. What was afterwards the main line was used until 1859, when a new line parallel to the old was constructed.

(2) *The Pennyvenie Road.* Opened 1884 to replace the Sillyhole Road. About 4 miles.

(3) *The Dalharco Road.* 2.5 miles. From north end of furnace bank. First to Jellieston No. 2 in the late 1860s, then to Dalharco No. 2. The latter closed 1894. A new branch opened from this line at Jellieston to the new pit at Houldsworth about 1899.

(4) *Cutler Sidings to Burnton.* About 2 miles. Constructed 1927 to supersede the first two miles of the 1884 Pennyvenie Road. The remainder of that route still in use.

(5) *The Carnochan Road.* 2.5 miles. By main line of G & SW Railway to Patna, then by branch descending steeply and crossing River Doon. 1858-75.

(6) *The Coylton Road.* By main line of G & SW Railway to Potterston Junction, 6.5 miles, then 5.5 miles over the DICo line to pits in the Coylton area. 1865-1935.

(7) *The lines on the Burnfoothill-Benwhat 'plateau'.* These consisted at first of branches splaying out from the top of the old Drumgrange incline and serving various pits. There was no connection with the incline serving Corbie Craigs pit. The reorganisation which occurred in the middle sixties produced a 'main line' running north and south from the new Drumgrange incline.

Narrow Gauge Lines

(1) Pennyvenie No. 1 to Beoch mines. 3 miles. *c.* 1870-1912.
(2) Sundrum No. 2 to Sundrum Nos. 3 and 4. $\frac{3}{4}$ mile.
(3) Brickwork to clay pit. $\frac{1}{2}$ mile.
(4) Pennyvenie No. 4 to Beoch mines. $2\frac{1}{2}$ miles. 1912-.
(5) Pennyvenie No. 4 to Beoch mines. $2\frac{1}{2}$ miles. Single line alongside (4) and used for transport of workmen. *c.* 1933.
(6) Chalmerston Nos. 4-7 to Burnton Washer. 1 mile. *c.* 1933-57.

Overhead Ropeways

(1) Bogton mine to Burnton Washer. 1 mile. 1930-50.
(2) Bing at old Burnfoot No. 11 pit to loading point on line to Houldsworth. 1.1 miles. In use 1940-50s.

Certain of the standard and narrow-gauge lines incorporated inclined planes, the working of which is dealt with later in this chapter.

Permanent Way

The permanent way of the DICo lines was very far inferior to main line standards. Rails and chairs were invariably obtained second-hand from the main line companies. Sleepers were largely scrap pieces from the DICo saw-mill. One spike to a chair was in many cases deemed sufficient. Ballast, where it was apparent, was engine ashes. In the days before ashpans were in use DICo lines had the four-foot full of ashes almost to rail level, while the sleeper-ends were almost without support. Chaired track was universal. I do not recollect seeing flat-bottomed rails at any point on the DICo system. The general standard of track condition has improved greatly in recent years but still leaves a lot to be desired.

Narrow-gauge rails were of flat-bottomed type, spiked direct to the sleepers. Prefabricated track of various kinds is now much in use.

Standard Gauge Motive Power

Horse haulage was used exclusively until the coming of the first engine in 1851. A number of years must have elapsed, however, before there were sufficient engines to undertake the entire standard-gauge haulage.

Up to the present, twenty-eight engines have worked at Waterside, the greatest number at one time being eleven. All were designed and built by outside firms. All were stationed at Waterside except one, or for a period two, which were in a shed at Burnfoothill. There is a story that one of those two engines on this elevated section was stationed in a shed at Corbie Craigs, but I can get no confirmation of this. No. 5 (I) was stationed at Coylton during the period 1865-74.

All engines at Waterside have been tank engines, water being conveyed in saddle, side or well tanks. Coal was supposed to be carried in bunkers on each side of the footplate, but in my experience it was more usual to heap the footplate only. Until 1913 no DICo engine had a back bunker. At the back of the footplate was a plate about waist high. This had a large aperture in the middle through which, I was informed, one was supposed to manipulate the back coupling. Again I never saw this done.

Under these conditions the amount of coal which could be carried was extremely limited. It was therefore customary for enginemen to replenish their supply from the nearest wagon which contained good coal. About 1910, however, this practice was forbidden officially and each engine except, I think, those on the Slag Hill job, was provided with a tender. This consisted merely of a wagon with one end removed. Sufficient coal could be carried for a full day's work, the fireman going into the tender from time to time to shovel a fresh supply by means of the convenient aperture on to the long-suffering footplate.

The two 0—6—0s had back bunkers and I was much surprised to see them also equipped with tenders. The throw from the floor of the wagon to the rim of the bunker is at least

5 ft. No water supply was ever carried in these tenders.

In the 1920s the back of the cab in each 0—4—0 tank was closed in. The centre aperture remained and would have created very draughty conditions, so a hopper is now affixed behind each aperture and coal supplied to the cab *via* the hopper.

A complication arose concerning the tender of the engine working between Waterside and Coylton. The G & SW authorities refused to permit this engine to *propel* its tender. So, when the Coylton engine was running cab first on the main line, the tender had to be switched round to the funnel end and *hauled* along with the rake and the van. As half the journeys between Ayr and Waterside were performed by G & SW engines propelling *their* tenders this prohibition seems quite unreasonable.

Numbering of engines. Engines of the DICo were numbered in order of arrival, with the exception of No. 5 (II), the circumstances of whose numbering have been explained. With the transfer to the ownership of Bairds & Dalmellington the numbers remained, and similar conditions prevailed during the period of West Ayr Area of the NCB. When, however, West and East Ayr amalgamated, it was necessary to renumber two of the Waterside engines. NCB had brought four additional engines to Waterside, giving them numbers of Waterside engines which had been withdrawn from service, in some cases very many years before. In my narrative I have had to distinguish between two engines bearing the same number. I have therefore appended the numerals (I) and (II) to the engines concerned. These are only for use in this narrative; it will be understood that no engine carried these numerals.

Painting of engines. To my youthful vision Waterside engines partook of the nature of cats in the dark. All were black! Clean enough, but black. I am assured, however, that green was the prevailing colour. Barclays favoured a pleasant shade of olive green, lined out in black, white and red, and repaintings in DICo days were in this colour. The exceptions were Nos. 5 (II) which came new in a blue livery, 15, in a luscious gamboge, and 20, whose green livery was of a much lighter shade, akin to that of the North Eastern Railway. B & D adopted black for all engines and this has continued under NCB management. In each case neat and effective lining-out is applied.

The name of the company, together with the number, was painted on the side of each tank. The number was not carried in any other position on the engine.

Engine buffers. As will be explained, a large proportion of DICo stock had buffers which were lower and closer together than the standard position. To engage both standard and low buffers, engine buffers consisted of large wooden slabs, faced with metal. The 0—6—0T No. 17 appeared in 1913 with spring metal buffers, but these were of large diameter. No other engine was so fitted until the second 0—6—0T nine years later. In recent years all engines have been fitted with spring buffers, the only exception being No. 23. These buffers are of normal size, there being now no low-buffered stock in use.

Engine lubricators. During the period of the First World War, rather strangely, the experiment was tried of fitting a mechanical lubricator to one of the DICo engines, believed to be No. 16. This was of The Vacuum Oil Co's manufacture. The results in economy and efficiency were so gratifying that over a comparatively short period all Waterside engines were so equipped. The Wakefield lubricator is now in use, but No. 16 retains her Vacuum Oil Co lubricator, while No. 20 has a 'Transport Lubricator' by Dunbar & Slater of Stoke-on-Trent.

Funnels to the north. All DICo engines, at least since the 1860s, appear to have worked with 'funnel to the north'. The exception was No. 10 (I), which worked with funnel to the south. At one time any engine undertaking the Coylton job, even temporarily, was duly taken to Dalmellington, the site of the nearest turntable.

Engine crews. At first the DICo engines were run by driver and fireman only, but from a period about the 1860s a third man, designated 'guard' or 'runner' was carried also. Both fireman and guard attend to coupling and braking, the driver being alone on the footplate for long periods. From about the end of the first war periodical examinations of DICo crews were carried out by main line railway inspectors as a test of their knowledge of the rules of the lines over which they were permitted to work.

Narrow Gauge Motive Power

Surface lines in narrow gauge were at first operated by horse haulage, with man or boy power for short-distance movements. The use of horses was never very extensive in the underground workings of the DICo. These were operated by engine worked 'dooks' or inclines. In 1912 the first application of endless rope haulage took place in Pennyvenie No. 4 drift mine. In this case, instead of being run in rakes, the hutches are clipped individually to the slowly-moving rope. Shortly after, the same system was adopted for the line from Pennyvenie No. 4 to Beoch.

No locomotives were used on any narrow gauge lines until in the period of B & D it was desired to continue the transport of workmen from the terminus of the standard-gauge line at Pennyvenie No. 4 to Beoch. This was quite a problem, as it could not be done over the road which was using rope haulage. Eventually a single line of narrow gauge was laid down alongside the existing double line. Primitive little vehicles provided scanty shelter for the passengers. Motive power was by a small petrol-driven locomotive. This working had not a long life, and succumbed to bus competition in the early 1950s. Diesel locomotives are now in use below ground in Pennyvenie Nos. 2 and 7.

Standard Gauge Vehicles

Wagon stock of the DICo may be divided first into two categories—for internal use on the DICo lines, and for work over the main line of railway to certain destinations. From the

B & D period, wagons 'for internal use only' were so lettered.

The wagons for internal use were likewise divided into two main classes—the older and smaller wagons with buffers set much lower and closer together than the standard, and those with buffers of standard height and spacing.

Low buffered stock. The low buffered wagons had probably altered little from the days of horse haulage. The main frames of these wagons consisted of two stout baulks of timber, set above the axles and passing just inside the wheels. These frames protruded beyond the wagon body at each end to form the buffers. There were no bearing springs. The axles revolved in large plummer blocks bolted to the lower side of these frames. On one side only there was a hand brake applying blocks to both wheels, the brake lever going up at an angle to a ratchet on the side of the wagon.

Drawgear consisted of a single flat iron bar pierced at each end with a round vertical hole. At one end a pin was inserted in this hole; to the other end was attached a chain of three links, terminating in a shackle—always referred to as a 'muzzle'. To couple two wagons the muzzle was placed over the hole in the adjacent wagon drawbar and its pin passed through muzzle and drawbar.

A number of accidents had occurred on the incline by reason of couplings or drawbars breaking, so the low buffered wagons working on the incline were fitted with additional short chains attached to the outside of the buffers.

These low buffered wagons were of various classes. The best known were probably the 'blue billies'. 'Blue billy' is, in some districts, a geologist's term for calcined ironstone, so the name is easily explained. These were neat little wagons with vertical sides and outside framing. They had two side doors and, I believe, two end doors also. Of the latter I cannot be certain, for another class were always called 'the wee *end* wagons'. Two other classes bore the names of 'The Maids' and 'The Princes', but I cannot get an adequate description. Certain wagons had sides sloping inwards. These may have been hopper wagons. Those most familiar to me were the high-sided wagons, sparred like a cattle wagon. These conveyed the coke from Pennyvenie ovens to the furnaces.

Low buffered stock was also provided for transport of goods from the DICo's main store at Waterside to the branch stores at Burnfoothill and Benwhat. There were several small vans and one wagon, which had a curved wooden top and was used to convey beer barrels.

All the low buffered stock, I believe, was built in the DICo wagon shop. All were painted a light grey. No lettering or numbering appeared on the sides. To the main frames were attached two cast-iron plates bearing the initials 'DICO' and the number.

Standard buffered stock. These were wagons of main-line aspect. In after years they were largely second-hand vehicles purchased from the railway companies. I am informed that such DICo vehicles were mostly built new by outside firms. At first the standard capacity was eight tons, and dumb buffers were in use, with brakes at wheel level as in present-day practice. Gradually ten- and twelve-ton wagons made their appearance, with spring buffers. Finest of all were the famous 'Fifteen-Tonners', the first of which came about the year 1906. These were very fine wagons and were employed largely on traffic to and from Ayr harbour. All standard buffered stock had spring drawgear and three-link couplings, and were painted red. The name of the company adorned the wagon sides, together with its number.

On the DICo lines there were frequent occasions when standard and low buffered wagons had to run in the same rake. This was done quite freely. It was amazing to see the buffers of a 'standard' wagon striking a low buffered wagon on its end panel, evidently without harm. Couplings were a difficulty, and some of the combinations employed to unite 'muzzle-and-pin' to 'three-link' would have gladdened the heart of Heath Robinson.

The First World War did not affect private owners' wagons, but in the second war those passed for main-line work were swept into the national pool. Our splendid fifteen-tonners vanished from Waterside and the Dalmellington line, never to return in any recognisable guise. I saw only three of them in after years. One was at Yoker on north Clydeside, one was at Sprouston on the Tweedmouth-Kelso line. The third I found when walking by the path from Trent Junction to Long Eaton station. It was deep in the heart of a bush-clump, away at the stop-block of a long siding, a far cry indeed from the Doon valley.

Those 'main-line' wagons of the DICo were inadequate to carry the traffic to and from Waterside, and many G & SW wagons had to be employed. All the pig iron was taken away in G & SW wagons—the usual low-sided variety used for this traffic.

Brake vans. No brake vans were used for any of the DICo mineral trains on their private lines. For the trains to and from Coylton, however, the G & SW insisted on a brake van, in which the guard travelled. Waterside wagon-shop constructed in succession several brake-vans for this service. In each case current G & SW practice was followed. The first was probably an open brake bogie. This was followed by a low-roofed van with raised 'doo-cot' at one end. Then came the type with open end platforms. These had outside framing. In later years a van obtained second-hand from the main line was in use, the last being an ex-L & Y vehicle with metal side panels and the small window in the side.

No account of the Waterside brake-vans would be complete without a mention of that strange edifice we called 'The Summer Van'. This was a vehicle which had started life as an open brake bogie. Later in its career, a wooden hood had been erected at each end, with seats, the occupants facing towards the open space in the centre in which stood the brake column. This 'Summer Van', painted red, spent a large period of its career idle in various out-of-the-way sidings. I recall it most clearly perched precariously at the end of the Cutler Tip.

The uses of The Summer Van, when it *was* in use, were somewhat varied. If the Coylton van was in need of overhaul it was used as a substitute. If the engineers got an emergency call to Coylton they would use the Summer Van to carry their gear. My uncle recalled one occasion when such a trip had to come to a halt half-way with the four van axle-boxes on fire! When workmen's trains began to run to Pennyvenie the Summer Van would eke out the rather meagre accommodation, while on the wedding day of Mr Walker, General Manager, on 8 November 1898 celebrations were held in a field about a mile-and-a-half out on the Dalharco line. An engine ran a shuttle service from Waterside to the field, conveying revellers in the Summer Van.

Poor old Summer Van. I remember my last sight of it. I was coming along the furnace bank on 20 September 1918. There was a short spur on the east side of the main track. At the end of this spur, jammed up against the abutment of the High Level line, was the Summer Van. Shabby, neglected and with a smashed headstock, it presented a dejected appearance. Certainly I never saw it out on the road again.

Conveyance of slag. The working of the slag traffic from the furnaces to the Slag Hill was for many years conducted by a somewhat laborious process. Flat wagons with no sides at all were employed. These were known as 'slag bogies', and the engine which hauled them to the Slag Hill was always called 'The Bogie Injin'. Beside each furnace a line of rails terminated in a bay, the sides of which were of wood sloped inwards to the top. The flat bogie was run underneath this wooden framework, after which a door of wood closed the remaining side, making a complete box whose floor was the bogie.

Boys now proceeded to line the interior of this box with a thick layer of fireclay. On completion the slag hole was tapped and the molten slag allowed to run into this 'mould', water being sprayed on it meanwhile. The fireclay lining soon hardened; the wooden framework could be removed and the bogie drawn out and left until its cargo should cool. Bogies were then taken three at a time to the Slag Hill, where they were tipped by the primitive method of having one rail shorter than another. When one wheel dropped off the road the bogie tilted and slid its block of slag down the hillside.

It would be about the year 1908 that the above process was replaced by the provision of 'ladles'. These were large metal crucibles sitting in bearings on a heavy four-wheeled vehicle. The slag was run into the ladle and taken in a molten state to the Slag Hill. There the wheels were scotched, the ladle uncoupled, and the engine, pulling on a light chain, tilted the crucible and discharged the contents. One ladle only was taken up at a time. Two ladles were arranged to tip at the end. The others were side tipping.

Workmen's trains. These would appear to have originated in the late 1890s. In previous years the great majority of the miners lived at a convenient walking distance from the pits. By the above period, however, the demand for labour at the Pennyvenie pits had outgrown the supply provided at Dalmellington. At the same time there was a serious decline in ironstone mining in the Burnfoothill area. Numbers of Burnfoothill men obtained work at Pennyvenie and probably got a lift on the wagons or engine of a train going that way. For these men a service was provided. It started with one or two 'home-made' vans, often supplemented by the Summer Van. The workmen's train left the foot of the incline, down which the Burnfoothill men walked, and ran up to Pennyvenie No. 1, with a return service at the time of termination of work. As traffic grew, something more was required, and a number of old carriages were obtained from the railway companies. From that period these services were always referred to as 'The Cairriages'.

There were three such services. One, as described, ran from the foot of the incline to Pennyvenie. This train had to be augmented until finally five carriages were in use. Its journey was later extended to the crossing of the new Burnfoothill road above Patna. Another service took Waterside men to Houldsworth pit, but here a single carriage usually sufficed. Burnfoothill, however, had a large number of men travelling to the distant Bowhill pits, and four carriages were in use. When Bowhill closed down in 1913 the Craigmark mines were starting up, and a service was given thence. This was on a smaller scale. The 'train' dwindled to a single carriage, though this had to be supplemented by an open wagon in which the hardier individuals travelled.

In the early 1920s the Pennyvenie train, even with five carriages, was packed to overflowing and my uncle Davie Larmer was sorely perturbed by its working. It was still the 'Old Road' to Pennyvenie and they were *hauling* those five carriages up that 1 in 37 with all three of the crew on the engine. Should a coupling break the carriages would be off down that headlong descent before anyone could get near their wretched 'ground-level' brakes, and it would be a wonder if they did not derail and go down into the glen. As is usual with matters affecting safety, it was long before he could make his protest heard. Eventually, the brake gearing was restored to the rear coach and connected to the original guard's compartment, in which the DICo guard was instructed to travel.

The use of 'The Cairriages' was not confined to workmen's trains. From time to time they were brought into use for the general public. What payment, if any, was made for such services I do not know, but if Dunaskin Lads were playing Craigmark Smithfield, the football team and supporters would be run from Waterside to Craigmark. Extensive use of 'The Cairriages' was made on The Hill. Political meetings, flower shows, football matches were catered for. If Burnfoothill Primrose were playing Benwhat Heatherbell, a special was run. If Rankinston Mountaineers were the opponents, Primrose and supporters were run out to Bowhill, from whence it was an easy walk across to Rankinston's ground. Whenever the public had to be conveyed the crew had the carriages dusted and clean newspaper spread upon the seats, that no clothing might be soiled.

I wish that I could record that the regular patrons of 'The Cairriages' were equally solicitous. It was long before the days when one began to hear the word 'vandalism', but it is only the truth to say that each of the old carriages lasted until it was *kicked* to pieces. When it had grown too decrepit for even these services it was shunted to some obscure siding and left to rot. Then another second-hand main line vehicle came to take its place.

By 1946 'The Cairriages' were already affected by bus competition. In that year I found the Pennyvenie train reduced to two carriages. Both had belonged to the North British Railway, and both were built at Cowlairs in 1897. One had been an open saloon, the other a six-compartment third. The Cairriages kept on until the early 1950s, when, with a bus for every pit and for every shift, they gave up the struggle.

How I wish I had got a note of some of those older carriages. The first were four-wheelers, then when six-wheelers came, some, if not all, had the centre wheels removed. All continuous brake gear was removed and hand brakes at ground level substituted. The carriages were painted red. I do not recollect any DICo lettering or numbering.

Narrow Gauge Vehicles

All but a very few of the vehicles used for narrow gauge traffic were open coal wagons and were always referred to as *hutches*. A hutch was simply a rectangular wooden box about 3 ft in depth, set between the wheels of a 2 ft 10-in gauge axle. There were no frames or bearing springs. Plummer blocks were attached to the floor of the hutch, as was the round metal bar which formed the drawgear. This was curled up at each end to form a hook, coupling being effected by small independent chains. At each top corner hung a metal handle for haulage by hand.

The only passenger-carrying vehicles employed in pre-NCB days were those constructed for the service between Pennyvenie No. 4 and Beoch. On a metal frame with a rather long wheelbase for its two axles, a covering was erected. This consisted of little but a roof about the height of a seated man. In a side wind such as has been known to blow in those latitudes there could have been little comfort, and the buses soon diverted the traffic to themselves.

Narrow-gauge vehicles to-day conform to patterns approved

by the NCB. I see that the hutches now have frames between the wheels, with the body set above the frames and extending over the wheels, thus providing for a broader and more capacious interior.

Regulation of Traffic

At all pits and works of the DICo, sidings were provided on a lavish scale, but the lines joining one to another were without exception single track. In these circumstances one would think that elaborate measures would be necessary to prevent collisions. As a matter of fact no block signalling, fixed signals or distance-controlled points were installed at any point on those lines.

This would seem to be dangerous to a degree, and it is certainly remarkable that there is no record over all those years of any collision between trains. Of course, certain lines presented no difficulty, as they were worked, very literally, by one engine in steam. The only real complications were on the Pennyvenie Road. This was very heavily graded for its first two miles. There were no actual passing loops, but the sidings of the Laight mine formed a loop—frequently occupied by stored wagons—and when the new washer was installed at Burnton a new loop and weighs were put in there.

Working on the Pennyvenie Road was to a rough-and-ready timetable. Driver A. would leave Waterside about 7 a.m. and go up to Pennyvenie. He *knew* that he must not leave for the return journey until Driver B. arrived. On B's return journey he *knew* that he must wait in Burnton loop until Driver C. went past. Special runs were arranged by the foreman on the furnace bank. He would get Driver D. ready at a time he *knew* to be propitious, and *perhaps* in the interests of safe working he *might* go up on the High Level and have a look. If Driver C's smoke was not in sight beyond the Laight Brae then there would be time for Driver D. to nip up and get inside at the Laight mine before C. got there!

It all sounds delightfully casual, yet there we have the accident-free record. One may ask why trains were not 'blocked' from pit to pit by telephone. But the present century was well advanced before there *were* any telephones between Waterside head office and the pits, and I fear that the clerical staff would not have welcomed their use for such a purpose.

The men on the Coylton Road necessarily worked to the G & SW system, at first of staff-and-ticket, then, from 1893-4, of electric tablet. Once on their own line from Potterston Junction, of course, they had the place to themselves.

While observing correct discipline upon the main line of the G & SW, the DICo men, in yard working about Waterside, were somewhat apt to continue their own easy-oasy methods. The Waterside signalman might have two or more G & SW trains shunting at his station when without warning there would appear beneath the Slag Brig a rake of about thirty wagons, pushed vigorously by a DICo engine which was probably out of sight round the curve. So about the year 1908 the G & SW people put a scissors arm on the signal post of Waterside down distant. When this arm was put to danger DICo men, in theory, held back. The combination of signal arms on this post used to puzzle some of my friends.

Rope-Worked Inclines

In the course of the DICo rail system there were encountered at various points gradients too steep to be worked by locomotives or horse haulage. In such cases an incline of uniform gradient was laid down and rope haulage installed. This rope haulage was confined to the length of the inclined plane only. It should not be confused with haulage by endless rope. The latter negotiated some steep gradients in the course of its circuit, but the problems they raised were not divorced from those of the circuit itself.

Two methods of rope haulage were employed by the DICo. Where the loaded wagons had a *descending* course, the method was that known as 'self-acting'. The loaded wagons, descending, hauled the empty wagons up. Where the *loaded* wagons had to ascend, haulage was by means of a stationary engine at the top of the plane.

Inclines worked by stationary engines were numerous in the underground workings of the DICo, but I can trace only one example of this working on surface lines. This was the incline which used to convey ironstone, limestone and coal from the sidings adjacent to the main line at Dunaskin to the furnace bank. Its working is referred to on page 24. Its use was probably discontinued soon after the opening of the route to the furnace bank via the Cutler Tip, and it would certainly be swept away in the clearance for the construction of the later furnaces in 1865.

Self-acting inclines were only to be found, as far as I am aware, on surface lines. I know of three on standard gauge lines. These were not contemporary. The third replaced the first two. There were also two on narrow-gauge lines.

Engine-worked inclines were single track only, dividing into two at top and bottom. The single rope was attached to the descending rake, which carried it down the incline. At the foot the rope was transferred to the ascending rake, waiting in a parallel road. This was then hauled up by the stationary engine. Such inclines, in underground locations, were called *dooks,* and the speed of descent of a train of hutches down a long dook had, I am told, to be seen to be believed!

Self-acting inclines had perforce to be of double track throughout to permit of up and down rakes passing at the half-way point. In certain instances elsewhere, however, such inclines were laid with *three* rails, the centre one being common to ascending and descending traffic. For a short distance at the half-way point the three rails became four to allow of passing. A close study of the Ordnance Survey map of 1858 would suggest that three-rail working was in force on the Corbie Craigs and Drumgrange inclines of the DICo, but this is not known for certain.

Early Self-Acting Inclines

The first of the Corbie Craigs pits commenced production in 1850, and the incline of that name must have come into use then or slightly earlier. From Corbie Craigs to the furnace bank, by the route taken, was about one-and-a-half miles. First came a level length to the crossing of the Dunaskin Burn, then a portion of gentle descent to the top of the incline. This appears to have been some twenty-six chains in length and with a gradient of about 1 in 12. From its foot the line was again level, crossing the Dunaskin Glen by a high timber viaduct and continuing along the hillside to the bank. Horse haulage was employed on the level sections.

Drumgrange incline was probably constructed about the same period. It served various ironstone pits to the north-east of the ironworks. These were on the same elevated plateau as the Corbie Craigs pits, but at that period the two groups had no rail connection. Drumgrange incline was in two different sections, in length some 22 and 16 chains respectively, with a strange little intervening level stretch which must have been worked by horses. This brought the ironstone to the level of the main railway in the valley, along which it must have been hauled to the engine-worked incline at Dunaskin for the lift up to the furnace bank, a very roundabout way of working, one would say.

The upper part of the Drumgrange incline must have been considerably steeper than the Corbie Craigs incline. This is not now easy to ascertain, as the track of the old incline is somewhat obscured by the construction of the later incline close alongside.

New Drumgrange Incline

This later Drumgrange incline was laid down about the middle eighteen-sixties. It was probably much more substantial than the two earlier planes and was equipped to handle heavier traffic. It began its descent at a point considerably higher than the former incline and came close alongside the older line, the two levelling out together at the foot. Here, however, the new line turned away from the old and made its way along the hillside to the furnace bank, thus saving much distance. The new incline was half-a-mile in length and inclined at 1 in 6. At the same time as it was constructed the

Corbie Craigs pits were joined by rail to those above Drumgrange, and all traffic was concentrated on the new incline.

The Corbie Craigs incline with its great viaduct, and the older Drumgrange incline, were then removed. The final part of the Corbie Craigs line, however, from the north end of the viaduct to the furnace bank, was allowed to remain as a storage siding. It is still in use for this purpose and still known to the traffic authorities as 'The Corbie Road'.

Narrow-Gauge Inclines

The two self-acting inclines on the narrow-gauge system were very far apart. One was on the line between Pennyvenie No. 1 pit and the Beoch mines. The line emerged from the screening plant at No. 1 and traversed a short length of level track before commencing the incline. This was quite short—I should say not more than 16 chains, after which level track and horse haulage took over again. When the standard-gauge line was extended to Pennyvenie No. 4 the Beoch line was carried over it by a lifting bridge. This had a short life; when No. 4 came into production the Beoch line was diverted to its screens and the section to No. 1 closed and removed.

The other narrow-gauge self-acting incline was at Coylton. Sundrum pit No. 2 was worked out, and Nos. 3 and 4 were operating at a higher level to the east. The screening plant at No. 2, however, was retained and the coal from Nos. 3 and 4 brought down to it by a self-acting incline. This would appear to have been approximately 27 chains in length and of somewhat gentle gradient. I did not see this incline when it was in use. Its pits were closed in 1934-5, when it would be removed.

Little is known of the working of the earlier inclines or of those on the narrow-gauge lines. The later Drumgrange incline (generally referred to as the *Burnfoothill* incline), however, continued in use until the year 1933 and so is well remembered by the people of the district, including men who took part in its working. This working may be described in some detail, as it is in many respects typical of the working of other such inclines on the DICo system.

Incline Working

The incline was of double track, with pulleys set between each pair of rails for the support of the rope. At the top, suspended between two massive brick buttresses, was an iron drum, some 5 ft in diameter. This was fitted with a hand brake, operating large wooden blocks set round the perimeter of the drum. Built over the drum, between the brick walls, was a shelter for the brakesman. It was much needed on wild nights up on the face of this west-aspect incline. Round the drum passed the rope. One end was at the top of one road; the other stretched the length of the other road.

At top and bottom of the incline the two roads became three. At the bottom the centre road was level but the roads on either side rose to a hump, with a final descent to the incline foot. *Ascending* traffic was shunted into the two hump roads, from which the attendants could work the wagons forward by gravity to whichever road was in use. *Descending* traffic was run out *via* the centre road.

A similar arrangement had been in operation at the top but in the reverse order. *Descending* traffic was shunted into the one hump road, which was in the middle, the wagons passing underneath the drum. The outside roads were level, and the *ascending* traffic was received on these. This worked very well until the small wagons previously in use were superseded by standard-size wagons of eight, ten, twelve, and finally fifteen tons capacity. None of these, it was found, would pass under the drum. So instead of the descending traffic being lowered easily down by gravity it had to be *inched* along the level side road by the engine, a brave man holding a scotch to stop the whole show going over the edge to destruction.

Runaways

And a runaway on the Burnfoothill incline *was* destruction! There were many tales of wild runaways even in the days of the small wagons. I never heard of a rope breaking, but couplings broke from time to time. The safety chains later fitted to the outsides of the wooden buffers probably saved a few smashes. But modern three-link couplings were not infallible. In the later years of operation two fifteen-tonners loaded with dross were being lowered when a coupling broke and they descended. Part of the journey was made by air; they flew over the Houldsworth line and never touched a fence-post. They were found, smashed to pieces, in the field beyond. After this accident an extra rope was supplied. This was attached to the coupling hook of the leading wagon and passed under the wagons for attachment to the main rope.

Ascending traffic did not escape unscathed. My father used to tell me of the famous night when the store vans derailed and went over into the glen of the Drumgrange Burn. The small wagon with the beer turned upside-down, the barrels knocked off the roof, and the beer joined the groceries and the pit-oil in a glorious hell-broth down in the glen.

The cause of this derailment I do not know, but a more recent one of a like nature and result was described to me by my uncle. Apparently the brakesman at the top had been somewhat ham-handed. He allowed the rope of the ascending rake to *lash*. At one lash it went over the outside rail and got underneath a sleeper. Fortunately this sleeper was so rotten that the end snapped off. So with the next and the next. Then came a more sturdy sleeper. It held, and the rope towed the rake over the edge to destruction.

After one fearsome runaway my uncle Willie Smith spoke to the man at the foot of the incline. 'What did you do?' he asked. 'I *ran,*' said the man, 'richt oot *there*!' pointing in a most emphatic right-angled direction to the rails!

A prominent landmark at the head of each self-acting incline was a semaphore signal on a wooden post. This remained at danger unless lowered by the man at the foot of the incline pulling a lever which operated a wire. A 'tow', as a train of wagons on the incline was always called, was got ready at the top, but no move could be made until the man at the foot lowered the signal as an indication that *his* tow was hooked on and ready to ascend.

(10a) *No. 17* (1913)
(10b) *No. 22* (1923)

(11 & 12) DALMEI

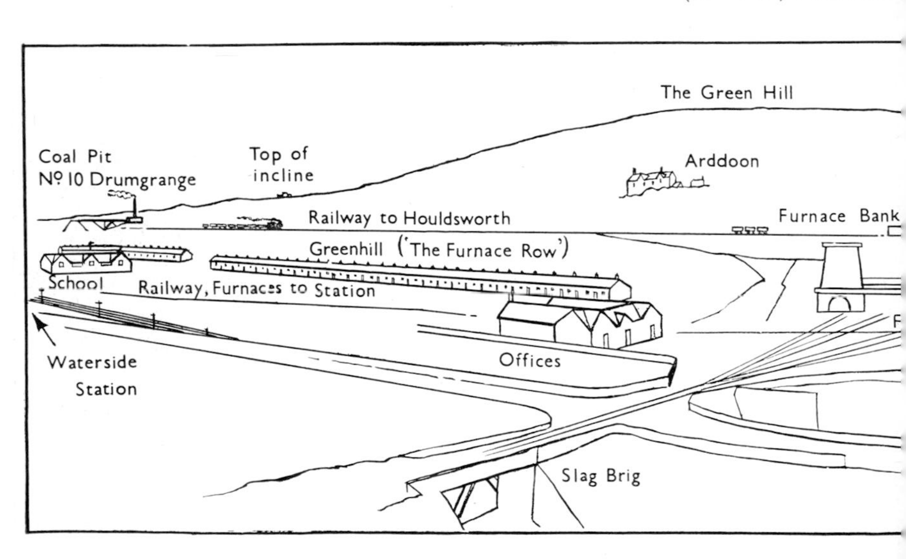
The Green Hill
Coal Pit
Nº 10 Drumgrange
Top of
incline
Arddoon
Railway to Houldsworth
Furnace Bank
Greenhill ('The Furnace Row')
School
Railway, Furnaces to Station
Waterside
Station
Offices
Slag Brig

RON WORKS, c.1903

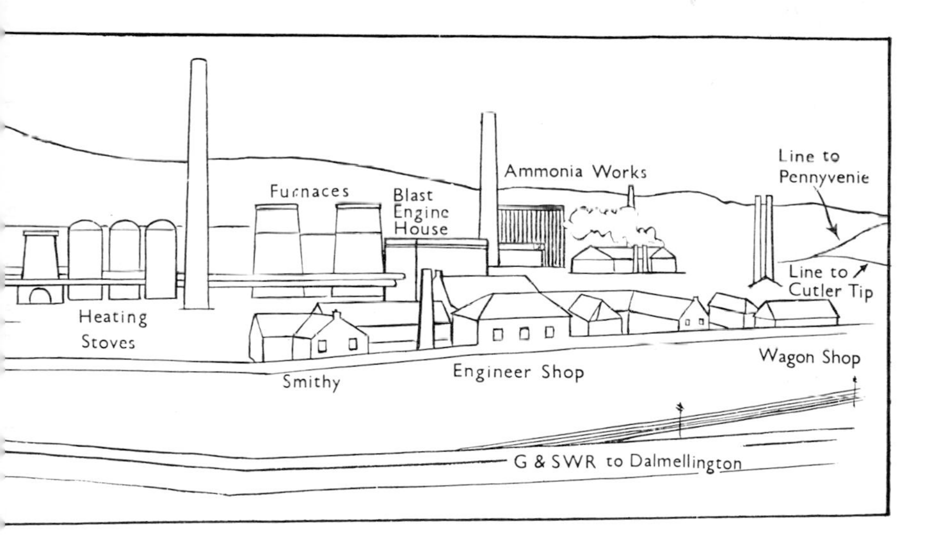

(13a) *Burnfoothill Incline*

(13b) *The Clay Pit. Last worked* 1920

(13c) *Accident to No. 19, Cutler,* 25 *April* 1929. *Left to right: James Kerr (Kaur) Horse Driver; John Kerr, Engine Driver; Thos Rowan, Traffic Foreman*

It is said that there used to be a custom to leave at least three wagons at the top of the incline in case the engineers had to go up with their gear in an emergency. These three loaded wagons, descending, could haul them up. On occasion this facility had not been provided, and hydraulic jacks had to be man-handled up that half-mile of 1 in 6. I have *walked* it, empty-handed, on several of my periodic visits to The Hill. On my first visit I reached the foot of the incline as a tow was ready to ascend. An office clerk called to me to join him on the wooden buffers of an eight-tonner. I was afraid to risk it. Half-way up I thought I had never done anything so stupid in my life. Oh it was a bruiser! Yet the Hill folks, young and old, walked it, up and down, summer and winter. Save for the wretched paths which led down to Burnfoot and Patna the incline was the sole means of access to this village.

This concludes the catalogue of inclines on the DICo system, but to complete the picture it is necessary to refer to that of the Summerlee Iron Co. at Kerse. This incline was longer than any of the DICo, about 50 chains, but was graded at about 1 in 11 only. It appears to have been laid down when the Ayr & Dalmellington Railway was put through in 1856 and to have ceased operation about the start of the eighteen-seventies.

CHAPTER 9

The Engines and the Men

List of engines in numerical order. This is followed by an individual account of each engine, those being given in order of arrival at Waterside, the accounts commencing on pages indicated.

No.	Builders	Year built	Builders' no.	Year arrived	Year withdrawn	Page	
1 (I)	Neilson & Mitchell	1851	47	1851	1882	123	
1 (II)	Barclay	1947	2244	1947	—	226	Reno. 10 (II), 1964
2	Neilson & Mitchell	1854	65	1854	c.1890	128	
3	Hawthorns, Leith	1856	138	1856	1924	130	
4	do	1858	174	1858	1916	136	
5 (I)	Neilson	1865	1129	1865	1899	145	
5 (II)	Gibb & Hogg	1899	5	1899	1955	188	To Mauchline 1934
6	Lilleshall	1866	90	1866	1911	147	
7	Barclay	1868	75	1868	1888	152	
8 (I)	Taylor	1868/71	none	1868/71	1912	154	
8 (II)	Barclay	1953	2335	1953	—	230	Reno. 24, 1964
9	do	1871	133	1872	1928	160	
10 (I)	Hawthorns, Leith	1867	unknown	1874	1923	166	
10 (II)							See 1 (II)
11	Hawthorns, Leith	1881	unknown	1881	1906	177	
12	Grant, Ritchie	1887	179	1887	1949	180	
13							There was no No. 13
14	Barclay	1906	1062	1906	1964	192	
15	Markham	1909	none	1909	1956	198	To N. Cumnock 1947
16	Barclay	1910	1116	1910	—	203	To Mauchline 1956
17	do	1913	1338	1913	—	205	
18 (I)	do	1913	1345	1913	—	211	To N. Cumnock 1947
18 (II)	do	1930	1985	1955	—	232	Originally Coltness Iron Co. No. 3
19	do	1918	1614	1918	—	213	
20	Hawthorn, Leslie	1918	3351	1918	—	218	To Mauchline c.1952
21 (I)	Grant, Ritchie	1920	435?	1920	c.1942	221	Sold to Cunningham, Leith 1932
21 (II)	Barclay	1949	2284	1951	—	229	
22	do	1923	1785	1923	—	222	
23	Grant, Ritchie	1911	531	1937	—	225	Originally Eglinton Iron Works No. 6
24							See 8 (II)

An engine built by Dick & Stevenson was hired from Barclay for a short period in 1899.

No. 1 (I)

0—4—0, with saddle tank, vertical sides, flat top, extending length of boiler barrel only.

Built Neilson & Mitchell, Glasgow, 1851. Makers' number: 47.

Only known dimensions: cylinders (outside) 10 in by 18 in
wheels: 3 ft
working pressure: 110 lb p.s.i.

Dome over firebox. Spring balance safety valve on top of dome. Regulator in dome. Handle on top of dome, working horizontally round a quadrant. Gab motion. No cab. No splashers. Plain parallel funnel, no coping. Top of funnel less than 9 ft 2 in from rail level.

This engine was not reconstructed at any subsequent period.

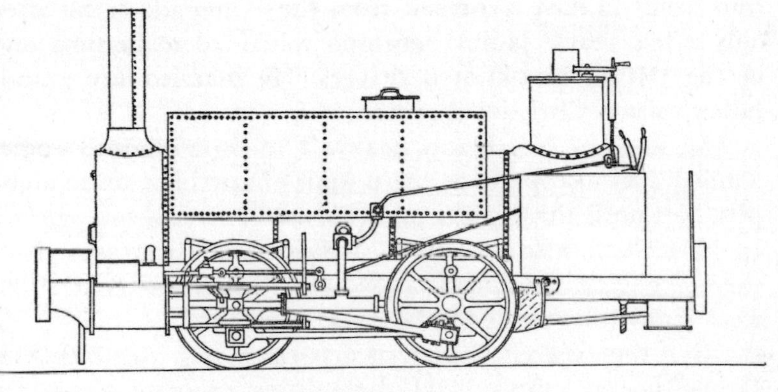

No. 1 (I)

This was the first locomotive owned by the Dalmellington Iron Company. 0—4—0 *tank* engines were not very plentiful in 1851. She was intended to work the coal traffic from Sillyhole pits to the iron works over the section of line constructed by the Ayrshire & Galloway Railway Company and opened in 1849. For the intervening two years horse haulage had been employed. This section of line was completely isolated from any other railway. Whether No. 1 was brought from Glasgow to Ayr by rail or sea we do not know. We do know that she was hauled up the main road from Ayr to Waterside by a team of horses. She travelled upon her own flanged wheels and is reported to have come up without difficulty. I am not surprised. In 1916 I saw a narrow-gauge Barclay, which could not have been much lighter than No. 1, go up the road from Dalmellington to Loch Doon on her own wheels. The only record of her passing was a pair of parallel grooves in the soft surface, which were ironed out in a couple of days of traffic.

A *locomotive* was of course a complete novelty in those parts, but a number of stationary steam engines were at work and a man named McCallum, described as 'an engineer of sorts', who was the first driver of No. 1, probably had experience of stationary plant. Trained firemen were equally scarce, but a courageous young man called James Ferguson, who had been a horse driver, undertook the duties of fireman. McCallum seems to have vanished from the Waterside scene after only a few years. James Ferguson remained to become one of the DICo's best-known drivers. He married my grandfather's sister, Christina Larmer.

The work of No. 1 was heavy. The little engine, single-handed, had to cope with the output of anything up to eight pits. Not until three years later did No. 1 have a companion. In 1854 No. 2, also a Neilson, arrived. McCallum was given the new engine and Ferguson became the driver of No. 1. The work if anything tended to become heavier and when, in 1856, the line they travelled was incorporated into the full Ayr-Dalmellington railway and the railway company restricted the hours during which the DICo could work their traffic, the two engines were toiling desperately hard. My grandfather Larmer was then traffic manager. To save line occupation he ran Nos. 1 and 2 coupled together, with as much as they could stagger under. To give every assistance he had a water-barrel mounted on the rear of the train engine, with taps and two pipes leading down to the rails. As soon as the train got started the taps were opened, and while the engines pedalled away on the dry rail the friction of haulage was slightly diminished.

I do not know how long Ferguson drove No. 1. By the early sixties he was on No. 2. No. 1 then goes about her work unreported until the late sixties, when two remarkable things happened to her.

Locomotives had almost entirely replaced horses on the 'valley' lines of the DICo, but those on the plateau 500 feet above were still using horse haulage. Some time about the middle sixties it was decided to reorganise these lines and to introduce locomotive haulage. There had been until then two separate groups of lines, stemming from the summits of the two rope-worked inclines at Drumgrange and Corbie Craigs respectively. Now a new incline, double line throughout and graded at 1 in 6 for half-a-mile, was laid alongside the Drumgrange incline. The new incline terminated at a point level with the furnace bank, to which a new and level line was constructed.

No. 1 was sent up to the plateau—the first engine in Ayrshire to reach the 1,000 ft contour one would imagine. But the manner of her ascending is a most intriguing problem in Waterside history.

My uncle Davic Larmer certainly told me of No. 1 working on Burnfoothill. A man called Jock Newall drove her there. He then went to India and was there for fifteen years. On returning to the British Isles he drove a pumping engine at Belfast harbour, finishing work on a similar pumping engine on the Caledonian Railway at Flemington.

A story has been circulated in recent years that No. 1 was taken up to the plateau not, as might be supposed, by the existing Drumgrange incline, but by the incline of the Summerlee Iron Company at Smithston two miles north of Patna. This had a gentler grading than the other. It is also related that No. 1 had to be 'partially dismantled' in order to be taken up.

This is a most interesting piece of information and I wish that I could set it down without qualification. But there are certain difficulties about doing so. The Summerlee company's lines, fanning out from the top of their incline, were far from making a junction with the DICo lines from Drumgrange incline. A considerable stretch of roadless moorland intervened. It is also peculiar that though my informant, a very reliable person, states that he had this story from my uncle Davie Larmer, my uncle never told *me* of it. This to me seems very strange, as we were discussing this matter in great detail, as witness my uncle's description of the career of No. 1's driver.

We can at least say that No. 1 (I) went to 'The Hill' and no doubt laboured as hard as she did in the valley. She left on The Hill one mark of her presence which was rather unwelcome. An engine shed was constructed there, and as No. 1 was the only engine available for measurement the shed was unfortunately constructed to dimensions suitable for her short stature. Later and larger engines had to suffer a truncation of their funnels until many years after when the walls were heightened.

No. 1 was replaced on The Hill by No. 6, a much larger and more powerful engine. This replacement must have taken place soon after No. 6's arrival at Waterside in 1866, for we find, in a year which by a consensus of opinion was 1868, No. 1 (I) returned once more to the valley for an event which was the most spectacular of her career.

The scene was Sillyhole level crossing. There would be no Sillyhole pits working by that time, but the coal from the Chalmerston and Craigmark pits would be gathered together there. No. 1 (I) was waiting to leave Sillyhole with a rake of coal for Waterside. It was a cold day and the rails were rather damp. The time was just after midday.

Jimmy Gill was driving No. 1 (I). Ivie Campbell from the Corbie Craigs was firing. He got out and sat on the front ready to sand ahead. There was a little upgrade into the cutting north of Sillyhole, so Gill held down his safety valve to get a good head of steam for the lift away. Many and many a time he had done this with impunity, but this was the hundredth chance. No. 1's sorely-tried boiler exploded. The dome ripped off from its rivets, and out of the tremendous cloud of steam and boiling water dome and driver went hurtling across the main line, high above the telegraph wires, to fall in the middle of the field beyond.

Gill was dreadfully scalded. The first to reach him was Mrs Young from the adjacent Tilework Cottage. She ran for a bowl of buttermilk and bathed his eyes. Gill said afterwards that this action saved his sight.

In the town of Dalmellington half a mile away the noise of the explosion brought people running to their doors to join in the rush to the scene of the accident. William Stewart, grocer and indefatigible collector of Dalmellington lore, told me that he was then a pupil at the parish school on the Burnside. They were playing at the midday interval when they heard the great noise and ran down the road. Andy Calderwood, another man with an excellent memory, recalled that he was passing the parish church which overlooks a wide stretch of the valley when he heard the explosion and saw the great cloud of steam. As he ran down the hill towards the crossing he saw ahead of him the Rev Thomas Walker, minister of Dalmellington, running also, bare-headed and in his carpet slippers, just as he had risen from his desk. It is remarkable that despite all this excitement—the story was still being related when I was a boy, forty years later—I have been quite unable to find any reference in any local newspaper.

The exact circumstances of Gill's flight I cannot state. The story given to me was that Gill was wearing a long muffler and that at the moment of the explosion this became entangled in the spring of the valve. It may be that he had merely hung on too long and too tightly. Whatever the cause, he went with the dome and was found lying beside it in the field. He always said that he 'stuck to his post'. Gill recovered and lived to drive again, and to take exactly the same risks as he had taken with old No. 1. In his old age he lived with his son, who was the teacher in Mossdale school, at New Galloway station. There, in the 1920s, he was visited by William Stewart from Dalmellington to whom he told once more the story of the explosion. No. 1 (I) likewise survived, was repaired, and worked for another fourteen years after that. She seems to have been on work round the furnaces. A most useful asset was her ability to pass through the Quarry Brig without lowering the funnel. It is very likely that this diminutive tunnel had been made to suit No. 1's dimensions. Like the Burnfoothill shed it was to prove an embarrassment to future engines.

No. 1 (I)'s final task was on the slag, at which she assisted or acted as substitute for her small companion No. 7. My uncle Davie Larmer, then a boy of eleven, saw her on this job in her final year, 1882. She was a fearsome object. Her frame was broken in at least one place, and they had her bound round with a great chain tightened with wedges. One of the connecting rod big ends had only half a brass. The vacancy on the other side was filled by a bolt with a large nut! Lairdie Bryden was driving. He had a stout heart.

No. 1 (I) was scrapped in that year, 1882.

No. 2

0—4—0, with saddle tank, vertical sides, flat top, extending over smokebox and boiler barrel.

Built Neilson & Mitchell, Glasgow, 1854. Makers' number: 65.

Only known dimensions: cylinders (outside) 12 in by 18 in
wheels: 3 ft
working pressure: 110 lb p.s.i.

Dome over firebox. Spring balance safety valve on top of dome. Regulator circular butterfly valve in dome. Handle on top of dome, working horizontally round a quadrant. Gab motion. No cab.

This engine was not reconstructed at any subsequent period.

No. 2 was an altogether larger engine than No. 1 and her size seems to have impressed the DICo. Ayr, twelve miles from Waterside, was still the nearest rail-head. No. 1 had been transported therefrom on her own wheels, but for this monster greater precautions were necessary. A special vehicle—evidently a primitive form of the modern 'low loader' was provided. No. 2 rewarded their prudence by breaking through the road surface somewhere about Boghall, where the outflow from Martnaham Loch makes the ground marshy, and a good deal of trouble ensued.

Driver McCallum of No. 1 was given custody of the new giant on its arrival at Waterside. Fireman Ferguson was promoted to be driver of No. 1. No. 2 joined No. 1 in the hauling of coal from Sillyhole and, of course, in other duties nearer home.

McCallum was not long in discovering that he had made a bad exchange. No. 2 proved a strong engine and a good runner, but she was one of those hopeless steamers which break men's hearts. All her days this malady afflicted her. Another discovery was that she was too high to pass through the Quarry Brig, so her funnel was hinged at the base and arranged to fold back down on the tank top, the first of several DICo engines to be so fitted.

I do not know how long McCallum ran No. 2, but by the early sixties Ferguson had advanced to her command. Apart from her journeys coupled to No. 1, and with the water barrel on the rear engine, I know singularly little about the no doubt many adventures of No. 2. Only two incidents have come down to this generation. Both took place in Ferguson's time.

My grandfather Smith was then in charge of, *inter alia,* the Minnivey pits. He was at one of them in the dark of a winter morning, speaking to one of his men near the pithead when there came a tremendous commotion from the direction of the pit bing. They ran to the scene of the uproar and there found No. 2 half way up the bing like a cat trying to climb a wall! Ferguson, coming in in the dark and taking a race at the steep gradient, had been turned into a dead end at points carelessly left open. How No. 2 was restored to the rails is not recorded, but I have no doubt that Ferguson merely brought her down the way she had gone up. He had tackled more difficult tasks on many occasions.

Another Ferguson exploit occurred on a trip into the brickwork. Ferguson's fireman was a young man called Thomas Rutherford, destined to be the driver of No. 10 on the Coylton Road, and universally known by his nickname of 'Nanny'. The runner or guard was, I believe, Mick News. They were going briskly round the curve approaching the Quarry Brig, pushing a few wagons ahead of them, and Nanny was up on the front of No. 2 ready to knock back the funnel at the last moment, when some of the wagons went off the road. Nanny jumped for it and fell over the fence into the field, while No. 2 left the road also, broke down through the wooden flooring, and landed in the Dunaskin Burn.

Ferguson probably drove No. 2 until about the end of the sixties. Who got her after he transferred to No. 9 I do not know. She was still giving trouble. For a while she was on the slag traffic. Then about 1879 she was laid aside for a contemplated reconstruction. A new boiler was made in the DICo shops, her wheels were turned, new tyres and axleboxes provided, and a new saddle tank made. And then something went wrong. Probably the onset of the great depression of the eighties made the authorities unwilling to repair this ailing engine with no guarantee that she would be any better. The new boiler was actually set in the frames but it was never bolted in. My father never saw No. 1, but when he came to Waterside in 1884 No. 2 was there in her partly-dismantled condition. About the end of the eighties Mr James Frew, who had come to Waterside as chief engineer, decided to utilise the new boiler for No. 5 (I), another Neilson engine with an indifferent reputation. The remains of No. 2 were moved to the yard beside the Slag Brig and were finally disintegrated about 1890. The new saddle tank was still intact in the late 1920s.

No. 3

0—4—0, with pannier tanks extending from front of smokebox to rear of boiler barrel.

Built Hawthorns & Co., Leith Engine Works, 1856. Makers' number: 138.

Only known dimensions: cylinders (inside) 13 in by 20 in
wheels: 4 ft
wheelbase: 6 ft
length over buffers: 20 ft 6 in
working pressure: 120 lb p.s.i.

Small dome, centre of boiler. Spring balance safety valve over firebox, with brass cover and tall funnel. Regulator in smokebox. Funnel long and parallel, with rather wide coping. No splashers. No cab, except a temporary wooden affair fitted in the 1915-21 period when on Burnfoothill section.

Subsequent reconstruction: 1882-3. New wheels, 3 ft 6 in diameter, substituted for originals. New side tanks fitted. 1903. Extensive overhaul and renewal. New boiler fitted by Barclay, Kilmarnock. Dimensions of new boiler: heating surface, tubes 456 sq. ft, firebox 50 sq. ft, total 506 sq. ft; grate area 9 sq. ft. Dome in centre of boiler. Regulator in dome. Ramsbottom safety valves over firebox.

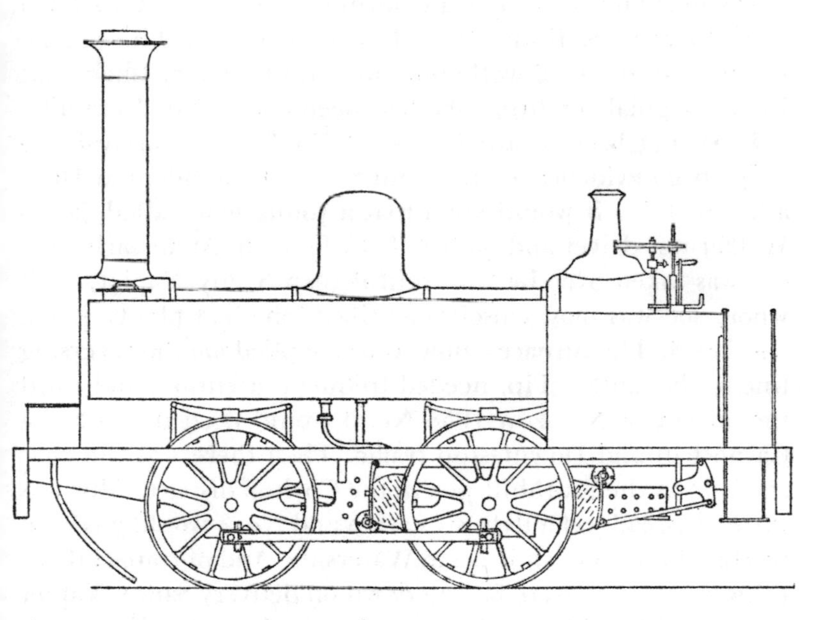

No. 3 in original condition

No. 3. We all knew her—with her *inside* cylinders. Nos. 3 and 11—these were the inside cylinder ones. Few could remember No. 3 as she came to the Doon valley, with her big 4 ft wheels and her tall, spindly funnel. No. 3, which came on *rails,* the first to do so. This dates her coming. The rails on the Ayr and Dalmellington line were not complete until about the beginning of May 1856. The first passenger train went up to Dalmellington on 7 August, preceded by No. 3 running ahead as a sort of herald.

No. 3 was an unusual engine, but she was not unique. I think there is little doubt that Highland Railway No. 17, which was obtained from Hawthorns in 1863 to work the Burghead branch, was similar. She had the same principal dimensions. No. 17 became No. 1A, and was given the name 'Needlefield'. William Stroudley rebuilt her during his tenure of office at Inverness, adding a small pair of trailing wheels. Then in the Railway Magazine of June 1925, page 482, there is a photograph of 'the first locomotive in South Africa'. This shows an engine built by Hawthorns in 1859 for the Capetown & Wellington Railway, then 4 ft 8½-in gauge. The engine shown is an 0—4—2 well-tank, but I think it very likely that in her original condition she had been one of No. 3's family.

It has not been recalled who got No. 3 on her arrival. To judge from evidence at the inquiry into the accident at Dunaskin in 1856, it would seem that a young man called James Walker was driver and Robert Dick fireman. At an early date she was taken over by that skilful man Sanny Napier, with whom she was most closely identified. She had plenty to do, had No. 3. The furnaces, now to be supplied *via* the reversing line at the Cutler Tip, needed frequent attention, and until the advent of No. 4 in 1858 No. 3 would need to work the Carnochan and Downieston traffic. Then there was the char traffic from the Raithhill pits in the Coylton district. This was carted by road to Hollybush station and No. 3 would go down to Hollybush to fetch it up to Waterside. And of course, if the railway company were falling down on delivery Sanny Napier and No. 3 would nip down to Ayr harbour for limestone.

Napier had a soul above the hauling of limestone, however. Failures of G & SW engines were not infrequent, and the DICo invariably came to the rescue. If it were a passenger train then Sanny Napier and his fleet No. 3 were the usual substitutes. They could run passenger time in very good style —too good on one occasion, when they failed to stop at Ayr station and went right out through.

A photograph of the Waterside furnaces, taken in 1871, shows No. 3 still at her accustomed tasks. She is on the high level line of the furnace bank. But she was soon after to get a very literal 'rise in the world'. The ironstone pits on Burnfoothill were at the peak of their production. One engine could not cope with the traffic, and No. 3 was rope-hauled up the incline to join No. 6 on the high plateau. Her tall funnel must have required drastic shortening in order to fit the Burnfoothill shed, though I have heard recently of a shed at Corbie Craigs, of what dimensions I know not. Apparently at one period one engine worked the southern part at Corbie Craigs, and the other the northern district around Bowhill. Then at a later date one engine only was in use in summer, but in the more rigorous conditions of winter the second was put in steam to assist.

I do not know who first drove No. 3 on 'The Hill', but when the 'summer and winter' era began it was customary for No. 6 to work in the summer by herself, then in winter No. 3 would be sent out to assist, with No. 6's fireman driving.

In the eighties it was Jimmy McGraw who was firing to Yorston on No. 6. I remember him very well in 'The Old Hospital' adjacent to Sillyhole crossing at Dalmellington, an old man with ruddy cheeks and fluffy white side-whiskers, a great cultivator of prize roses. But I learned afterwards that this placid old rose-grower had a period in his hot youth when he found the big-wheeled No. 3 very much to his liking and proceeded to conduct the traffic on Burnfoothill at a speed which was not seen again in that region until the days of aeroplanes passing overhead.

Of course there were rows about it. The permanent, so-called, way on Burnfoothill was several degrees worse than that of the DICo lines down in the valley, which is saying a good deal, and I have no doubt that McGraw and No. 3 were off the road about as much as they were on it, but it was one glorious smash at Burnfoothill which caused the biggest row.

It was a Saturday night in winter, and McGraw and No. 3 were coming in from Corbie Craigs with a great rake of char —I think they had thirty-three on. To get these to the 'drum-head'—the top of the rope-worked incline—it was necessary to draw forward in front of Burnfoothill houses and then shove back to the drumhead. This was on a heavy rising gradient, and you could put only about a dozen wagons up to the drumhead, so McGraw stopped the rake clear of the points and left his guard to get down brakes while he took the first ten or so forward for a race at it. The crowd of them had been far too long in the beer-store at Benwhat; the guard's fingers were all thumbs, and just as McGraw came storming back to charge the grade to the drumhead the rake came creeping down and fouled the points. There was a crash you could have heard ten miles away. One wagon reared up and fell on its side, its open mouth against a kitchen window in Burnfoot-hill; the window burst in and the kitchen was filled with char.

Of course they all got the sack, but enginemen were scarce; before long 'all was forgiven' and they were back on the job.

This wild work, however, irritated William Prentice, General Mining Manager. These big 4 ft wheels, he reckoned, were a menace on The Hill. The company had got recently from Messrs Hawthorns a very nice little engine, No. 11. She had wheels 3 ft 6-in diameter and was doing very useful work. Prentice thought that if they could get two similar pairs of wheels for No. 3 it would improve her hauling capacity and prevent these wild cowboys from trying to break records and everything else in sight. So this was duly done, and in the engineer shop at Waterside No. 3 was duly fitted with her new wheels. But, alas, like many another good idea it did not work out in practice. The smaller wheels entailed a greater number of revolutions in order to cover the same distance. I have no doubt that McGraw and Co. tried to go as fast as ever, and they promptly ran No. 3 out of breath. The boiler which had supplied the 4 ft wheels refused to meet the increased demand of the 3 ft 6-in. No. 3 got a bad reputation for steamnig which remained with her until she was fitted with a new and presumably more efficient boiler.

By the end of the century the mining of ironstone on the Burnfoothill plateau had declined so much that the services of two engines were no longer required. So in 1899 No. 3 returned to the valley and took the place of No. 5 (I) which had recently been scrapped. This was on the Slag Hill job. Her neighbour was No. 12, and when I was a boy the 'Bogie Injins' were always Nos. 3 and 12.

By 1903 No. 3 had reached the respectable age of forty-seven, and many things about her were in need of renewal. So in that year her overhaul was taken in hand. The primary requirement was a better boiler, and this was fitted by Barclay of Kilmarnock. The engine's original boiler had had 63 2-in tubes. The new one had 112 1¾-in tubes. No. 3 went back to her Slag Hill job in a much more efficient state. I think that No. 8 deputized for her during her absence.

Bob Shaw and Hughie Brogan were the drivers on the Slag job in the early part of the present century. No. 3 seemed destined to finish her days on this humble task, but in the middle of the First World War she was, most unexpectedly, recalled to her old post on Burnfoothill.

The Hill engine at that time was No. 15, which had gone there new in 1909. Now No. 15 had a steel firebox and tubes, and these did not prove any more of a success on Burnfoothill than they did elsewhere in Britain. So about 1918 No. 3 was sent up aloft. I have a note in a diary for that year that Nos. 3 and 15 were *both* on The Hill. I take it that replacement of No. 15's firebox and tubes was pretty much out of the question in war-time, while No. 3 herself was by that time in a very poor state. The management probably approved the keeping of both engines on The Hill, with crossed fingers lest they both break down at once!

No. 3's firebox had got very bad. There were three bad cracks in the outer shell. I remember my uncle Davie Larmer telling me of an occasion when he had been up trying to cobble up old No. 3, and when he had got her a bit better they went out on a trial run to 'Ben Braniachan', otherwise the Craigmark mines Nos. 3 and 4. Alec Beattie would be the driver then. But poor old No. 3 was still weeping sadly—the *inner* firebox was paper-thin—and short of destination she failed for the necessary steam to put them over a small hump. They stopped for a blow-up. My uncle got down for a look round. The firebox leaks were hissing away dismally. Then he noticed that they were in a shallow cutting through peat. He got the bucket down, crumbled some peat into it, filled up with water, and made a sort of mulch. Then he fed it to the boiler through the injector overflow. He said it was amazing how each leak stopped hissing almost with a *click* as the peat got to it.

No. 3 was on The Hill for a goodly spell—probably until No. 15 was overhauled—and when she returned to the valley there was no more Slag Hill job. The furnaces had closed down. So for a while No. 3 lay derelict, then about the end of 1921 my uncle had another go at her. In April 1922 my friend Tommy Hopes had a most pleasant two days firing to my uncle on No. 3 when they were running her in. Hopes's description of his driving her in from the Houldsworth didn't savour of any deficiencies in speed—age and smaller wheels notwithstanding! But there was not really much life left in the old engine. She did very little work thereafter, and was withdrawn and scrapped in 1924. In 1939 Wallace Boyns, Chief Engineer, offered me the makers' plate off No. 3. I didn't accept his kind offer. I think I must have been suffering from temporary mental black-out!

No. 4

0—4—0, with side tanks extending the length of the boiler barrel, and cut away above each wheel.

Built Hawthorns & Co., Leith Engine Works, 1858.

Makers' number: 174.

Only known dimensions: cylinders (outside) 16 in by 24 in
wheels: 4 ft 6 in
wheelbase: 7 ft 6 in
working pressure: 120 lb p.s.i.
length over buffers: 22 ft 6 in
weight in working order: 26 tons 5 cwt

Dome over firebox, with brass funnel. Spring balance safety valve on dome. Parallel funnel with coping. Cab fitted *for one day only*. (See narrative.)

Subsequent reconstruction: New boiler fitted by Grant, Ritchie & Co., Kilmarnock, 1898. Dome in centre of boiler and safety valve over firebox.

Truly No. 4 was a remarkable locomotive. Her acquisition was a matter of great moment, as well it might be, for she cost £2,050. The chairman announced 'We are getting an engine which will do the work of eighty horses. . . .' Yes, perhaps in theory, but those eighty horses were working at scattered points over an area maybe six miles square. No. 4 couldn't be everywhere at once.

Dimensionally, of course, she was enormous—a great, sprawling elephant of a thing, ill-balanced in her machinery and equally so in her huge frame, perched on its 7 ft 6-in wheelbase. In overall length she was only four inches shorter than No. 10, which was a 2—4—0.

In her details No. 4 had one very remarkable feature. The steam pipe was carried from the dome to the smokebox in the usual manner. There it divided in two branches, one to each cylinder, and each branch had a separate regulator. These were coupled by a connecting rod, and a wiper shaft from the actuating spindle engaged this connecting rod. As wear developed the connections got a bit slack and it was possible, by a judicious working of the regulator handle, to shut off one regulator before the other. And thus, during periods of light steaming it was possible to take No. 4 hopping along on one leg! When Grant, Ritchie fitted the new boiler, however, they cut out such frivolities and put the regulator in the dome.

It is strange that Hawthorns should have designed such a large engine for the 0—4—0 wheel arrangement, for 0—4—0 *tank* engines were still somewhat rare in 1858. She was not unique, however. I am informed that No. 3 of the Coltness Iron Company was similar, but that her ungainly antics had resulted in her being considerably modified. A pair of small carrying wheels had been fitted underneath the footplate and she had been given a tender. In this guise she used to do a daily trip over the Morningside branch of the North British Railway as far as Bathgate. Her driver was James Frew and her fireman John Yorston. These men had interesting links with the Doon valley, for James Frew, son of the above James, came to Waterside to be chief engineer, while John Yorston came to the DICo as a driver, spending most of his driving career on the 'elevated lines' on Burnfoothill.

So No. 4 proceeded to do the work of eighty horses, and very soon it became apparent that she could give work to another eighty at repairing what she had damaged. These poor little light rails were put in in the days of exclusive horse haulage. This great monster, walloping about like a bull in a china-shop, was breaking them right, left and centre. She had to be warned off various sections for a time. However, there was work in plenty. The coal-pits in the Patna area, the Downiestons and the Carnochans, were producing copiously, so No. 4 was put on to this job. With the same restrictions as on the Sillyhole section, where DICo traffic was allowed to operate only at certain times of the day, it was good to get an engine which could haul plenty of coal and haul it *quickly*. No. 4 was all right for that.

Quite the most prominent driver of her early days was Matthew Leggat. He was a young man when No. 4 came—only twenty-four years of age. He married my grandfather's sister, Margaret Larmer. Rob Dick, who was a good deal older, used to fire to him. He was a keen young chap, Leggat, game for anything. They tell of one day when he was on the Carnochan job and the G & SW goods came up from Ayr and stopped just short of Dalharco. She had two engines on. Load: sixteen of limestone and four vans. The train engine had failed—a broken valve spindle. She limped inside at Patna.

The pilot (it must have been a very small engine) confessed himself unable to take on this train unassisted. 'All right', the Patna stationmaster said. 'Wait till Leggat comes up from Carnochan, and if he hasn't too many on we can combine the two trains.' Presently up came Leggat, and as he came through the bridge they signed to him to stop and began to count the rake. By the time the fiftieth wagon hove in sight they gave up and signalled him to go on. However, Leggat stopped and came back. 'What are you wantin'?' he said. They told him about the broken-down goods with its twenty wagons. 'Hing them on,' said Leggat. 'But good heavens', they said, 'you've got *seventy-four* on!' 'I ken,' said Leggat. 'Hing them on!' Then the wee pilot piped up and said he would go on assisting Leggat. 'I don't need a pilot,' said Leggat, and forthwith hauled those ninety-four wagons single-handed to Waterside. Granted the gradients are pretty slight, but it was a great piece of work.

They tell of another time that Leggat was down at Patna with No. 4. Shunting at Dalharco Junction, some of the wagons got away down the main line. Leggat was alone upon the footplate, but without a moment's hesitation he uncoupled, shunted out and set off in pursuit. Five miles almost they went, pell mell, before he got within reach of them. He was on the viaduct; ahead there was a slight hump at Pleasantfield cutting. If they got over that he would never catch them —they would be right away for Ayr and probably disaster. He caught them almost at the top of the hump, buffered up, climbed round to the front, coupled up and brought them to a stand.

It was probably for that Patna job that No. 4's crew petitioned for a cab and got it. A large cab was affixed to No. 4, and the first day they got it they were shunting on the furnace bank when they side-swiped a man coming out of another road. There was a considerable pile-up, and my grandfather Larmer, Traffic Manager, came along, full of wrath. They said they couldn't see for the cab. He said he would damned soon sort *that,* so he got a man with a cold chisel and they cut the rivets and tossed the cab down the banking.

Leggat was up on the furnace bank one day with No. 4. He was going down to the Brick Row for a rake of limestone, and his men had cut down through the works to get the wagons ready. So Leggat, all alone on the footplate, came to a set of points which had to be *held* for the road he was going. Leggat gave No. 4 a puff of steam, dropped off, ran ahead, and held the points. As soon as she was over he let go and chased her. Now just at that point they had been emptying limestone, the piles of which had left very scanty clearance for anything passing. Leggat overtook No. 4, and just at the lime-heap he tried to get along to the footplate end. No. 4 caught him in a tight place, twirled him round, dropped him behind her with two broken ribs, and then footed it down the 1 in 40 to the Cutler Tip with great alacrity.

The shepherd and his wife, in the Boathouse, were standing at their front door. They got a ringside seat for the show. No. 4 went flying off the end of the Cutler Tip. Ninety feet till she struck the bed of the burn. She sat down level on her wheels and all that was damaged was a blow-off cock, which hit a stone and was knocked off. Thereby she emptied her boiler and burned firebox and tubes. They had to lay a track down the side of the Tip and haul her up over sleepers.

I remember my uncle telling me of an adventure with No. 4 near the same spot. His aunt Aggie was in the Cutler at the time and he used to go in the mornings to fetch milk before he went to school. Another boy was on the same errand—I think it was The Ghost Nichol. It was winter weather and the mornings were still dark. Here at the saw mill they found a fine wee light bogie that the fencers used to use for taking their materials along the line to the job. So they got the bogie, had a nice downhill run to the back of the Brick Row, pushed the bogie up the 1 in 40 to the Cutler Tip, and ditched her.

Then when they returned with their milk cans they had a grand rush down the long descent to the Brick Row. All had gone well till this morning when they were rattling down the bank and one of them happened to look round. . . . There was a thing like the Demon King right on their tail! This was No. 4. She had dropped a plug up on the bank, and they were flying for the shed before the steam would be out of her! My uncle took off the one side and The Ghost off the other, and No. 4 went *SCRUNCH* out through bogie, milk-cans and everything!

Uncle Davie's first job was in the 'weighshouse' up on the furnace bank. He was clerk there to Willie Watson. There might be anything up to half-a-dozen engines shunting about the bank at one time and when dinner-hour came the men just left the engines where they sat and went home. Old Willie Weir was traffic foreman on the bank, and the sight of an engine doing nothing used to send him nearly frantic. So the enginemen would be scarcely down off the bank when he had his head in at weighshouse door. 'Are ye there, Davie? Awa' an' get Shaw. Tak' Nummer Fower an' awa' an' get me a rake o' limestone f'ae the Brick Raw.' My uncle was fifteen years of age. Shaw, the grease-boy on the bank, was fourteen. The pair of juveniles would get this great unwieldly No. 4 and toddle away down quite unconcernedly to the Cutler Tip and the Brick Row and bring up fourteen or fifteen of limestone.

One day they were on their accustomed dinner-hour job. They were hauling, tail-first, up the first leg of the V. It was raining heavily and No. 4 started to slip. Both boys began to sand from the wooden boxes on the footplate. Shaw's was handy enough. He could sit astride it and drop sand down the pipe. The one on the driver's side was more awkward, in at the back of the reverser. To reach it my uncle had to bend over the quadrant with his back to the face-plate. The solitary gauge-glass, set at an angle, had, of course, no protector. He thinks that as he stooped some rain may have dripped from his jacket-tail on to the hot glass. BANG she went off, and promptly filled the seat of his trousers with powdered glass!

However, they were not disconcerted to any extent. Davie got the cocks snapped shut. They had now no water-level indicator, but they put on the injector at the usual place on the second leg of the V and reached the bank safely. But before my uncle could resume work he had to take off his trousers and pick the glass out of them!

No. 4 would be on the (1884) Pennyvenie Road by then. That was when No. 4 fairly came into her own. John Caldwell was her driver then, a worthy man, but no one would recognise him by that name. 'Cur-*waal*' was the Scots rendering of this surname in our parts, and I don't see why I shouldn't call him that. The work that Curwaal did with that engine was prodigious. He could come out at five in the morning and be up on the bank by six, go into the sidings at the north end and catch twenty empties, *shove* these up to the head of the Laight Brae, pull the pin and let them go. The runner could travel down the bank with them to Craigmark and stop them on the level by dropping brakes. Meanwhile Curwaal would tear away back down to the bank, go into the sidings at the *south* end, and catch another twenty. These he would *pull* up the Laight Brae, go gently down the far side, and couple up with his first half at Craigmark. He would take the forty empties right up past Pennyvenie No. 2, slip those he was *pulling,* and they would run back down into No. 2. Those he was *shoving* he would shove up into the sidings at No. 1 pit. Then he would catch the loads which were ready and drop down with them past the entrance to No. 2 pit. The crew would go in and run out the loads from No. 2, he would back on to them, and right away, over the Laight Brae and the Quarry Brig to the furnace bank. Then he would go and have his *breakfast*! Some railway organisations would be quite content nowadays to allot that as a whole day's work!

Then poor Curwaal fell ill. It was T.B. There wasn't much to be done about it in those days. About the same time No. 4 went on the sick-list also. Her boiler was sorely strained with the heavy work. She may have had a working pressure of 120 lb officially, but of course no driver ever thought of tackling the Laight Brae till he had held down the spring balance and he had about 135 to 140 on the gauge. My father, as a boy, used to come down the Pennyvenie Road on No. 4 and others, and it was his job to hang on to the valve till they had got her well up. Then they would charge the bank. They kept the injector shut off, and they would top the bank with 90 lb of steam and the water just in sight. Then, of course, on with the injector and bring the temperature down with a run. No wonder boilers gave trouble.

Well, No. 4 was very bad. Tubeplates were bulged. She was needing urgent shopping, but they couldn't spare her out of traffic. Curwaal was off; next in turn was Hammy Frew. His correct name was Robert, but few people knew that. I think he had been firing to Curwaal. At all events the authorities judged that Frew was not sufficiently experienced to tackle the Pennyvenie Road *plus* No. 4 in her then parlous condition. James Ferguson with his No. 9 was on the pig-iron job about the works. He was transferred to No. 4 on the Pennyvenie, while Frew went to No. 9 on the pig iron.

Uncle Davie Larmer was by then serving his apprenticeship as an engineer. He had been up at Pennyvenie pit on some job or other, and came home to Waterside by the evening rake, No. 4 and his uncle, James Ferguson. There were on the footplate the uncle and nephew, together with old Adam Campbell, the pit joiner. Fireman and runner were back on the rake. They had twenty-nine on.

Things went quite normally at first. They took it gently along to Craigmark, and my uncle probably held down the safety-valve. Then with a full boiler and a more-than-full head of steam they let her at it. They were about a third of the way up when the front tubeplate bulged and two tubes dropped inside. . .

DICo engines didn't use ashpans in those days. *Down* through the fire went a torrent of steam and hot water, hitting the ground and enveloping the whole engine. My uncle made out along the gangway to the front end, where he hung on, dodging the eruption which was coming from the funnel and the smokebox door. The old joiner *fell off*, and tumbled over the fence into the field. Ferguson stood to his post. He whisked round, yanked out the pin, and let the rake go. The crew could get brakes down and hold them. Then with what steam was left he put her over the top of the Laight Brae. He then ran by gravity down to the Quarry Brig. My uncle dropped off and held the points. They ran by gravity to the Cutler Tip and my uncle once more held the points and they ran down to the Brick Row. They had then only 150 yd to go to the shed, and No. 9 came down and hauled them in.

I have always thought that that was a piece of quick thinking. Many a man in those appalling circumstances would have shut off, sat down, and sent someone to walk in and fetch assistance—a full hour's job. My uncle said that Ferguson was a *sight* when they got in. He was soaked to the skin. He was wearing one of those old felt hats with a low crown and a wide brim—we used to call them 'wideawakes'. Also his thick hair had grown rather long, and the ends were curling up where they met his collar. The brim of his hat and the up-curl of his hair were lying full of grey ashes!

That would be about the year 1890. I don't think Ferguson was very long on No. 4 then—she probably did go in for overhaul, then Hammy Frew got her, and he had her for a long time. When I was a small boy, Nos. 4 and 9 were working the Pennyvenie Road. Frew had No. 4 and The Squirrel (Adam Ferguson) had No. 9. Then Willie Boyd had No. 4 for a spell. Jock Kaur followed him. I think Geordie Guthrie had her at the finish.

The first morning that big No. 17, the first 0—6—0, took a rake down from Pennyvenie I was on the footplate. I remember that when we came to the bank they wouldn't let our engine go over the weighs, so it was old No. 4 that had to take our rake and weigh it. That was in August 1913. I don't remember seeing her again. Some time about 1915-16, unnoticed in the great turmoil, the old veteran slipped away. It is quite probable that over the heads of Waterside men crouching in the trenches before an attack went parts of old

CONTRAST IN FUNNELS

(14a) *No. 18*(I). *Boiler mountings cut down to fit Quarry Brig*
(14b) *No. 23* (*ex Eglinton No. 6*). *Driver, Kennedy Bryden*

(15a) *No. 15. On footplate, Wm Hutchison, Cleaner*

(15b) *No. 20. Left to right: Harry Graham Jnr, Fireman; John Hendrie, Driver; Robert Bryden 'Teuch', Guard*

No. 4 which they knew so well, fashioned into weapons for the destruction of their enemies.

No. 5 (I)

0—4—0, with saddle tank, ogee sides, flat top, extending from front of smokebox to rear of boiler barrel.

Built Neilson, Glasgow, 1865. Maker's number: 1,129.

Only known dimensions: cylinders (outside) 12 in by 20 in
wheels: 3 ft 6 in
working pressure: 120 lb p.s.i.

Dome over firebox. Regulator in dome. Handle on top of dome, working horizontally round a quadrant. Motion: Stephenson's link, driving rocking arms which actuated valves on top of cylinders. No cab.

Subsequent reconstruction: About 1884, fitted with new boiler which had been intended for No. 2. Nothing is known of the dimensions of this boiler.

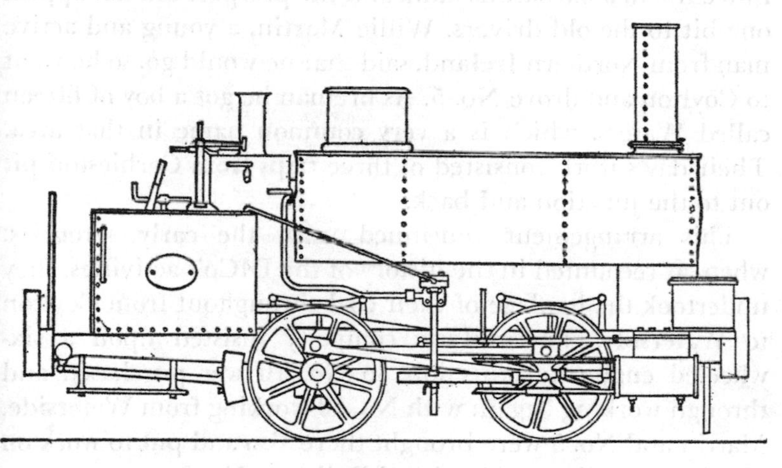

No. 5 (I)

A fifth engine was clearly needed for this new venture in the Coylton district. The engine working this new branch would require to be isolated from the others at Waterside. The work was not very heavy. Hawthorns had rather frightened the DICo, I think, with those two big and expensive high-steppers.

They went back to their old friends Neilsons, now a very big firm indeed and doing plenty of business in small tank engines, besides much bigger stuff. No. 5 was of a standard which Neilson had developed at this time. She had the now very characteristic valve gear with the rocking arms and valves on top of cylinders. Neilson had been 'plugging' this for some years. According to some authorities it was not a source of strength in pulling. Certainly in No. 5 strength was sadly lacking. No, she was a weakly engine, from her pulling and running to her exhaust. My father used to give me imitations of the exhausts of all the DICo engines. He would come to No. 5, and he would say 'Oh 5 had a poor, *fushionless* bark!' A most expressive Scotticism. However, she went to Coylton (to south Ayrshire people 'Culton') and Willie Martin got her.

As I have indicated, the engine for the Coylton Road had to be isolated there to work only between Coylton and the junction with the main line. Her driver would require to go into exile in a barbarous land, and the prospect did not appeal one bit to the old drivers. Willie Martin, a young and active man from Northern Ireland, said that he would go, so he went to Coylton and drove No. 5. As fireman he got a boy of fifteen called Waters, which is a very common name in that area. Their day's work consisted of three trips from Carbieston pit out to the junction and back.

This arrangement continued until the early seventies, when, as recounted in the history of the DICo's activities, they undertook the haulage of their coal throughout from Coylton to Waterside. The railway company insisted upon a six-wheeled engine for this job, so No. 10 was purchased and through working began, with No. 10 working from Waterside. Martin and No. 5 were brought there also and put to work on the line to Jellieston No. 2 and Dalharco No. 2.

On this job her reputation did not improve—there were some heavy little snaps on the Dalharco Road. No. 5 was cursed with the affliction of *priming*, which was not a help. In 1881 No. 11 came new and Martin transferred to the new engine with few regrets I have no doubts. No. 5 then drifted away to menial tasks and eventually joined little No. 7 on the Slag Hill jobs.

No. 2, the larger of the two earlier Neilsons, had been in need of heavy reconstruction about the year 1880 and several new component parts had been got ready for her. She was laid off, and then for some reason the intended reconstruction never took place. About the year 1889 the boiler which had been intended for No. 2 was fitted to No. 5. Whether it was any improvement I do not know. No. 5's indifferent reputation continued to pursue her. Father remembered her coming up the (1884) Pennyvenie line to work Craigmark pit. It was a very steep grade up out of the pit, to say nothing of the Laight Brae beyond, and No. 5 used to make very heavy weather of it.

Bob Shaw had her then. He certainly had her that night in the summer of 1897 when the engineer shop was burned. Her fiery ordeal is described at some length in Chapter Five. No. 5 (I) had not very long to go after that. When I arrived in the world, 10 June 1899, she was probably still to the fore, but by the December of that year she had gone utterly, one of the four DICo engines which I never saw.

No. 6

0—4—0, with saddle tank rounded to contour of boiler. Tank extended over boiler barrel only.

Built: Lilleshall Engineering Co., Oakengates, Shropshire, 1866. Maker's number: 90. This is the number in the maker's records, and did not appear on the affixed plates.

Only known dimensions: cylinders (outside) 14 in by 21 in
wheels: 3 ft 8 in
wheelbase: 7 ft
length over buffers: 20 ft
working pressure: 120 lb p.s.i.

Dome in centre of boiler, protruding slightly above tank. Ramsbottom safety valves over firebox. Shields over slide-bars. Allan straight-link valve gear. Funnel parallel, with neat coping. Weatherboard.

Subsequent reconstruction: Shields removed from slide-bars at an early date. Safety valves removed to top of dome. Large cab replaced weatherboard about 1896. New boiler fitted by Barclay, Kilmarnock, 1906. No record of the dimensions of this boiler. Cab removed, 1909, and funnel hinged at foot, to fold sideways.

The circumstances of No. 6's coming have been dealt with already. The second set of blast engines, dated 1865, and this engine built in 1866 show the sequence of events. An old cash-book of the DICo lists payments to 'Lilleshall Co's engineers'. On 1 March 1866 Charles Machin and George Fisher receive £1 each. On 10 April 'Lilleshall men for starting the blowing engine on 7th inst., £2'. On 18 May 1867 'Sam Maddox and H. Whitehead, Lilleshall Co.' are paid £1 apiece. On 3 June Isaac Baillie receives £2. We do not know if any of those transactions refers to the men who brought No. 6 on her long journey up from remote Salop. It would be fascinating to know.

I am informed that the Lilleshall Company first built locomotives for their own use, as they were having trouble with those supplied by other builders. The home product proved much more satisfactory; building for outside purchasers began and was carried on to a total of some thirty-six engines. This firm appears to have been one of those which allotted works numbers in sequence to all kinds of machinery manufactured. No separate list was kept for locomotives, so the number 90 for engine No. 6 is no indication of the number of locomotives turned out.

An interesting feature of the Lilleshall company was their affinity to Crewe practice, particularly during the Ramsbottom era there. The safety valves and the Allan valve gear will have been noted. The funnel shown in the 1886 photograph is believed to have its original coping, but earlier productions of Lilleshall went the length of fitting the Ramsbottom funnel with its ornamental top. This is shown in the illustration of the engine *Ravenhead* in *Chronicles of Boulton's Siding,* page

248. The Ramsbottom safety valves and the shields over the slide-bars will also be noted.

No. 6 went to Burnfoothill, if not at the start of her working life at least very shortly after. It seems likely that she relieved little No. 1, for which the work had grown altogether too heavy. Jock Newall may have got her then; I do not know. In 1871 the engine driver on The Hill was a young man of twenty-nine, one William Weir later 'Aul' Willie Weir', traffic foreman on the furnace bank. The fireman was a mere boy, one John Thomson, aged seventeen. There is no mention of any 'guard'. The pair of them must have done a power of running about.

The heavy work, often under dreadful conditions of weather, must have had its effect, for in 1871 it is recorded that No. 6 'wasn't doing very well' and No. 9, brand-new, was sent up in her place. But poor No. 6 had to return after a very short time, No. 9 having almost wrecked the entire permanent-way on The Hill. Who drove her in the late seventies I do not know, but about the beginning of the eighties there came to The Hill one John Yorston, and Yorston and No. 6 became another never-to-be-forgotten association.

I have already mentioned John Yorston in dealing with No. 4. He was a neat little man with a remarkably fair complexion and blue eyes with a sort of dancing light in them. He married Christina Ferguson daughter of James Ferguson of No. 9 fame, and so in a round-about sort of way became a relative of mine.

Johnnie Yorston was a most reliable and conscientious man. Of a truth he had need to be, for many an emergency would require to be dealt with on the spot without any engineering assistance from the valley. The weather he worked through must have passed description. My uncle Davie Larmer told me of going up to The Hill one bright frosty morning with the temperature well down to zero Fahrenheit. He was approaching the engine-shed when he saw coming from another angle a strange figure. It was garbed from head to foot in dark clothing, puffs of smoke were arising from it, but it had *no face*! The mystery was revealed when he found this to be old Johnnie. For the rigours of The Hill footplate Auntie Kirsty had knitted for him a species of Balaclava helmet. Instead of following the later pattern so well known in the First World War, where an opening was left for the face, she had left only three small slots, two for his eyes and one for his pipe!

My cousin John Hamilton Smith, son of my uncle William Smith, General Mining Manager, recalls an experience of his early boyhood which illustrates very vividly the free-and-easy ways of DICo transport. Uncle Willie and a young assistant, Bob Leggat, were going up to Burnfoothill and they took my cousin with them. No. 8 Corbie Craigs was in process of sinking and my uncle wanted to check the depth of water in the shaft. They arrived at Burnfoothill just at the enginemen's breakfast-time, so my uncle told Johnnie Yorston to go home for breakfast as usual, then he and Bob Leggat got on to old No. 6 and ran her to No. 8 Corbie Craigs and back with the much intrigued small boy as passenger.

I understand that it was my uncle Willie Smith who first called attention to the enormity of making enginemen work on The Hill with a mere weatherboard for shelter. So about the year 1896 a great cab was fitted to No. 6. It appeared to be similar to that provided for No. 10 on the Coylton Road. Neither could claim any aesthetic quality. It always seemed to me a singularly futile fitment, with its whole back open to everything from the south and east, but old Johnnie Yorston said that there never was a wind blew on The Hill but that cab provided *some* shelter.

Of a truth he had need to be a philosopher. It could be very dreadful up there. I remember my uncle Davie Larmer telling me of one night they were just finishing work in the engineer shop down at Waterside when word came that The Hill engine was off the road. They gathered up some gear and went out into a blinding blizzard! My uncle had never seen the snow so fine and powdery. Thrice as they climbed the incline he had to turn his back to it to get breath. Up on the top conditions were beyond imagining. John Talman, good man, had been promoted from the post of store manager at Benwhat to the similar post at Lethanhill. With no road between the villages, his furniture had been loaded in wagons and taken across by rail. Close to Burnfoothill shed the road crossed the railway on the level. The snow had packed hard in the flange-grooves and No. 6 had ridden off at the crossing and taken most of the train with her. On one wagon was the American organ covered by a sheet. The sheet had flapped loose, and every crevice in the precious organ was drifting full of snow!

However, they had tackled hard jobs before and they did this one. Five hours they were at it, then at midnight they came down the incline on a most marvellous night of clear moonlight in which they could see for miles!

No. 6 had easily the longest service on The Hill of any DICo engine. Of course she came down to Waterside for overhaul from time to time. On one of these occasions, probably about the year 1908, I saw her for the first time, up on the blocks in the engineer shop, with her wheels run out. After such overhauls my uncle, with two of his apprentices acting as fireman and runner, would spend maybe a week shunting around the furnaces. He said that No. 6 was a strong engine but she had no turn of speed whatever. Also her motion was very 'low set' and sometimes on the furnace bank she was apt to catch on heaps of ore or limestone spilled in the four-foot by ill-fitting hopper doors.

My view of No. 6 was of her later aspect. Towards the end of the century she was getting into very bad condition. The outside shell of the firebox had a 23 in crack on the top and side. She was laid up in 1898, and a new boiler seemed a necessity. However, Nos. 4 and 10 were in like condition and new boilers had been ordered for them. A third boiler was out of the question, so the engineer shop had to get busy and patch her up as best they could. So she ran until 1906, when Barclay of Kilmarnock fitted her with a new boiler at last. Thereafter she worked on The Hill until the year 1909, when she was replaced by another English engine, No. 15, built by Markham of Chesterfield. Johnnie Yorston remained as driver until No. 6 left The Hill. Harry Graham was then fireman and Jimmy Stevenson guard.

Poor No. 6. They got her down to Waterside. They stripped her great cab off her and they hinged the funnel to fold down sideways. These humiliations were necessary if she was to work through the Quarry Brig to the brickwork. For thence forward No. 6 was to be a mere drudge around the furnaces. She had a spell on the Slag Hill, relieving Nos. 3 or 12.

It was in the dark of a winter evening in 1911. I was walking through the iron works with my cousin Davie Larmer (Junior). Down about the saw mill this wee waif of an engine went shambling past. They had two firebars out and were dropping their fire as they approached the shed. I was astonished when Davie told me it was No. 6. She did not last long after that and was broken up in the same year. The comparatively new boiler was sold intact.

No. 7

0—4—0, with saddle tank, vertical sides, slightly rounded top, extending length of boiler barrel.

Built Andrew Barclay, Kilmarnock, 1868. Maker's number: 75.

Only known dimensions: cylinders (outside) 10 in by 18 in
wheels: 3 ft
heating surface: tubes: 267 sq. ft
firebox: 33 sq. ft
total: 300 sq. ft
grate area: $5\frac{1}{4}$ sq. ft
working pressure: 120 lb p.s.i.
weight in working order: 15 tons

The above dimensions of heating surface and grate area are for Barclay's standard engine of the size and period, and are not guaranteed individually correct.

Dome in centre of boiler, protruding through tank. Spring balance safety valve over firebox, with cover and discharge pipe. Plain funnel without coping. No splashers. No cab.

This engine was not reconstructed at any subsequent period.

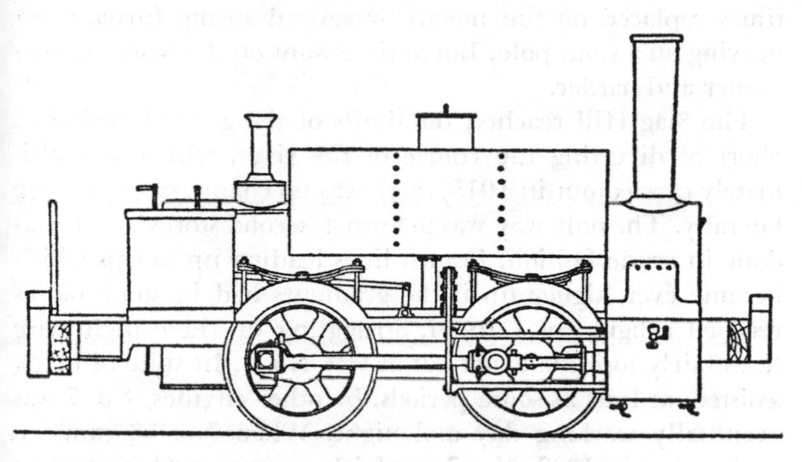

Barclay's No. 31 of 1865. Stated to be similar to DICo No. 7 except that No. 7 had no wheel-splashers

By 1868 the disposal of slag from eight furnaces had become a big job. The Slag Hill, between the main road and the River Doon, reached by bridges over main line and road, was already assuming large dimensions. The 'slag' job had probably been attended to by any engine which had nothing better to do. Now it was necessary to have an engine which must attend to this duty exclusively. But the task, though constant, did not involve any long run or heavy haul. A quite small engine would suffice. The firm of Andrew Barclay of Kilmarnock was getting a good name. They were standardising a small engine which seemed very suitable. So No. 7 was purchased.

She must have been a very small engine. She shared with No. 1 the distinction of being able to pass through the Quarry Brig without any structural alterations. In fact, she must have resembled No. 1 quite a bit. With her weight of fifteen tons, she was certainly not sore on the wretched track, always of a temporary' nature, which straggled out on to the Slag Hill.

Tom Bryden is remembered as her driver for a long time.

She was always on the slag job—the first engine to receive the exclusive title of 'The Bogie Injin'. It was well within her powers at first, and on her frequent derailments she was sometimes replaced on the metals by several strong furnacemen heaving on a stout pole. But as time went on the work became harder and harder.

The Slag Hill reached the limits of the ground available. Short of diverting the course of the river, which was ultimately carried out in 1915, there was no chance of expanding laterally. The only way was to form a 'second storey'. This was done in crude fashion, branch lines leading up to tips which became ever higher until the gradients had in some places reached a figure of 1 in 14. Struggling up these nightmare lines fairly tore the heart out of wee No. 7. In spite of being assisted, at least at some periods, by other engines, No. 7 was eventually working day and night. When No. 12 came to replace her in 1887, No. 7 was fairly worn out. She was then withdrawn and was scrapped in the following year.

No. 8 (I)

0—4—0, with saddle-tank, vertical sides and flat top, extending above boiler barrel only.

Built J. & A. Taylor, Ayr, at some time in period 1868-71.

Only known dimensions: cylinders (outside) $13\frac{1}{2}$ in by 21 in
wheels: 3 ft 8 in
wheelbase: 6 ft
working pressure: 120 lb p.s.i.
length over buffers: 21 ft

Dome over firebox. Spring balance safety valve on dome. Shields over slide-bars. Screw brake applying blocks to both pairs of wheels. Parallel funnel with neat coping. No cab.

Subsequent reconstruction: (very early in career) funnel shortened and coping removed. Saddle tank reduced in height. Funnel hinged to fold down sideways. (Later) shields removed from slide-bars. Was not reboilered at any period.

I wonder how many locomotives have been built in the town

of Kilmarnock. Probably four thousand or more. Twelve miles away is Ayr, a town equal in size to Kilmarnock and which in its day had a number of engineering firms—Messrs J. & T. Young employed 800 men at one time. Yet in the town of Ayr there have been built, as far as I can trace, but *two* locomotives. In 1863 J. & T. Young built a very small 0—4—0 saddle tank for the firm of Taylor, Gordon, who operated a number of small pits in the country lying immediately east of Ayr. About seven years later J. & A. Taylor built a locomotive for the Dalmellington Iron Company.

The circumstances of this transaction I do not know, but Taylors seem to have done a great amount of work associated with mining undertakings—haulage and winding engines—and were very likely introduced to the DICo through these activities. No clue to the locomotive's year of building has so far emerged. The makers' plates, affixed to the sides of the coal-bunkers, state merely: 'J. & A. Taylor, Engineers, Ayr'. This engine was allotted the DICo number 8. No. 7 was delivered in 1868, No. 9 in 1871, so we have a period of four years to cover the date of No. 8's advent. I think it worth remarking that in her early days No. 8 was working on the steeply-graded line to Pennyvenie. This line was opened in 1868, and it may be that No. 8 was built in that year with a view to working the line.*

For No. 8 was a sturdy, big engine—far removed from the tiny little No. 7. Her construction must have been a very big undertaking for J. & A. Taylor. They were good and sound engineers but they had no experience of locomotives, and No. 8 suffered therefrom. For one thing, they seem to have had no means of building in strict alignment, and No. 8 was definitely 'off the square'. DICo got her trued up a bit at successive overhauls, but she was always somewhat tight to gauge. She could never be run with the standard thickness of flange. There was a wee bit at the top of one of the roads in

* From certain features in photograph, Mr R. H. Inness states 'no earlier than February 1869'.

the Waterside engine-shed where the gauge was tight, and if No. 8 was put into that road she always rode up on the rail. But she was stoutly built and a strong engine. My Uncle Davie used to say 'She would go on long after you thought she was *bate*'.

No. 8 had need of power, for the Pennyvenie Road to which she was early assigned was a brute to work. It left the Sillyhole Road just south of the farm of that name, crossed the level meadows to the Chalmerston pits, and then ascended very steeply through the wood beside the Dalmellington-New Cumnock road, curving round until at the Collier Row, opposite the present pit baths of Pennyvenie Nos. 2 and 7, the the grade became even steeper for the half-mile to Pennyvenie No. 1.

Rob Dick had her on the Pennyvenie Road at an early period, with the famous Jimmy McGraw firing to him and Mick News as runner. After a short time the crew got rather fed up with the heavy work involved, and they applied for an addition to their pay in view of the amount of braking they had to do. The application was apparently made to William Prentice, General Mining Manager, who took one look at it and turned it down flat. So this day McGraw and News saw Prentice get on to the footplate with Rob Dick at Pennyvenie to travel to Waterside, and they resolved to give him a 'gentleman's hurl'. So instead of dropping off at the Collier Row and getting brakes down they climbed up on the rake and let her go.

She *went*! By the time they got down through the wood, Prentice was getting a bit worried about his chances of survival. As they passed Chalmerston No. 3 he jumped for it. He was quite lucky. He struck the spot where the smithy folks had been dumping their ashes, and he went into the heap, right up to his neck in the soft, powdery cinders. Rob Dick stuck to her and by some miracle she took the sharp curve on to the Sillyhole Road, but Dick said he was out through Minnivey Brig before he got a grip of them.

No. 8 was probably superseded on the Pennyvenie Road by

No. 9. What she did then I cannot say for certain. I know she had a spell on the Coylton Road with old Davie Culbert. Then when about 1881 No. 9 was laid off for a protracted overhaul her driver, James Ferguson, was given No. 8 as a substitute.

Hughie McCartney was firing to Ferguson at that time—Hughie who in after years drove the Peckett 0—4—0 for the Ayr Harbour Trust. They had gone down to the Brick Row for a rake of limestone, and No. 8 was hauling it tail first along a piece of line that the DICo called straight when the crooked old creature put her hind foot over the rail. She tottered to the edge of the embankment, tipped sideways and slid down till she stuck, canted at a precarious angle. Both of them fell off the footplate; Hughie rolled to the bottom of the slope. When he got himself picked up the first thing he saw was Ferguson, poking about among the grass in the lee of the tilted engine. 'Man, Hughie,' he says, 'I've lost the fancy cover aff ma pipe.' 'Pipe! ' Hughie says, 'Come tae hell oot o' that afore the damt aul' thing comes doon on the tap o' us! '

No. 8 had another playful characteristic. Her screw brake was *left-handed,* that is to say to apply it you had to wind it *anti-clockwise*. Some folks were caught that way. My grandfather Smith was one. He was up at Pennyvenie No. 1 this day. No. 8's crew had gone into the engine-house to eat their piece, and No. 8 had been left rather too near the pithead. With a change of wind the pithead crowd were in process of being kippered, and just as my grandfather crossed the lines Simpson, pitheadman, came to the top of the stairs and bawled 'For God's sake somebody shift that injin! We're gettin' smeakit oot up here! ' So Grandpa obligingly mounted the footplate, gave her a few puffs of steam, and away she rolled down towards the dead-end. Then he applied the brake. . . Of course, nothing happened. No. 8 rolled along, and he was perilously near the 20 ft drop down into the field when he remembered. . . I was told that old Happy Young was caught the same way up on the furnace bank and pitched into something.

One night in the late 1880s my uncle Davie Larmer went out for a stroll after tea. I think he was still a clerk in the weighshouse then. He walked down by the engine-shed and found there Rob Dick. Rob was getting on in years and had not been keeping very well—had grown very stout. So he was just a spare driver by that time. He asked my uncle if he would come and fire to him that night as he had to go up the Sillyhole Road to the level crossing below Dalmellington with J. P. Walker, General Manager, and my grandfather Smith, who were going to a parochial board meeting. So my uncle, aged about 16, readily consented. Someone was clearing the empties out of the Sillyhole Road and word was left that it be kept clear for their return after the meeting.

It was No. 8 that they got—she was spare engine at the time. Away they toddled up to Sillyhole crossing, and the two gentlemen alighted and walked the other mile up to the parochial office. Old Dick and my uncle probably went in and had a yarn with 'Alec of the Gates'—Alec Stewart, a stalwart man of Banffshire, only two weeks in the service of the G & SW when one winter morning at College he slipped on a frosty sleeper and had both legs taken off. About nine o'clock the two returned from their meeting and they set sail for home.

Now the Sillyhole Road was getting into pretty poor shape. It had got no maintenance since its disuse as an access road to the various pits and maybe not much attention even before that, so old Dick was taking it pretty gingerly. This didn't suit the general manager at all. 'Come on, man! Come on!' he says. 'We're not going to be out all night!' So old Dick shook her up and No. 8 began to rattle and clang along.

It was my uncle who saw it first. They had just cleared the Cutler Brig and the light of the furnaces was in their eyes when it loomed up—the high end of a wagon! My uncle made one leap, snapped the regulator shut and slammed over the reverser, then with one almighty BLAM they were into it!

Poor old Dick got the worst of it. He had been standing right behind the reverser and the handle caught him in the pit of the stomach. For the general manager there was a bit of poetic justice. He was wearing a very light-coloured raincoat. The tallow-kettle came off the flame-plate, hit him amidships, and tipped its contents down the front of his coat.

They must have hit it a pretty solid bang, for when my uncle got down to see what was broken he found that the ponderous 'tool-kist' which sat up on the top of the tank had been hurled off and was lying across the main line—and the late passenger not yet up! It was far too heavy for him to lift unaided, and there was no help. My grandfather was trying to get Rob Dick revived, and the general manager was too busy vituperating and scraping his coat. So uncle Davie had to get about half the tools unloaded and up on the footplate before he could lift the kist itself. Then his passengers departed for home and he was left to push these wagons clear, then go round about them and replace them in the Sillyhole Road. After which he had to take No. 8 to the shed, dump her fire, and probably see Rob Dick home.

In her latter years No. 8 had long spells of being spare engine. I remember her pottering about the furnaces, working the brickwork, or running pig iron down to the station. It was for the brickwork job that her tank was cut down in height and her funnel hinged at the base. Once it was reported that her safety valve was not functioning properly. When the engineers took off the dome-cover they found a mass of *fish-bones*! When the crew had been in at Waterside Store getting the provision-vans for Burnfoothill they had been pinching herrings. Then they strung them across inside the dome-cover and cooked them in the steam!

I last saw No. 8 on a fine summer day in the year 1911. My father and I had gone out to 'The Big Mine', later called Pennyvenie No. 4, to see the progress of the construction of the mine and the new railway leading to it. And here, shunting wagons of spoil, was No. 8. Jock Kaur had her on this job —an engine on construction work was always called 'Clay Billy'. That day it was not the genial Jock who was in command, but a very quiet man with a red beard whom father identified with some difficulty as John Weir, who at one time had driven No. 5 (II). This was No. 8's last job. She was broken up in 1912.

No. 9

0—4—0, with saddle tank, vertical sides, flat top, extending from front of smokebox to rear of boiler barrel.

Built Andrew Barclay, Kilmarnock, 1871. Maker's number: 133.

Only known dimensions: cylinders (outside) 14 in by 22 in
wheels: 3 ft 9 in
wheelbase: 5 ft 8 in
heating surface: tubes: 582 sq. ft
firebox: 61 sq. ft
total: 643 sq. ft
grate area: 9.5 sq. ft
working pressure: 120 lb p.s.i.
length over buffers: 20 ft
weight in working order: 25 tons 2 cwt

The above figures for heating surface and grate area are for Barclay's standard engine of the size and period, and are not guaranteed individually correct.

Dome in centre of boiler, protruding slightly above tank. Spring balance safety valve over firebox. Brass cover and discharge pipe. Parallel funnel with very narrow coping. Regulator in dome. No cab.

Subsequent reconstruction: Extensive renewal, 1885. New boiler made in DICo shops—the first made there to be butt and strap jointed. The heating surface figures for this boiler are not known. It was similar in dimensions to the original.

No. 9. Ferguson and No. 9! Who in Waterside had not heard of that immortal partnership?

No. 9 was another Barclay. The DICo had evidently had enough of adventuring with untried manufacturers. Barclay's No. 7 was a good sound job, if small. They had a 'line' in

BARCLAY SIXTEEN-INCH, OLD AND NEW

(16a) *No. 14* (*built* 1906), *at Minnivey dump,* 27 *May* 1963
(16b) *No. 21*(II) (*built* 1949) *at Pennyvenie,* 27 *February* 1963

(17a) *Nos. 23 and 22 on first leg of climb, October* 1962
(17b) *No. 1*(II) *on second leg of climb, No. 23 banking*

14-in engines, and one of those was indicated. Barclay's records show 1872 as the year of delivery. No. 9's plates bore the date '1871'. This is quite understandable. No. 9 was a standard job, built and put into stock to await a customer.

She was no beauty. A side view gave one the impression of a pile of iron boxes, plentifully supplied with snap-headed rivets and surmounted by a funnel that had about as much grace as the funnel of a tar-boiler. I wonder if this was her original funnel. For No. 9 had a queer start. She was sent up on to the plateau at Burnfoothill, and had to have a short funnel fitted in order to get into Burnfoothill shed.

Yes, Burnfoothill was a queer move for this powerful new engine. Prentice, the mining manager, was then reported to be favouring the Burnfoothill people to the exclusion of all others. Of course, the ironstone mines were probably at their peak in the early seventies, and No. 6, the Burnfoothill engine, had been doing poorly. So No. 9 was sent up. About a week later they had to send her down again.

You see, the lines on 'The Hill' were still to a great extent laid with the light material put in when there was horse haulage and little three-ton wagons. No. 6, with her long 7-ft wheelbase, had not done much damage, but No. 9, with her twenty-five tons see-sawing up and down on her short wheelbase was absolutely knocking everything to glory. Rails were being broken all over the place. After No. 9 went back down the incline they had twenty platelayers working on 'The Hill' to restore order.

No. 9's place was certainly where there were substantial rails and sleepers. The Sillyhole Road and the branch off it to Pennyvenie were both laid more recently. Their traffic required a strong engine. So No. 9 was given to Jimmy Ferguson and put on that job.

My father was then living in Dalmellington, but he did not attend the board school there. My grandfather held the view that as manager he should set a good example and have his children taught in a DICo school. So my father had to walk a mile-and-a-half to Craigmark, the nearest DICo school.

One day about the year 1879 (he was then eight years old) he was to go on a visit to Waterside. He was instructed that on getting out of school he was to walk down the Sillyhole Road to the junction of the branch leading to Craigmark pits. One can picture his lonely little figure plodding along, school bag on back, and waiting at the junction till No. 9, with his father on the footplate with Ferguson, came down with her rake. Grandpa jumped down and hoisted father aboard, and he remembered Ferguson looking down at him and saying 'What are ye gaun tae mak' o' this yin, Dauvit?'

That was father's first run on a DICo engine. Rather strangely, I made *my* first DICo run with my father almost thirty years later, again on *Number Nine*. We came down from Pennyvenie to Waterside. I think John Ireland was driving. And over the years father and I retained as our most vivid memory the ear-splitting exhaust of No. 9.

It was terrific. I don't know what size of mouthpiece they had on her blast-pipe. It sounded to me as if it had been about 1½-in diameter, and that someone had bashed it in with a hammer after that! Ferguson in his later years was almost stone deaf—in his own home. Put him on the footplate, with No. 9 kicking up her appalling din, and he could hear you speaking all right. I don't know if they had been trying to make No. 9 *steam*. Barclay's engines had no great reputation at Waterside for steaming. They seemed to be made for a heavy bout of work—as in a shunting yard—and then an ease off. The four or five miles of continuous heavy work which some of the DICo jobs involved seemed to drain the boiler far too quickly. Maybe someone had been trying to get steam where there was none.

The inevitable back pressure didn't seem to affect No. 9's pulling capacity. They were lifting a huge load from Pennyvenie one night, and my grandfather Smith was on the footplate with Ferguson. 'Jimmy,' he said, 'I believe if you had a rope roon Ailsa Craig you could shift it!'

Strong but crude—that was No. 9, and one of the crudities was her regulator valve. It was just a large flat valve with no pilot-valve to ease the pressure. The effort to open it under a full head of steam must have been dreadful. No wonder Ferguson died when he was but sixty-five—his heart and chest muscles racked by that awful regulator. I remember my grandfather telling me about one night when they were ready to leave Pennyvenie and it took the efforts of three of them—Ferguson, my grandfather and James Hill the Pennyvenie manager, to get No. 9's regulator open!

Ferguson worked No. 9 for about ten years—mainly on the Pennyvenie, Chalmerston and Craigmark jobs—and by that time she was utterly worn out. So she was shunted into a siding adjacent to the engineer shop, and there she lay. Summers passed and winters came, and still No. 9 lay idle and rusting. No one in authority seemed to be able to decide what to do with her. Then one day the general manager stopped to have a look at her and he sent for old Bob MacGregor, the chief engineer and asked him point-blank what was wrong with her.

'Weel,' old Bob says, 'she's needin' a new b'iler, an' she'll need new cylinders, an' the frames are dune.' 'Good heavens, man, it's a new engine you're needing!' says the manager. But No. 9 was rather a favourite of old Bob's, and this rather got him on the raw. 'No, it's *no'* a new injin we're needin!' he says, in his crabbit kind of way. So it wasn't long before the reconstruction of No. 9 was put in hand, and the engine which went back into traffic in 1885 (four years she had lain idle) *was* very largely a new one, with very much the good and bad qualities of the old.

Jimmy Ferguson got her once more. He had her on the pig iron jobs about the furnaces for a bit, then I think that there was so much work on the Pennyvenie Road (the 1884 one) that both Nos. 9 and 4 were on it.

My uncle had begun his engineering apprenticeship in 1888, and if he had to go to a job up at Pennyvenie he usually travelled with his uncle Ferguson. He told of one cold, dark winter morning. They were going up tail first and pulling the rake. My uncle was curled up on the coal bunker, his arm wrapped round the brake-handle; Ferguson was standing in the middle of the footplate, his back to the fire. He was wearing white moleskin trousers, which were much in favour by workmen of those days. They rolled briskly down the Laight Brae and were just on to the level at the back of Craigmark when there was a loud BANG and they hit something very hard. Uncle Davie, his arm round the brake, was not dislodged, but he was conscious of something *white* flying past. This was Ferguson's moleskins! They had hit a wagon that had run away from Pennyvenie. Ferguson went right over the back plate and landed on hands and knees on the floor of the wagon! But that was just 'one of those things'. Ferguson got up, shook himself, climbed back on board his engine and went on, shoving the wagon.

Wandering wagons seem to have been lying in wait for Ferguson. One of his Pennyvenie nights my uncle was coming home on No. 9. They got over the Laight Brae and down past the Sheep Brig, and they were just coming on for the top of the Quarry Brig when there was a terrific crash and next moment a thick shower of lime-dust fell upon them. An empty lime-wagon had got away from the furnace bank. She must have had a slight application of the brake, for she had gone down to the foot of the dip and a little way up the Laight Brae and had then stopped. The smash broke the buffers and the wagon was locked to them, with the plummer blocks broken and the two pairs of wheels shoved together and screeving against one another. Ferguson thought he might knock the wagon clear, and he opened up, but she ran in front of them right up on to the furnace bank.

Oh he was a tough nut, was old Ferguson. They tell a famous story of him when he was on the pig iron and he was coming down to the station with a load. Just opposite the platform the line from the furnaces came through a gate which marked the boundary of DICo property. Now it was a grand short cut to come down from the Furnace Row, through this gate, across the G & SW sidings and main line, and you were right at the Store. Ferguson was coming along when down from the Furnace Row came The Quey's* wife. She saw Ferguson coming but thought she had time to get through the gate ahead of him. She was just a wee bit late. She was just clear of the rail when No. 9's big broad buffer took her in the rear and tipped her down the banking. Old Ferguson took a look back, saw her gathering herself up, and resumed his duties. 'Stippitest things in the waurl',' he remarked to his fireman 'weemen an' hens—weemen an' hens!'

One dark night Ferguson was just getting in after a hard day's work when they came running for him to go away down to Coylton—The Nanny had broken down. So away Ferguson went with No. 9, away the long road into Coylton in the dark, got coupled on to Nanny's rake, and away for Potterston Junction. They were getting back somewhere about Martnaham Loch when old No. 9 says 'Da-dump'. 'God,' says Ferguson, 'I'm ower a man!' 'Da-dump.' 'God, twa men!' 'Da-dump.' 'God, *three* men!—Naw! It's a *flock o' sheep*!' It was, too. They killed about a dozen before they could get pulled up. The fireman got down for a look and was promptly *sick*! Old Ferguson waded about the gory battlefield, cutting their throats, then they heaved the sheep up into the front wagon. At Waterside, Ferguson stopped at the platform, hauled along the flat barrow, dumped the carcasses on to it and left word for the porter to take them across to the Store.

James Ferguson died in April 1897. I think that he had been off duty for a fairly long time before. Only sixty-five, and they called him '*Auld* Ferguson'. 'The Aul' Deuce' or 'Deucey Ferguson', that was his nickname. He was a great man.

The Squirrel got No. 9. He was another Ferguson, Adam of that ilk, but no relation of James. The Squirrel's folks came from about the Brick Row. He was on the Pennyvenie Road, but, still in the nineties, The Squirrel had No. 9 on the Coylton Road for about six weeks while No. 10 was getting an overhaul.

Nos. 4 and 9 ran the Pennyvenie Road until 1906, when

---

* 'The Quey' was one of the Rutherford family. See page 170.

the first Barclay 16-in, No. 14, came. The Squirrel got her, but No. 9 kept on as her neighbour. John Ireland drove her then. No. 16, the second of the big Barclays, came in 1910. No. 9 went for overhaul, and they must have taken this one very seriously for they *painted* her. It was the only time during my boyhood that I ever saw one of the existing engines of the DICo *painted*. Baillie of Ayr did it. I remember seeing her on the pig-iron job; she was a sort of grass-green, with scarlet connecting and side rods. My recollection says there was no lettering, but I may be wrong in that. No. 9 kept on for a long while on this pig-iron job, then about the end of the First World War she reached the 'last ditch' of old Waterside engines, the Slag Hill job. No. 9 was getting into a pretty sore state. There was a bad crack down the right wall of her inner firebox. The engineers had it packed with little wooden wedges, and when the wood got soaked and the boiler was hot, wonderfully little water escaped. But when the fire was dropped and she got cold overnight, No. 9 was like a spray-bath. In the morning the kindler had to go into the firebox wearing a suit of oilskins and build a wall of coal up the right side of the box to keep her from drowning out the fire before it got started.

Nos. 9 and 12 were on the slag until about the end of 1920. Then No. 9 was laid off, we thought for good. But the furnaces closed down and the blast engines could no longer supply steam to the steam-hammer in the smithy. So No. 9 was brought round behind the smithy, connected up, and supplied steam for the hammer at a pressure of 80 lb p.s.i. She was finally withdrawn and scrapped in 1928.

No. 10 (I)

2—4—0, with two well tanks. No back bunker.

Built Hawthorns & Co., Leith Engine Works, 1867. Makers' number: no record.

Only known dimensions: cylinders (outside) 15 in by 21 in
tubes (length): 10 ft 5 in
wheels: leading: 3 ft 6 in

coupled: 4 ft 6 in
wheelbase: 5 ft 9 in + 7 ft
working pressure: 120 lb p.s.i.
length over buffers: 22 ft 10 in
weight in working order: 30 tons

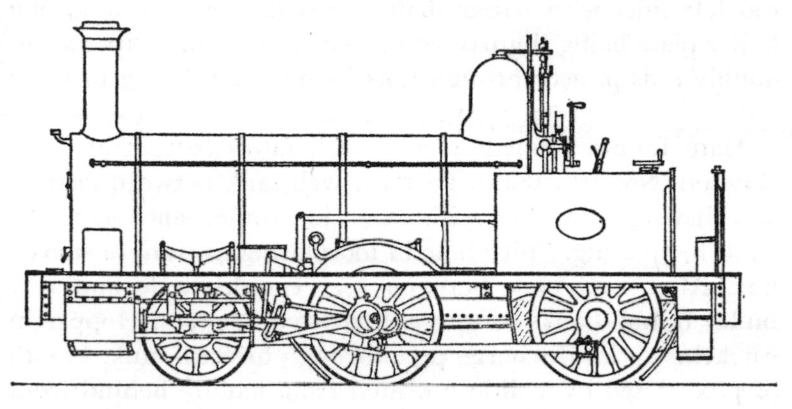

No. 10 (I) in original condition

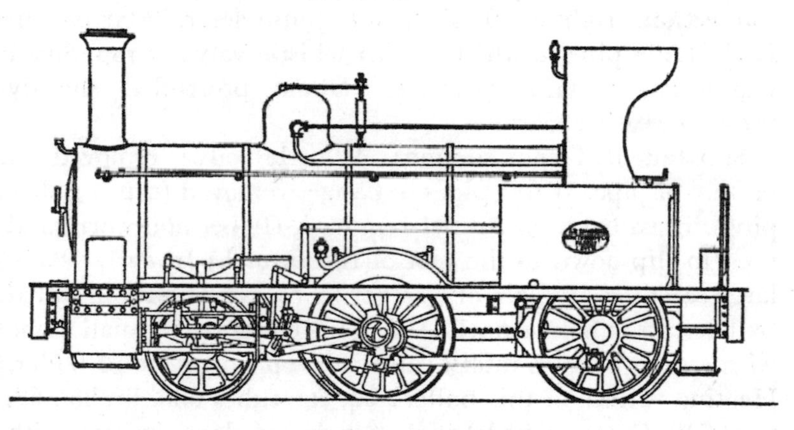

No. 10 (I) as rebuilt, 1898

Boiler fitted tightly on top of forward well tank. Large dome, with copper cover, over firebox. Spring balance safety valves on top of dome. Funnel parallel, with neat coping, and brass band underneath coping. Smokebox door rectangular, hinged at top. Giffard injector left side. Cylinders horizontal. Valves worked horizontally, but valve faces, set above cylinders, inclined inwards towards blast pipe. Gooch's valve gear, outside. Valve rod coupled to lower arm of rocking shaft working in bracket on top of slide-bar. Link (about 6 to 8 in long) from top arm of rocking shaft to valve spindle. Reversing lever and rod left side, with wiper shaft across top of well tank, one boiler plate being slightly set in to clear it. From wiper arms, double rods passed through slots in side footplating to valve rods.

Main frames formed sides of well tanks (patent of S. D. Davison, No. 312, 1859). Forward well tank between leading and driving axles, but with extension under smokebox and front footplating. Filler hole in footplating in front of smokebox. After well tank between rear coupled axle and rear buffer beam. Tanks connected by two 3-in pipes. Hopper in smokebox, with discharge pipe through forward tank. Mouth of pipe closed by a slide operated from handle behind front buffer beam. Water pipes to flanges of leading wheels. Steam connection, right-hand side, for pulsometer, Martnaham Loch. Long pipe to whistle, with whistle valve at top. Small weatherboard with spectacles. Dome protruded slightly through weatherboard.

Subsequent reconstruction: Whistle valve removed to bottom of pipe. Water pipes to flanges removed (causing slipping). Brass band on funnel removed. (It became worn, and used to slip down to the foot of the funnel.) In early 1890s, large cab fitted in place of weatherboard. New boiler installed by Barclays at Kilmarnock 1898. This boiler had a small dome with spring balance safety valves on top, in centre of boiler. Heating surface of this boiler: sq. ft: tubes 680, firebox 62, total 742. Grate area: 10 sq. ft. Smokebox door circular, with central bolt. Trouble with injector later, so Waterside fitted a connection to the injector from the side of the dome, with external control rod from cab. Went again to Barclays, Kilmarnock, for extensive overhaul in 1908.

For many years I had been of opinion that No. 10 (I) was a

solitary specimen of her kind. However, Mr R. H. Inness, of Darlington, tells me of what would appear to be a similar engine. This 2—4—0 well tank, then named *Hawk*, worked at a colliery in Durham and was reported to have come from a Scottish colliery second-hand. *Hawk* was afterwards rebuilt as an 0—6—0 side tank, in which guise she was seen by Mr Inness. There are also many points of resemblance to the engine *Miers*, described in *The Locomotive*, 1940, Vol. XLVI, page 64. *Miers* was an engine with a very chequered career, including a head-on collision with a passenger train between Tralee and Limerick! No. 10 (I) was hardly so adventurous, but she had her share.

My first close-up view of No. 10 (I) was in the engineer shop at Waterside, some time in the early 1900s. I was much intrigued by her makers' plate, which bore the date in Roman numerals—MDCCCLXVII. When she arrived, someone at Waterside asked if that was the name of a new foreman Hawthorns had got!

1867. Years and years ago, someone at Waterside told me that No. 10 (I) was built for *passenger service in the north of Scotland*. The story was vague, and I had long since dismissed it as one of those fables inseparable from locomotive history, but quite recently I was impressed by a coincidence in dates which I had not observed previously.

In 1863 the Highland Railway got from Hawthorns of Leith an 0—4—0 side-tank, which they put to work on the newly-opened Burghead branch. I have already spoken of this engine as closely resembling DICo No. 3. In *1867* William Stroudley, then locomotive superintendent of the Highland, rebuilt the 0—4—0T with a pair of trailing wheels.

Might we postulate a sequence of events? The 0—4—0T, product of Hawthorns, gives trouble through unsteadiness. Hawthorns offer to build a more suitable engine. They build in 1867 a 2—4—0T. The price asked, however, is considered by the Highland to be excessive. Their locomotive superintendent offers to cure the unsteadiness by alterations to the 0—4—0T at much less cost. The Highland approve this plan and the 2—4—0T is left on Hawthorns' hands, to be purchased by the DICo seven years later. We can hardly know the truth now, but it is an interesting speculation.

Seven years. That is what I was told. Seven years she lay in stock. That would make her date of purchase 1874. This links up with the G & SW working timetable for 1 December 1874, which shows a DICo working from Waterside to Potterston Junction each evening at 8.15. Rather strangely, no return working is shown. It may be that with variable amounts of work a return time could not be predicted. In any case, the return trip would be much later than the last G & SW working for the day.

No. 10 (I) was certainly No. 10 to the operating staff. To the public she was 'The Nanny', or 'Coylton Nanny'—'Culton' in the vernacular.

This is one of the strangest pieces of nicknaming that I am aware of.

Thomas Rutherford may not have been the first driver of No. 10 (I), but he had her from a very early period. Now Tom Rutherford belonged to a family whose male members rejoiced in an extraordinary series of nicknames. There were The Bear and The Quey and The Fiddler and The Cobbler and The Huggie—and Nanny. Tom was 'Nanny', and so well-known was he that presently the folks used the name also for his kenspeckle engine. Coylton people went one better, and to this day a Coylton man will point out to you the course of the now-vanished *'Nanny Line'*.

He was a big, stoutly-built man, 'Nanny'. In latter days he grew excessively stout and had some difficulty in squeezing through the narrow opening to the footplate. I remember one day when my mother was taking me to Ayr by the 12.45. At Waterside we were joined by my Aunt Agnes (Uncle Davie's wife) and another lady whom I did not know. We stopped at Patna and to my great interest along the loop came The Nanny, to stop with her footplate at our carriage window. Whereupon the lady, who was none other than Mrs Thomas Rutherford, solemnly presented her husband with the key of the house, as she was going to Ayr for the afternoon.

When The Nanny began on the Coylton Road the Sundrum pits were opening up, and with Carbieston still hard at work there was plenty to do, especially as most of the Coylton coal was coming up to the Waterside furnaces. Two runs had to be made each day, Waterside to Coylton and back, a daily mileage of about forty-eight. The first run left at varying times between 6 and 7 a.m., returning about noon. The second left soon after 1 p.m. and was back about 4.45.

The return journey involved some heavy work. First you had the very steep ascent from Meadowhead pit to Coylton Hillhead, then when you had descended to Carbieston you would get some more from there. The journey out to the junction was not very difficult, but the grade was against the load all the way. From Potterston there were four-and-a-half miles of very heavy pulling up to Patna, with a final two level miles to finish. No. 10 (I)'s load was thirteen eight-ton wagons of coal up there, together with brake-van and, in later years, with tender.

The first time that my uncle travelled back from Coylton with old Nanny he thought he was the greatest old fidget of a driver he had ever seen. Nanny kept fiddling with his regulator, adjusting his cut-off, altering his injector feed, opening and shutting his firedoor. When my uncle got more experience he began to realise that the old man was trying to *save every drop of water*.

You could depend on a fill-up at the tank beside Martnaham Loch. There was another at Purclewan about a mile short of Potterston, but in times of drought it was frequently dry and could not be depended upon. On the main line there was nothing before Waterside. Nanny's tanks were not very capacious, and despite old Tom's careful handling there were many occasions when they had to drop their rake at Patna and run for Waterside with the tanks dry.

They tell many a tale of Nanny and his similarly-named engine. Away back in the seventies and eighties, when staff-and-ticket working was still in vogue on the Dalmellington line, an engine and saloon had been up to Dalmellington on inspection duties. Some of the Top Brass were anxious to get back to Glasgow quickly, and were very annoyed when the signalman at Holehouse Junction held them up, as Nanny had the staff and had probably entered the section from Potterston. By force of numbers they overcame the signalman's scruples and he let them go. Well, they met The Nanny head-on, but fortunately in open country north of Hollybush, so that both trains had plenty of warning. They ran forward and ordered old Nanny back to Potterston. 'Na, na,' says old Tam. 'I have the stawf. You fellas have nae richt here. Back ye go yoursels!' And back they had to go to Holehouse, with their tails between their legs.

It would be in the early nineties that No. 10 (I) got her cab, of a similar pattern to that installed on No. 6. It was neither a thing of beauty nor, in backward gear, a joy forever. No. 10 (I) had no more back protection than the customary waist-high plate at the back of the footplate, and that great cab must have simply *scooped* the wind into it on the downhill journeys.

I remember Uncle Davie telling me of one of those early-morning trips. He was going down to an engineering job at Coylton pits. They were going tail first, with a great string of empties—I think he said they had thirty-three and the van. He was huddled into the right-hand corner of the cab. It was just breaking day, and as they came past Hollybush station he looked back along the train. He idly counted the wagons as they came through the overbridge. *Thirteen* came through, then no more. . . . 'Look out, Tam!' cried my uncle, 'You've broken away!' Old Tam came hobbling across the footplate, took one scared look, then *over* went that regulator, and *down* that line they went as hard as the old thing could dance!

At Potterston old Steel the signalman was out to get the tablet and then, as they drew slowly past him on to the branch he would take the wagon numbers. This morning they came walloping down, nearly knocked him down with the tablet, and went tearing away on to the branch with old Steel shouting and gesticulating after them! Round they went, screeving round the curve through the wood, then, horrors, came Purclewan gates. So they had to *stop* and run and get those gates open, fumbling with them in the half-light, with always a frightened look over the shoulder to look out for the rest of the rake coming. In again, and away as hard as they could, but here within half-a-mile came the *main road gates*! Stop again, out and get them open, and while they were at it someone gave a shout that the rake was coming. It was, but it was coming slowly, and it stopped before it hit the first portion. There had been some pit joiners in the van, and when the cry got up that they were broken away the guard turned the joiners out to climb along the wagons, get the brakes down and jump on them.

I don't know who was guard that morning. Possibly Tammy Rowan—he had a long spell as guard on the Coylton Road. Willie Hamilton fired a lot on the Coylton.

I was speaking of old Steel at Potterston. He was a great character—a stout old man of stout opinions. Steel used to cut hair, and Nanny went to him for a hair-do at extremely long intervals. This day Steel was cutting Nanny's hair and they began to argue about something. They fell out, and Steel put Nanny out of the box with one side of his head cropped close and the other with the hair hanging over his collar. Mrs Rutherford had to borrow a sharp pair of scissors and complete the job when he got home.

Between Potterston and Coylton there were several sidings. One, a short little thing, was at the road crossing at Purclewan. You can still see the earth bank which formed the buffer-stop. Farmers got traffic delivered there, mainly coal. In broken weather a farmer would maybe find himself with extra workers, taken on for the harvest, and nothing for them to do. Here was a chance to get some coal in. He would go out and stop Nanny. 'Can you spare us a wagon o' coal?' 'Oh aye,' and the wagon would be duly shunted into the siding. Then when he got home at night old Nanny would stump across to the general office. 'There five poun' I got for a wagon o' coal I sell't tae Purclewan.'

Another siding was at the east end of Martnaham Loch, just at the road crossing. It dealt with the traffic from a saw-mill set up there and may have been in use only for the duration of its operation. Then before you came to Low Coylton there was the bing of old Carbieston pit. When it closed down they left some of the sidings, and Nanny used to make up his train there. Going down in the mornings they would leave the brake van at Carbieston in order to lighten the ship as much as possible, for old No. 10 (I) could bring only about seven loaded wagons up from Meadowhead pit, and two runs up to Carbieston were necessary to get their train together for Waterside.

No. 10 (I) got her new boiler in 1898. She would likely be re-painted then, and my uncle records the colour as a dark green with the boiler clothing bands picked out in red and white lining. Her large, ungainly cab remained, but of course the new dome was no longer over the firebox. It was away out in the middle of the boiler. Not long after they got the new boiler James Frew the chief engineer was coming up with them from Coylton. They were about to start from Meadow-head pit down in the hollow. Ahead loomed the 1 in 50 bank up to Coylton Hillhead. Frew smiled. 'Aye, Tom,' he said 'You'll not be able to hold *those* valves down!' They started up the bank, and presently Frew became aware that the driver was no longer on the footplate. He looked through the window and there was old Nanny sitting astride the boiler, his arms tight down on the spring balances, continuing the treatment as of yore!

Of course, all DICo locomotive boilers were subject to these strains, but The Nanny's boilers got into an exceptionally bad state. Many a time leaking stays would drown out the fire and they would come to a stand, preferably within easy reach of the inns at Coylton. An SOS would be sent to Waterside and away my uncle would go to the rescue. He kept an old *barrel*-hoop hanging up in the engineer shop. This he took with him on all such expeditions. There must have been some special virtue in this wood. Small parings would be taken off and tapped in at the edges of the defective stay with his trusty horn-handled knife. My uncle was a man of quick temper at times, but for work like this he had infinite patience. His whole soul was in his work. He did not long survive the leaving of it.

Tam Rutherford was on the Coylton job until about 1908 or 1909. He was getting rather infirm by that time, so they gave him a job as spare driver at Waterside, and he worked away up to the period of the first war. Jimmy Geddes got his job on the Coylton. I think he had been Nanny's fireman. I know that Jimmy Geddes was driving No. 10 (I) in the autumn of 1910 when they were building the new houses at Broomknowe, Dalmellington, and The Nanny used to come up the Sillyhole Road in the afternoons with a rake of bricks and other building material.

By the middle of 1914 The Nanny was getting into a very poor state. She would probably have been replaced then, but of course war broke out and replacements were soon impossible. Jimmy Geddes must have had a sore time of it through the first war, with his tottering old engine, the rapidly-deteriorating track, and his increasing ill-health. Tom Bruce was his fireman in the last days of The Nanny, and the guard was John Weir.

John Weir had been the driver of No. 5 (II) for a long time. But John never seemed very happy as a driver—I think he was nervous. So he relinquished the cares of driving to go running on the Coylton, and they say that in DICo service there was no one to equal him for the agility with which he could jump up into a wagon.

During how much of the First World War No. 10 (I) was in active service I cannot now say. I can remember several occasions when I saw her place being filled by No. 15 and, I think, No. 12. Then, late in October of 1918, there came No. 20 and the old engine was officially replaced.

Poor old Nanny. They put her out of the shed to make way for the newcomer. They shoved her into the bank at the back of the saw-mill. Soon she would be sold for scrap, at a good price. But just then the war finished, and with so much surplus war material no one wanted scrap. Five years she lay there in a state of gradually increasing decay and squalor until one day some humanitarian put her out of her misery. That was how they treated priceless locomotive treasures in 1923.

I need not talk. For three years while she lay neglected but still intact I possessed a camera. I never thought of photographing her. Now, when such a photograph has become a virtual necessity to this history, not one can be traced.

Thanks to two craftsmen at whose skill I marvel we *can* see what she was like. My uncle Davie was still fit and active. The 1898 boiler had been retained at the works and was in use as an air reservoir until at least the start of World War II. This boiler he carefully measured up. Then from his incomparable memory came details of all the strange and ingenious mechanism of that great old machine. All this was correlated and set up by my friend David Newlands, now of Montreal. His preliminary drawings were checked by my uncle. I think that the finished product is a very faithful representation.

On one of the few fine days in the summer of 1965 I stopped my car at the east end of Martnaham Loch. Little or nothing remained to mark the position of the timber-cutters' siding, but the track of the line to the west was quite discernable. I followed it for some distance as it skirted the loch, winding round and through the little clumps of woodland. It was quietly beautiful down in that little valley, and it was nice to think of the old Nanny, wending her way through this sylvan scene that she knew so well. Waterside and the roaring furnaces and the molten slag seemed very remote, still more remote the years of humiliation behind the saw-mill. Here in this pleasant country—her own country—may we leave her, our dear old Nanny, on the Nanny Line.

No. 11

0—4—0, with saddle tank rounded to contour of boiler, but flat on top, with shallow beading. Tank extended over boiler barrel only.

Built Hawthorns & Co., Leith Engine Works, 1881.
Only known dimensions: cylinders (inside) 14 in by 21 in
wheels: 3 ft 6 in
wheelbase: 6 ft
working pressure: 120 lb p.s.i.
weight in working order: 22 tons

Dome over firebox. Ramsbottom safety valves on top of dome, with columns set transversely, and no projecting lever. Funnel, plain with no coping, tapering—wider towards top. No cab. No splashers.

This engine was not reconstructed at any subsequent period.

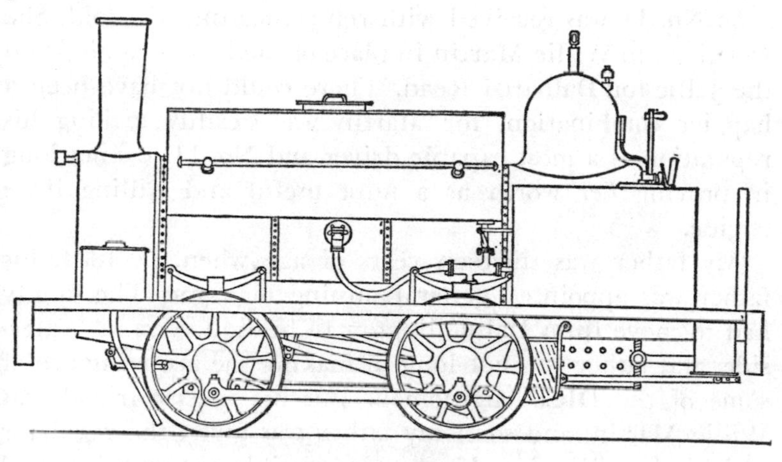

No. 11

Nos. 3 and 11—the two *inside* cylinder engines. That was always the comment. About the end of the seventies, Hawthorns seem to have designed this little inside cylinder saddle tank as a 'stock job', and several have been traced, the dimensions varying a little over the years. The design was certainly of the simplest. As I heard it phrased 'Nummer Eleeven hadna much mair machinery aboot her than a wagon'. But she was good.

John Hunter, General Manager, bought her. He was on a visit to Hawthorns' works one day, saw this engine for sale and purchased her for his company. £1,100 she cost. Her makers' plate bore the date 1881. The makers' number has not, unfortunately, been remembered. There is no tradition of her having lain in stock as No. 10 did, so we may take it that she came to Waterside in 1881 or possible early in 1882.

Her arrival excited little enthusiasm. Old Bob MacGregor, Chief Engineer, was probably a little hurt at having this engine bought and thrust upon him without consultation. '*Anither* inside cylinder yin!' he says. 'As if we hadna enough bother wi' the yin we hae!' Not very complimentary to poor old No. 3 which, knocked about by those wild cowboys up on The Hill, was more sinned against than sinning.

So No. 11 was received with reluctance into the fold. She was given to Willie Martin in place of the feeble No. 5 (I) on the Jellieston-Dalharco Road. There could not have been a happier combination, for Martin was steadily making his reputation as a most capable driver and No. 11 was not long in proving *her* worth as a most useful and willing little engine.

My father was thirteen years of age when, in 1884, his father was appointed general mining manager. The family had to move from Dalmellington to headquarters at Waterside, and father was not long in making the acquaintance of some of the DICo enginemen. But his special friend was Willie Martin, and soon my father was given the regulator and was handling No. 11 at every possible opportunity. And handling a DICo engine on those jobs was quite a different matter from my own efforts, with 'all mod. con.' on the G & SW, thirty years later. With only a screw hand-brake (and of course a reversing lever) one had to execute movements which would have raised the hair on the heads of main line men. Villainous track, awkward roads, heavy drags—he used to give me vocal impersonations of No. 11 starting a rake out of Dalharco. He loved little No. 11. Even when he had gone to Glasgow University I am sure that many a night he would pause from his studies in his poor, gas-lit lodgings, and think of those halcyon days when he belted a rake out to 'The

Fit o' the Incline' with the game wee Hawthorn.

One day, probably at dinner-time, Martin was alone on No. 11 when my father, then about fifteen, joined him. Martin had brought up a rake of limestone from the Brick Row to the bank, and it was now to be propelled up to the 'Limehoose', where the crusher was. It was a steep gradient, a sharpish curve and a rather blind one. Martin asked my father if he would take her while he, Martin, went up on the front wagon and signalled him.

J. W. Smith was nothing loth. He was laying at it, full open, full back gear, and watching Martin away on the front of the rake. Just as they cleared the High Level bridge he caught a glimpse out of the tail of his eye—between two wagons he saw the white hair and the broad-brimmed hat—his father! Grandpa was not there when they returned but Martin had spotted him also, and both were a little apprehensive. That evening my grandfather called his son into a room apart and began a gentle inquisition. He was not surprised or angry at my father's presence on the engine—the DICo engines were anyone's mode of transport, nor was he disapproving of my father *driving*. He had done some of that himself. It was the fact that my father had been *alone* on the footplate that had shaken him. 'Now,' he said 'suppose Martin had fallen off and you had run over him, what would *I* have been able to say to the management?' That was unanswerable and my father could only express contrition, but, as with his son so many years later, such warnings had only a temporary effect. A week later you were 'back on the job'. My parents used to say *'Don't let me see you* doing so-and-so'. I didn't!

No. 11 remained on the Dalharco Road for many years—probably till Dalharco closed in 1894, but she had another assignment. If the regular Coylton engine, No. 10, were laid off for any reason, No. 11 got the job. In my account of No. 10 I told of the pulsometer which was installed at Martnaham Loch, and how No. 10 had a special attachment for supplying steam to the pulsometer. I think I am correct in saying that No. 11 was the only other engine at Waterside which had this fitment, and I remember also that it was on the right-hand side. If No. 11 was sent on the Coylton Road, therefore, it was necessary for her to go up to Dalmellington to be turned on the table there.

On this Coylton job sometimes Nanny took her himself, sometimes Martin went with her. On one of those spells in the early nineties No. 11 was in wretched order. Martin reported the trouble and diagnosed 'broken piston rings', but he was not believed. For some reason Martin could not 'get on' with the chief engineer, who blamed Martin for the condition of the engine. Well, one evening No. 11 came tottering up from Coylton, and when she came within earshot of Waterside at the 'Drumgrange distant' she had an exhaust beat such as those at Waterside had never heard before. She got her train in, then they hauled her to the engineer shop and drew the pistons. The state of the rings was beyond description. My uncle Davie was gathering up the fragments in his bonnet—some of them no bigger than a small marble. To have kept the engine going at all under such conditions was the work of an expert. But the unfortunate misunderstanding between two competent men continued, and finally Martin left Waterside and went to work in Lanarkshire.

Who succeeded Martin on No. 11 I do not know. She would continue to work Jellieston until that pit closed in 1902. After that she was about the works—on the pig-iron job, I think. By 1906, after twenty-five years of hard work, everything about her was in need of renewal. It was hard to part with this gallant little warrior, but the management probably took a wise course in deciding that she had amply repaid their outlay, and in that same year No. 11 was withdrawn and broken up.

No. 12

0—4—0, with ogee-shaped saddle tank, extending over both smokebox and boiler barrel.

Built Grant, Ritchie & Co., Ltd, Kilmarnock, 1887. Makers' number: 179.

Only known dimensions: cylinders (outside) 12 in by 20 in
wheels: 3 ft 8 in
wheelbase: 5 ft 5 in
length over buffers: 18 ft 11½ in
working pressure: 140 lb p.s.i.
weight in working order: 22 tons

No dome. Regulator in smokebox. Spring balance safety valves over firebox with shapely brass cover. Funnel parallel, with neat coping. No cab.

Subsequent reconstruction: Working pressure reduced to 110 lb p.s.i. New funnel fitted, similar to original but with a broader coping and a ring in front by which it could be lifted off in order to pass through the Quarry Brig. Safety valves replaced by Ramsbottom pattern before First World War. About 1921, fitted with new cylinders, 12½ in by 20 in by Grant, Ritchie. 1937, original boiler tested and pressure raised to 140 lb p.s.i. Another funnel fitted, believed to be the one put on No. 9 when she went to Burnfoothill in 1871. Cab fitted.

No. 12 was a bargain. £750 for a 12-in four-coupled tank with 140 lb pressure. It is unbelievable, these days. And it was all new material—bits and pieces left over from various contracts. She had the frame of a 14-in. She came at a time of desperate need, for little No. 7 on the Slag Hill job was fairly worn out. No. 12 was given a week on the Dalharco Road to supple up, and then went on to the Slag.

Then a strange but interesting decision was made. James Frew, Chief Engineer, was of the opinion that this 140 lb pressure, hitherto unknown on the DICo locomotives, was quite unnecessary for this short haul work that No. 12 had to do. A reduction in pressure would reduce the cost of boiler maintenance. He had her valves adjusted to blow off at 110 lb p.s.i.

This was a courageous action, and time was to prove that it was a wise one. Fifty years later the *same boiler,* with the blessing of the boiler insurance firm, had its 140 lb pressure *restored.* Nor was this the end. No. 12 went to her grave in 1949, still with the same boiler. Sixty-two years. It may not be a record, but it is a most creditable achievement.

Another remarkable thing about No. 12 was the business of her funnel. She was a neat little engine, but apparently the top of her saddle tank was too high to allow of the customary folding back of the funnel on to the tank top. So this somewhat mad scheme was evolved of installing a block and tackle apparatus on the wall above the Quarry Brig. Each time No. 12 had to go through this tunnel the funnel had to be *unbolted,* hooked by its ring to the block and tackle, and hoisted up clear of the arch. There it would hang until No. 12 returned from her lawful business in the glen.

On the Slag Hill job No. 12 was neighboured first by No. 5 (I), and then by No. 3. Tom Bryden would be driving at the first, then Bob Shaw and Hughie Brogan were the pair.

It was in No. 12's early days. Tom Bryden had her, and he had gone for lunch (we called it 'dinner' in those days). Jimmy Gill, the hero of No. 1 (I)'s boiler explosion, was a spare driver then. Gill had recovered from his terrifying experience. His only blemish was an inability to exert any force with his right arm if the task were behind the line of his body. This was noticeable when he was bringing over a reversing lever and the movement had to be continued until the lever was well behind him. Gill was employed in substituting for any driver off ill, or at dinner-time, taking over any engine whose driver had gone home to eat.

Well, my grandfather David Larmer was in charge of the furnaces then, and he told Gill to take No. 12 and bring him up twenty-five empty pig-iron wagons from the station.

It was a heavy pull up from the station. Gill would get the pig-iron wagons in the head shunt at the Patna end of the station. Twenty-five was too many for him, so he would bring up a dozen. These wagons had to be weighed—a weary process, and to save the long hang on the grade while the wagons were being hauled up it was customary to pull them up over the weighs and then let them down into the storage siding which ran along in front of Greenhill Row, weighing them on the way down. After which you went down for the remainder.

Well, after he had given his orders my grandfather returned to his office and was sitting at his desk when he heard the exhaust of an engine, loud but *terribly* slow. He puzzled over

'The Quarry Brig', West portal

this, then went to the door. There was Gill and No. 12. He had the *whole twenty-five* hung on, and he was weighing them *on the way up*! Grandpa thought there was something very strange in this, so he hobbled along and on to the footplate.

Gill, who had been blown up with No. 1, was standing there pumping away at his regulator as he worked them slowly over the weighs. The lever of the safety valve came out through a slot in the brass cover. Gill had one or two iron wedges jammed into the slot to hold her down. I think No. 12's steam gauge was numbered up to 180, and the needle was getting well on for that figure! Grandpa thought that he had better remove himself to a place where he had a better chance of survival, and did so with some alacrity.

No. 12 was probably the best-known of all the 'bogie injins', but she did other things besides the prosaic trips to the Slag Hill. When my father and mother were married in 1897 they lived in a flat next to the parish church, now The Kirk o' The Covenant, at Dalmellington. In the late autumn of that year Willie Paterson, my father's cousin, spent a weekend with them. On the Sunday they walked the three miles to Waterside to visit their parents, intending to walk back in the evening. No buses or trains on a Sunday in those days. By late evening the rain was simply pelting down. Waterside had no vehicles for hire. So Grandpa Larmer got out into the tempest and sent Bob Shaw with No. 12 round to the furnace bank just behind their house, and the three wayfarers got up on to her footplate.

I have often thought of my mother on that terrible journey —not a particle of shelter on that footplate except for the waist-high back plate. I think she told me she was wearing a sort of cloak, and Grannie gave her a shawl to wrap round her head. The men-folk would just need to take it. Father said that Bob Shaw was doubtful if he could take them very far, for someone might have lowered the 'drawbridge' which carried the hutch-line from Craigmark No. 2 to No. 1. However, when they came to it the 'bridge' was safely hoisted out of the way, and they passed on. They alighted at the crossing of the road to Chalmerston farm, and would have another three-quarters of a mile of mud and potholes to negotiate before they got home.

On the G & SW every signalbox was issued with a report book, and from 7 May 1895 every out-of-course occurrence had to be recorded therein. Waterside signalbox had its report book, and on Tuesday 8 March 1898 we have the following entry:

> Engine No. 193 of 6.30 p.m. Passenger Ayr to Dalmellington broke down here, on arrival at 7 p.m. got D. I. Coy's Engine No. 12 to take it to Dalmellington and left here 7.29 p.m.
> Peter Stark on duty.

When I was a small boy my father told me the story of that night. He was in the train. Many a time I got him to recount it to me. He told how a messenger was dispatched post-haste to the iron works and how No. 12, her tail to Dalmellington, coupled up to No. 193, a James Stirling 0—4—2 of the 187 Class which looked a perfect giant beside the little Grant, Ritchie. No. 12's drawbar was not so high as No. 193's, and when the little engine began to pull she eased up on her front springs to the accompaniment of violent slipping. However, they eventually got away, and the populace of Dalmellington gave them a cheer as they came in with No. 12 at the head. Unfortunately I do not recollect who was driving No. 12 on that night.

The incident seems to have marked the end of an era. As far as I can trace this was the last occasion on which a DICo engine was called upon to haul, or assist in hauling, a main-line train. I do not recall any instance of it in my time. It is rather a pity. The old friendly custom of giving a helping hand was a nice expression of the link between the iron company and the railway company forged in the old pioneer days.

No. 12 continued on the Slag Hill job until the ironworks closed down. I think Hughie Brogan and 'Bangor' Brown who had been his guard would be the final drivers. Just before the finish she was joined on the Slag Hill job by the little No. 21, also a product of Grant, Ritchie.

I think No. 12 lay idle for a long time after the ironworks closed. I have a recollection of seeing her behind the engineer shop. But she must have been overhauled, for on 8 November 1923 I have a note that my uncle was running her in, with Jimmy McDowall and Tommy Hopes for his crew. Then, or shortly afterwards, she was sent up to Burnfoothill and was there for a long time.

Alec Beattie was the driver on The Hill then. There was no official 'fireman'. Jimmy Stevenson and John Campbell were both rated as 'runners'. It could not have been a very hard job. All the ironstone pits were by then closed down; the only thing working on The Hill was the dual mine, Nos. 3 and 4 Craigmark, out at Ben Braniachan. There was, however, a fair amount of traffic in the sending of blaes from the old ironstone bings for use in the making of bricks.

No. 12 was not continuously on The Hill. She came down for overhaul on one occasion and went back with her new cylinders, half-an-inch larger in diameter. As usual with The Hill engine they fitted her with a 'cab'—a homemade affair of wood resembling a packing-case. They needed it, up there.

No. 12 was the last engine to work on The Hill. Alec Beattie was still her driver at the finish, and Jimmy Stevenson was with him. John Campbell had gone as engineman to the new Bogton mine at Dalmellington. No. 12 was brought down the incline by Wallace Boyns, Chief Engineer, my uncle Davie, and John Graham, Engineer. They were pursued by the curses of a poor half-witted man whose dim mind seemed to perceive in this departure the beginning of the end for the moorland village that was his world.

This seemed the end for No. 12 also. For some four years she did little. Then came a surprising rejuvenation. The ironstone pits at Rankinston had closed down in 1913, but the steeply-graded branch railway which had led thereto with its 'zigzag' formation had remained in place. Some years before a company had opened or reopened an anthracite mine. In 1937 this was taken over by Bairds & Dalmellington, and No. 12 was fitted out to work its traffic to Rankinston station.

No. 12 had still her original boiler of 1887. This was duly inspected by the insurance company and pronounced fit not only for its pressure of 110 lb but for its original rated pressure of 140. To this figure the valves were adjusted. A stumpy funnel was fitted, together with an overall cab.

I visited her at Rankinston on 6 May 1939. I must say I was somewhat shocked. I remembered No. 12 as a rather pretty, sprightly little engine. Here she was, with no shelter but that of a dusty bing, dirty and neglected, an ugly, snub-nosed little drudge, with no grace or beauty left in her. I don't think I ever saw her again. Nevertheless No. 12 survived adverse conditions and returned to Waterside, *still* with her original boiler, in 1947. I believe she even did a little work at Waterside. But she had done enough, and in 1949 she was finally withdrawn and scrapped.

HIRED ENGINE

0—4—0, with saddle tank.
Built Dick & Stevenson, Airdrie. Makers' number: Unknown.

I know no more about this engine than the fact that she possessed a whistle! I have already referred to the circumstances of her hiring—Barclays coming to the rescue of the DICo in their extremity by the loan of this engine. Her history has now been forgotten, except that she had reached Barclays' works by way of part-payment for a new engine, or some like financial transaction.

The hired engine came to Waterside some time about the Black Week of the Boer War in late 1899. She was in extremely bad condition. The guns of HMS *Terrible* had been much in the news by their use to defend Ladysmith, and after a few days' experience of the hired engine she was christened 'The Wee Terrible'. Oh she was bad. They took her from the sheds to the furnace bank. By the time they got half-way, at The Cutler Tip, steam was down to 40 lb and they had to have a rest. Then they went on. On the second leg of the climb someone got on the line ahead and my uncle blew the whistle. The whistle promptly vanished into outer space!

She was 'Terrible', all right. They worked away for about

three weeks and then returned her to Barclays, with compliments.

No. 5 (II)

0—4—0, with saddle tank, vertical sides, slightly rounded top, extending over smokebox and boiler barrel.

Built Gibb & Hogg, Airdrie, 1899. Makers' number: 5.

Dimensions: cylinders (outside) 14 in by 22 in
wheels: 3 ft 6 in
wheelbase: 6 ft
heating surface: sq. ft: tubes 567, firebox 55, total 622
grate area: 9.5 sq. ft
working pressure: 140 lb p.s.i.
length over buffers: 21 ft 2 in
weight in working order: 28 tons

Dome on back ring of boiler, protruding slightly above tank. Ramsbottom safety valves above firebox. Funnel tapered, wider at top; very narrow beading. Balanced slide valves (Frew's patent). Steam brake. Overall cab with back standards, but back of cab open above waist line.

Subsequent reconstruction: Back of cab closed in, with circular windows, c. 1922. Upper part opened again after transfer to Mauchline. Extensive overhaul at Barclays, Kilmarnock, 1939. Then repainted and lettered: 'Bairds & Dalmellington, Ltd, Mauchline Collieries No. 2'.

No. 5 (II) was never a very prominent engine at Waterside. She was never a very popular engine. But she was a remarkable engine. No. 5 (II) brought the New Look to Waterside. Thirteen years before, No. 12, slim-lined, with ogee tank, slender funnel and cabless footplate, had seemed the acme of fashion. Now, beside this bulldog of an engine with short funnel and overall cab No. 12 looked like Stephenson's *Rocket*.

No. 5 (II) was the first Waterside engine to be fitted with a cab when new. The cab had a narrow escape from extinction.

James P. Walker, General Manager, inspecting the new arrival, eyed this fitment with disfavour. 'You'll have to get *that* off her!' he ordered the chief engineer. My Uncle Davie Larmer, standing in the group, was very wroth and spoke up hotly, asking why the enginemen should be denied this shelter now generously provided. 'Oh, they canna see for the shuntin,' says J.P., still living forty years in the past. Rather surprisingly my uncle's protest carried the day. The cab remained.

I have already dealt with the circumstances of this engine's acquisition and of her numbering. She was, as I have said, only the fifth locomotive that Gibb & Hogg had built, and the hand of inexperience was apparent in several of her aspects. She was, when she arrived, a hopelessly bad steamer. A journey from the shed to the furnace bank, light engine, necessitated a stop at the Cutler Tip for a blow-up. This trouble was eventually cured, I know not how.

I wonder if there was some affinity between the firm of Gibb & Hogg and the Caledonian Railway. Into this land of green engines came No. 5 (II), attired in what is described to me as a livery of 'Caley blue', whatever that elusive colour may have been. Another point of resemblance is in the lamp irons high upon the side sheets of the cab. That was a true Caley characteristic.

No. 5 (II) had balanced slide valves, the only Waterside engine to be so fitted. These were the patent of James Frew, Chief Engineer of the DICo (Patent No. 20,855 of 1890). The specification is highly detailed, and shows several varieties of the valve for use in different conditions. All, however, have one feature in common, that of having *inside* admission of steam.

Balanced valves with inside admission are not unknown—Murdock's slide valve of 1784 was of this type—but they are certainly extremely rare. Frew's balanced valve was quite well known in his native Lanarkshire. I am told that two of the Coltness Iron Company's locomotives were so fitted, and that there were several instances of its application to winding and other stationary engines at collieries. In 1947 I visited the newly-installed shaft at Pennyvenie No. 7. The winding engine was an elderly machine which had seen service at Drumsmudden and Corbie Craigs No. 8, and I was informed that it was fitted with Frew's balanced slide valve.

Engineers who overhauled No. 5 (II) spoke of the extremely heavy 'door' which closed the entrance to the valve chest. Enginemen remembered their ability to notch up No. 5 (II)'s reversing gear while the regulator was open. My uncle stated that No. 5 (II), once she got over her steaming difficulties, was a very strong engine for her rated ability.

John Weir got No. 5 (II) when she came out. This seems rather surprising. John was not by any means 'in his turn' for this new engine. The fact that his father, old Willie Weir, was traffic foreman on the furnace bank may have had something to do with his rapid promotion. It may be also that the older enginemen fought shy of this unfamiliar machine.

John Weir was a quiet, unimpressive man. I do not think he was happy as a driver. A DICo driver had a heavy responsibility. However, John drove No. 5 (II) for about ten years after which he reverted to the position of guard on the Coylton Road.

No. 5 (II)'s first job was on the Jellieston Road (Dalharco had closed down some years before). She would also do some of the work in connection with the sinking of the big new pit at Houldsworth and the making of the railway thereto. When the Houldsworth opened in 1901, No. 5 (II) went on to that job. There was a large output from this pit, particularly in its first ten years of life, but the gradient was in favour of the loaded wagons and No. 5 (II) was able to handle it satisfactorily.

About 1910 John Weir was succeeded as driver of No. 5 (II) by Robert ('Rab') Young, who had an extremely long connection with this engine. Shortly afterwards changes were made in the working of the Pennyvenie traffic.

Up to 1908 traffic from Pennyvenie Nos. 1, 2 and 3 had been handled by two engines working from Waterside. In that year pit No. 1 closed down, and in 1912 Pennyvenie No. 4

(generally called 'The Big Mine') was opened some distance east of No. 1. The sidings at the former No. 1 pit were retained for storage purposes.

Under the new arrangement one engine only worked between Waterside and those sidings at old No. 1. A second engine, however, went up first run in the morning, hauling 'The Cairriages' with the workmen. This second engine remained at Pennyvenie during the day, shunting Pennyvenie Nos. 2 and 3 and working down the No. 4 traffic to the No. 1 sidings. In the evening she returned to Waterside with 'The Cairriages', to which were generally attached the high, sparred wagons with the daily output of coke from the ovens at Nos. 2 and 3.

To No. 5 (II) fell this new Pennyvenie job, and Rab Young was on it for some years. Among his other duties he had to bank trains from Pennyvenie to the top of the Laight Brae if the load exceeded the capacity of the 16-in Barclay which was the train engine.

In 1913 came the great No. 17, and there was a general change-round. No. 14 and The Squirrel went to the 'Big Mine' job, while No. 5 (II) returned to be a hewer of wood and drawer of water at Waterside. With the coming of the eight-hour day after the First World War and the introduction of 'link' working, No. 5 (II) was again taking her share of both Pennyvenie and Houldsworth workings. Early in 1925 I was interested to see Rab Young and No. 5 (II) back on 'The Cairriages' from Pennyvenie.

About this time No. 5 (II) had a rather surprising interlude. She was sent for a spell to the Burnfoothill shed. My intrepid uncle went out with her to the foot of the incline. He had some time to wait until they were ready with a sufficient counter-balance of loaded wagons from the top. He had got a good head of steam, and as he meditated upon the 1 in 6 going soaring away up from beneath the sheep bridge he wondered how far No. 5 (II) would go up on her own. So he tried. In vain. No. 5 (II) got only some twenty yards up the incline when he could not even hold her on the grade and she came slithering back down to the foot.

Then on 27 September 1934 came a still greater adventure. Bairds & Dalmellington now possessed the Mauchline collieries, about a mile-and-a-half north of that town. A steeply-graded branch line connects the collieries with the main line at Garrochburn signalbox. B & D had usually three engines at Mauchline, and No. 5 (II) was ordered to be transferred there. She was taken in freight trains to Mauchline, where the engine of the train from Ayr coupled off and made a special run the short distance to Garrochburn, hauling No. 5 (II). My uncle travelled on the footplate all the way, and was somewhat intrigued by the passage of Mossgiel tunnel—a novelty for a Waterside engine.

I saw No. 5 (II) at Mauchline Collieries on 6 May 1939. She had recently had an extensive overhaul at Barclays' and had been painted Barclays' usual dark olive green shade. She had also been re-lettered and re-numbered. My uncle was able to assure me that this was the first time that No. 5 (II) had been painted since she came new! By the time I first saw her —say about 1905—there was no trace of her early 'Caley' blue. She was well-cleaned, but as black as the rest of them. Blue does not last, and the usual oily rag of the DICo, though it removed the dirt, removed also the paint.

No. 5 (II)'s companions in 1939 were Mauchline No. 1, a 14-in Barclay No. 1821 of 1924, and No. 3, built in North British Loco. Hyde Park Works in 1903, No. 16182. No. 1 was stated to have come from the Caprington pits near Kilmarnock.

Two more Waterside engines followed No. 5 (II) to Mauchline—Nos. 16 and 20. No. 5 (II) never returned to Waterside, and was reported to be withdrawn and broken up in 1955.

No. 14

0—4—0, with saddle tank, vertical sides, slightly rounded top, extending over smokebox and boiler barrel.

Built Andrew Barclay, Sons & Co., Ltd., Caledonia Works, Kilmarnock, 1906. Makers' number: 1062.

(18a) *Mauchline No. 2* (*ex DICo No. 5*(II)). *Worked Houldsworth Road* 1900-1912

(18b) *Coltness No. 3, later NCB West Ayr No. 18* (II). *Worked Houldsworth Road,* 1954-1964

(19a) *Nos. 22 and 17 at Cutler sidings,* 17 *September* 1964
(19b) *Contrary winds at Minnivey,* 6 *April* 1965. *Nos. 24 and 17*

Dimensions: cylinders (outside) 16 in by 24 in
wheels: 3 ft 8 in
wheelbase: 6 ft
heating surface: sq. ft: tubes 781, firebox 72, total 853
grate area: 11.7 sq. ft
working pressure: 160 lb p.s.i.
water capacity of tank: 850 gallons
length over buffers: 22 ft 2¾ in
weight in working order: 33 tons

Dome in centre of boiler, protruding slightly above tank. Ramsbottom safety valves on top of dome. Steam brake. Cab over footplate with rear supporting standards, but back of cab open above waist line.

Subsequent reconstruction: Back of cab closed in, with circular windows, c. 1925.

No. 14 began the Barclay era. True, there had been Barclay engines at Waterside before—thirty-eight years before. But there was little resemblance between the somewhat crude Nos. 7 and 9 and this dapper little engine of 1906. In the previous fifty-five years two Barclays had come to Waterside. In the succeeding fifty-five years there came ten Barclays.

Nor was No. 14 so very *little*. She was the first Waterside engine to have 16-in cylinders since No. 4 of 1858. Her weight in working order and her working pressure were both greater than any previous Waterside engine.

I was only a small boy then, but I remember No. 14's coming very distinctly. One of Barclays' men came with her, and for a week he and my uncle Davie Larmer ran her in—on light-engine trips or on short hauls around the furnaces. Two young men from the engineer shop acted as fireman and guard respectively.

I can't remember which of Barclays' men came with No. 14. It wasn't Bob Wallace. He came with more than one subsequent engine. They ran her all week; and on the Saturday Barclays' man was to finish up, and he wanted to catch the

6.5 p.m. train from Dalmellington. It was a through train to Kilmarnock.

But they had still to get her turned. Barclays always delivered their engines with funnel to the south. DICo engines always worked with the funnel to the north, so they had to take her to Dalmellington to turn on the G & SW table there. They ran down to Waterside station and asked the stationmaster, Mr Kerr, if they could have a tablet for Dalmellington. Kerr said 'yes'—if they'd let him drive! So Kerr got the regulator and he drove like Jehu the son of Nimshi; when they got back to Waterside they had four hot axle-boxes!

Then appeared James Frew, Chief Engineer, and he said that before Barclays' man left they must have a trial trip hauling a full load from Pennyvenie—the job for which No. 14 was destined. Well, time was getting short for Barclays' man catching that 6.5, but away they went, hot boxes and all, to Pennyvenie, where they shunted out a full load of coal.

The return journey was easy to Craigmark, then of course came the 1 in 44 of the Laight Brae. My uncle was driving. On the footplate with him were James Frew and the Barclay man. The fireman and guard were back on the rake. No. 14 was still terribly tight, and going up the Brae she began to grunt badly at the fore-end. As they approached the summit, my uncle got the tallow kettle, and asked Frew if he would take her. 'And watch yourself,' he said to Frew. 'You've a big heavy train on there. Don't let her get away with you.'

Out along the gangway he went and stood down on the front step. Frew shut off as they topped the hill, on which my uncle whipped the siphons out of the cylinder lubricators and gave her a dose down each pipe. That didn't take long, but as he straightened up and raised his head he knew. . . He hurried along back to the cab. 'You're away!' he said.

Frew was as white as a sheet. He had the steam brake on, and he and Barclays' man were twisting desperately at the hand brake. My uncle looked around. They had no tender. Next to the footplate was a twelve-ton wagon. Uncle Davie went down on the engine step, kicked off the wagon brake, put his foot on it, and felt for the pin. There was no pin on it.

Frew made for the reverse lever, got the catch out. Uncle Davie grabbed him. 'Don't, for God's sake!' he cried. 'She's so tight. You'd tear the inside out of her if you reversed her now. Nothing for it but to let her go!' It was a rake of triping* that they had. Back on the wagon-tops, in a blizzard of coal-dust, the two amateur brakesmen were huddled, their jackets round their heads. Such a descent of the Laight Brae was never seen.

The question was 'Would she take the curve and points above the Quarry Brig?' If not, they were done for. They would go down forty feet into the glen. Uncle Davie stood at the regulator. He had more than one problem in hand. The bank over the Quarry Brig was the bottom of the dip. The rake, all buffered up, was lying heavy upon him. If he hit the steep upgrade to the furnace bank like that he'd break his rake in two or more portions. As well be hanged for a sheep as a lamb. He took off his hand brake, opened the regulator gently. Roaring like a tornado, No. 14 tore down to the Quarry Brig, rocked wildly over the points and went charging up to the furnace bank at a pace that the furious Tom Rowan, foreman on the bank, had certainly never seen in his life. They were scarcely at a stand when he was up at them, his face two or three tones redder than usual.

'By hivvins Frew, don't you ever get on to my men for comin' doon that hill ower hard! You were comin' doon there like a madman! Yap-yap-yap! . . .' The engineer answered not a word. It was some time before his nerves recovered from that wild descent.

After her baptism of fire No. 14 settled down to a hard-working but peaceful career. They gave her to Adam Ferguson ('The Squirrel'). If he wasn't exactly in the first rank of scientific drivers, the old Squirrel had gained plenty of experience on the Pennyvenie Road with No. 9 and others, so would

---

* Unscreened coal.

know the tricks of the trade. For some years No. 14 was neighboured on the Pennyvenie Road by one of the elder brethren, Nos. 4 or 9. Then in 1910 her sister engine, No. 16, came new to join her.

The two were not long on the Pennyvenie Road together. No. 1 Pennyvenie pit closed, and in 1912, No. 4, commonly known as 'The Big Mine', opened. A new arrangement commenced whereby the first engine to go up in the morning spent the day at The Big Mine. She worked traffic down to the old sidings at the site of No. 1 and shunted out traffic from Nos. 2 and 3, returning to Waterside in the afternoon. The other engine worked only between Pennyvenie Nos. 2 and 3 and Waterside.

No. 5 (II) was taken from the Houldsworth job and put to this Big Mine one. No. 16 did the Pennyvenie-Waterside trip. No. 14 went to replace No. 5 (II) on the Houldsworth. Once again it was for a brief period. In 1913 No. 17, the first six-coupler, arrived. No. 16 was displaced to the Houldsworth, No. 14 going to the Big Mine job. She was there, still with the Squirrel driving, when Tom Bruce began his footplate career on her in April, 1914.

In my schoolboy diary for the year 1910 I have a brief note, now almost indecipherable, of an adventure of No. 14 on 28 August of that year. I have spoken of the building of the houses at Broomknowe, Dalmellington. The building material was sent up the old Sillyhole Road. The usual engine was No. 10, the 2—4—0, and the old track, virtually derelict from 1886, stood up surprisingly well to her. But one afternoon someone who didn't know much sent No. 14 up in her place. No. 14's thirty-three tons on two axles was too much. As she took the curve into the Sillyhole siding the road spread and she dropped down. Our evening walk was enlivened by the spectacle of my Uncle Davie and his more or less merry men engaged at their not unfamiliar task of re-railing.

The Squirrel had a long spell on No. 14. He had her until about 1921, when he went on the Coylton Road with No. 20. Just about that time No. 14, sorely worn, was laid aside for overhaul. In front of the engineer shop she was partially dismantled. But the furnaces had closed, fewer engines were required, and there she lay. Then she became a sort of 'stand-by' job for redundant apprentices. My friend Tommy Hopes spent many days working at her, generally all on his own. When, as was usual in those depressed years, he was paid off on completing his apprenticeship, the work on No. 14 was not yet finished.

No. 14's overhaul must have been completed soon after Tommy's departure, for on 20 March 1925 I travelled on her from Burnton Washer to Waterside. Will Guthrie had her then, with Willie Clark firing to him and Will Kaur as guard. We drew thirteen wagons of singles out of the Washer, weighed them, and awaited the passing of 'The Cairriages'. They came along a bit late, it being pay-night, with Rab Young and No. 5 (II), and we followed them 'on sight' to Waterside. Willie Clark had a good fire in, but for some reason we had only 135 lb of steam when we hit the bank. Will Guthrie drew her up two notches and laid his regulator wide open. The noise was terrific. Twice on the bank Willie Clark tended his fire, and part of the way he had his injector on. We topped the bank with 110 lb of steam. No. 19 was lying in the loop at the old Laight Mine. Our fireman and guard dropped off, got some brakes down, and climbed on the rake. Before the Quarry Brig we stopped to lift brakes, then charged up to the furnace bank with the usual uproar.

Will Guthrie had a far longer spell on No. 14 than The Squirrel. I think he was still driving her in 1954 when, by direction of the NCB authorities, she was removed to pastures extremely new. The great new pit at Killoch near Ochiltree was in process of sinking, and there No. 14 was taken. Her transit was necessarily by road, as there was then no rail connection to the pit. Pickfords transported her on a low loader, exactly one hundred years after the last Waterside engine had been so transported—No. 2, coming from Ayr. No. 14 worked at Killoch all through the period of sinking and erection of buildings. Diesel units were provided for internal shunting when production of coal began, and after a period of disuse No. 14 was returned to Waterside in 1961. After an overhaul she went out and did a certain amount of work. There was, however, no pressing need for her services, and having reached the respectable age of fifty-eight years she was withdrawn and scrapped in 1964.

No. 15

0—4—0, with saddle tank, vertical sides, rounded top, extending over boiler barrel only.
Built Markham & Co., Broad Oaks Works, Chesterfield, 1909.
Makers' number: none shown on date plate.
Only known dimensions: cylinders (outside) 14 in by 21* in
wheels: 3 ft 6 in
wheelbase: 6 ft
working pressure: 140 lb p.s.i.

Dome in centre of boiler. Ramsbottom safety valves on top of dome. Steel firebox and tubes. Steam brake. Funnel tapering outwards to top, with very narrow beading. Cab with overall roof and back standards, but very scanty weatherboard in front, with no side sheets and only a hand-rail, waist high, across back of footplate.

Subsequent reconstruction: New front and side sheets added to cab. Waist high plate placed behind footplate. Steel firebox replaced by a copper one. At a later date, back of cab closed in completely, with circular rear windows. 1938, extensive renewals, including new firebox.

One shouldn't believe all one hears. I was told at Waterside that Markham built only *two* engines, and No. 15 was the second. An article in *The Locomotive* of 1946, Vol. LII, page 20, reveals that Markham built *nineteen* engines in all. No 15 was, curiously enough, their fifteenth.

Markham & Co. were constructional engineers and makers of mining machinery. They dabbled in locomotive construc-

* The article in *The Locomotive* gives this as 14 in by 20 in.

tion in somewhat erratic fashion. During the years 1889 to 1897 inclusive they built eleven engines. To these were given makers' numbers running from 101 to 111. No more were built until 1909, when six appeared, followed by one in 1913 and one in 1914. None of those later engines carried any makers' number. The DICo engine was the fourth of the 1909 batch.

No. 15 created quite a sensation when she arrived in all the glory of her gamboge livery. She was really a lovely job and must have presented a tremendous contrast to poor drab, ugly old No. 6, shuffling wearily about on The Hill. For it was to The Hill that this new beauty went, to replace old No. 6. Even from the high ground south of Dalmellington I could catch the little splash of colour as her bright side-tank caught the sun on some curve. Men called her 'The Butterflee', and no name could have been more apt.

Bright colour apart, No. 15 was not a masterpiece of symmetry. Her short, rather box-like saddle tank, with its high dome and safety valves on top, was not particularly neat, and I never liked a 'stove-pipe' funnel, no matter how delicately it was tapered. To me she was a deceptive engine. She looked slender and light. Actually, in after years she was to prove herself capable of hard and continuous work.

Of course Johnnie Yorston got her, and she could not have fallen into more capable hands. There was still a fair amount of work left on The Hill, at least for one engine single-handed, and No. 15 must have been very nice to work once they got more adequate shelter on her.

8 October 1910 was a red-letter day for me. I had never before visited Benwhat or Burnfoothill, so on this fine Saturday afternoon my father and I climbed the long, steep ascent until, away on the moor beyond the 1,000 ft contour, the grey stone houses of Benwhat stretched their impressive length. As we approached there appeared from the direction of Burnfoothill the still-bright livery of No. 15, pushing some vans for the Benwhat store. There we ran her to earth. Johnnie Yorston was driving and Harry Graham firing. They joined

us in the back entrance to the store, and I was somewhat shocked when my teetotal parent stood the engine crew a bottle of beer apiece while we consumed our lemonade. I do not remember a guard. For a brief run to Benwhat with the store vans on a Saturday afternoon maybe a guard was superfluous.

So having thus paid our fare we were conveyed on the engine, now returning light, to Burnfoothill. I remember how, half-way, we overtook the manager, John Pollock. Yorston stopped to pick him up. He applied the steam brake by a mere turn of the wrist and my father, with memories of the screwing and reversing of his young days, said 'Man, it's a handy thing that, Johnnie'.

Yes, he was a nice wee man, Johnnie Yorston, but he was getting old and about 1913 he had had enough. Then came the problem, for none of the Waterside drivers wanted The Hill job. Matters had almost reached an *impasse* when Jock Henderson, who had been firing to Willie Craig at Dalmellington on the G & SW for some time, applied for it and of course got the job.

There was however a vast difference between firing on the G & SW and driving for the DICo on The Hill, and after a comparatively brief period Jock Henderson reverted to the firing, this time of the pit boilers at Pennyvenie.

Once again The Hill job was vacant. Now as brakesman at the incline there was a very good and steady man called Alec Beattie. Alec had been an engineman at Waterside, so he was persuaded to fill the vacancy. Harry Graham, fireman on No. 15, was given the post of incline brakesman. A young man named John Campbell became fireman. Jimmy Stevenson was guard, and this very competent crew remained on Burnfoothill until almost the end of the elevated lines.

The period of the First World War found No. 15 in rather a poor state. It was the inevitable trouble with a steel firebox, aggravated by The Hill weather and by Paddy Henderson's maladministrations. No. 15 had to go down to Waterside shops for a long spell, and old No. 3 came up to the scene of her labours of thirty years before. Things were pretty difficult just then. No. 10 on the Coylton Road was in a bad way, and after No. 15 had been fettled up she had a quite long spell on the Coylton job, for which she proved very suitable. She was even fitted with the steam connection for the pulsometer at Martnaham Loch, but it was placed on the left side so that turning was not necessary.

No. 15 returned to The Hill, but she still gave trouble. In 1918 both Nos. 3 and 15 were on The Hill, the one hardly more reliable than the other. It was not until some time after the war was over that it was possible to get a copper replacement for the firebox.

It was during the period of the two engines on The Hill that Tommy Hopes was sent up to execute some repairs to No. 15's saddle tank. It was drained and Tommy got inside, but there was still some water left in the channels at the sides. While Tommy worked he became aware of a ghostly 'plop-plop' in the darkness beside him. Presently he discovered that a colony of frogs had taken up residence in the tank, having come in through the not too discriminating water supply!

Work on The Hill was falling off rapidly, and by 1921 it was considered that old No. 12, released from the Slag job, would provide sufficient power. On her previous spells at Waterside No. 15 had proved her worth for far more extensive duty, so about this time she was brought to the parent shed. I think her first job was on The Houldsworth. In 1929 Tom Bruce had her, with Davie Ferguson and Willie Bryden as his crew.

Old John Young, whom they called with some truth 'Happy', was not a regular driver, but he would act as substitute for any man off sick, or in any emergency. He had a spell on No. 15 in the early thirties. Coming in from The Houldsworth one day they had a fair load, and the crew hadn't been too lavish in the number of brakes they pinned down. So No. 15 was walloping down towards Jellieston when an old cow took it into her head to stroll leisurely across the line. Old Happy did his best, but he couldn't stop. No. 15 hit the cow a hearty slap on the rump, but the speed at which she ascended the cutting-side proved that there were no bones broken!

It would be about this time—though I cannot remember who was driving—that my Uncle Davie one day got an SOS from the furnace bank that No. 15 was in distress. He went up and found No. 15 immobile. A swift examination confirmed the driver's diagnosis of a broken crank-axle. So they got the side-rods off her and scotched the driving wheels with bits of old rail and things until they were locked in place. Then No. 17 was brought up and No. 15 was taken in tow, very gently, with the driving wheels sliding.

They were about half-way down to the Cutler Tip, with my uncle walking alongside No. 15, when from her interior there came a sharp crack . . . No. 17 stopped. At first my uncle thought—or hoped—that one of the scotches had slipped. No. The unbelievable had happened—*the other axle had broken*!

Well, there was one that wasn't in the book. What could they do? There was just *nothing* they could do except go on and hope for the best. So they went on, very slowly, to the Cutler Tip. Then came the crucial test, for on the other leg they had to *push* her. Well, believe it or not, No. 15 was pushed down that 1 in 40 quite successfully. The only difficulty was at the fork of a crossing. She *would* take the wrong side of the fork. However, patience and pinching and blocking got her past each one and they got her without derailment to the engineer shop siding. It may not be a record, but you don't bring an 0—4—0, with both axles broken, home on her own wheels every day!

Tom Shaw got her in the thirties. She was then working in a link with No. 20 and the 16-in Barclays. They had various jobs on the Pennyvenie Road, the Houldsworth and the Coylton Road. The Barclays, however, were too heavy for the Coylton, so Nos. 15 and 20 got more than their share of that duty.

By that time the Coylton traffic was pretty light, at least that conveyed to Waterside. Nevertheless, it was a long run for a little 14-in engine with limited water-capacity. Potterston Junction, at which the Coylton branch joined the main line had, of course, to regulate their running according to the margin of time ahead of a main line train. Jimmy Birch kept rigidly to the book, but Jimmy Callow would sometimes let them have a go, and wee No. 15 would come peppering up the valley with a long trail of black smoke behind her, while away ahead at Patna the column of white steam showed that the passenger was already in and rarin' to go.

So No. 15 laboured until and during the Second World War. In that first terrible winter of 1939-40 she was trying to battle through to Pennyvenie No. 4, hauling two carriages full of miners, and with No. 22 banking vigorously in rear. The snow had caked hard at a field level-crossing, and No. 15 derailed and waddled some distance into adjoining territory, which fortunately was fairly level. Then in 1947 she was on the Houldsworth Road, which drifted up fantastically. With a snow plough mounted on a loaded hopper wagon No. 15 did valiant work in clearing the way.

In NCB days No. 15 was transferred to the New Cumnock district. A friend photographed her there about 1950. She never returned to Waterside, but was withdrawn and scrapped in 1956.

No. 16

0—4—0, with saddle tank, vertical sides, slightly rounded top, extending over smokebox and boiler barrel.

Built Andrew Barclay, Sons & Co., Kilmarnock, 1910. Makers' number: 1116.

Dimensions and description are identical with those of No. 14.

Subsequent reconstruction: Back of cab closed in, with circular windows, c. 1923.

Nos. 14 and 16 were the first engines to work at Waterside which were, in all but possibly some minute details, identical.

No. 16 must have come early in the year 1910. I remember that it was cold weather. My grandmother Larmer was then living with us in the Schoolhouse at Dalmellington. Uncle

Davie brought No. 16 up to Dalmellington to turn, and he came across the field to see his mother. I remember her chiding him for wearing only his thin dungaree jacket on that cold day. Grannie died in the May of that year, so the cold weather could not have been in the latter part.

No. 16 was given to Alec Young, who bore the rather strange nickname of 'Hanuel'. Why, I do not know. Alec took No. 16 to the Pennyvenie Road. For a little while Nos. 14 and 16 worked together, then No. 14, as related, went to the Houldsworth and No. 5 (II), driven by Alec Young's brother Rab, came to work at the Big Mine, shunting out traffic which No. 16 took to Waterside.

If the load for the Laight Brae exceeded No. 16's capacity it was the custom for No. 5 (II) to follow at the end of the rake and bank them up the Laight Brae. The big rake went down about one o'clock. We boys would be out of school at the lunch-time interval, and from the Ayr road we could see No. 16 going down with very big loads. Assistance by No. 5 (II) was a daily occurrence. From a distance of a mile, with the keen eyes of youth, we used to count the rake. Came the great day when those two quite small 0—4—0 tanks wrestled *fifty-three* wagons over the Laight Brae! Fifty-three, and not a few of them would be fifteen-tonners! I can remember how we listened to the great struggle, saw the hillside shrouded under a pall of black smoke as they battled their way up the 1 in 44. What we didn't know was that Alec Young and his brother were not on speaking terms at the time, and that as soon as they got to the top with their immense load Rab just shut off and scuttled away back to Pennyvenie and left them to it. There must have been some pretty frenzied work by fireman and guard getting down enough brakes to hold them down the 1 in 37.

Then in 1913 came the first six-coupler, No. 17. Alec Young's good handling of No. 16 made him the inevitable choice for the great new engine. I travelled to Waterside on No. 17 the morning she brought her first rake from Pennyvenie. My father and I returned to Pennyvenie on No. 16. In charge was the rubicund and smiling Jock Kaur. He got No. 16 then and ran her, I think, until the second six-coupler came out in 1923. He was a genial soul, Jock, but he wasn't an Alec Young.

No. 16 went to the Houldsworth Road in 1913. After the First World War, with the introduction of the eight-hour day she went into a species of link working, taking turns on the Houldsworth and the Pennyvenie. In 1923 Jock Kaur went to the 0—6—0 No. 22. I think Rab Young got No. 16 then. About 1929 she was running with Rab Young as driver, John Hendrie fireman and Francie News guard.

Except for periodic overhaul little of note seemed to happen to No. 16 until 23 October 1951, when she was the principal victim in a collision with runaway wagons at Waterside engine shed. I have recorded this event in detail in dealing with No. 1 (II). No. 16 was somewhat damaged about the back plating of the cab and her handbrake column was broken through.

On 11 June 1956 No. 16 went to Mauchline Collieries, probably to replace No. 5 (II), which had become Mauchline No. 2 and had been withdrawn in the previous year.

No. 17

0—6—0, with side tanks and rear bunker.
Built Andrew Barclay, Sons & Co., Ltd, Kilmarnock, 1913.
Makers' number: 1338.
Dimensions: cylinders (outside) 18 in by 24 in
wheels: 3 ft 9 in
wheelbase: 6 ft + 5 ft 6in
heating surface: sq. ft: tubes 887, firebox 93, total 980
grate area: 16.3 sq. ft
working pressure: 160 lb p.s.i.
water capacity of tanks: 900 gallons
coal capacity of bunker: 35 cwt
length over buffers: 28 ft $2\frac{3}{4}$ in
weight in working order: 45 tons
Dome in centre of boiler. Ramsbottom safety valves on back

ring of boiler. Steam brake. Large circular spring buffers. Overall cab with rectangular windows back and front.

Subsequent reconstruction: Flanges turned off driving wheel tyres, c. 1919. Footsteps removed from position alongside slide bars to front buffer beam.

With the output of three large pits to haul up a gradient of 1 in 44, it was inevitable that the DICo should aim at something more powerful than the Barclays standard 16-in. As soon as Pennyvenie No. 4 was into full production the step was taken. Those who were responsible for the maintenance of the permanent way must have had some qualms. One does not go light-heartedly from a thirty-three-ton engine to one weighing thirty-six per cent more.

No. 17 came in the August of that last complete year of peace before the First World War. Her coming was a great event. 'The Big Yin', they called her. I had not seen the great engine, and returned one Saturday from an expedition among the hills to be told, to my chagrin, that she had been at Dalmellington for turning. I had missed her! However, my uncle had left a message that on the Monday morning she would be bringing her first loaded rake from Pennyvenie, and that if my father and I could be there about 8.30 we would be accorded a place.

So on a lovely summer morning at an unaccustomed hour we walked out the wooded road to Pennyvenie and found No. 17 already arrived and preparing for the return journey. I had not much time to contemplate the new monster when I was assisted into the cab and dumped up on the top of the left-hand tank, close to the hot boiler. I can smell yet the warm oil and the new paint. The cab began to fill up. There were ultimately *eight* persons in it. There were Alec Young driver, Will Guthrie fireman, the guard, James Frew Chief Engineer, Tammy Rowan Traffic Manager, Bob Wallace of Barclays, my father and myself. There were certainly plenty of us to see her through any trouble. And trouble there was!

It was not the weight of the train. At that early hour of a

Monday morning a load of nineteen wagons was all that we could muster for a test. With these we set off confidently. I didn't know much then and in the crowded conditions couldn't see much, but half-way up the Laight Brae there was a hurried consultation and we came to a stand. No steam! It was a sorry come-down. There we sat for all to see, with our poor little rake that old No. 4 could have walloped over the top without difficulty.

Then my uncle, crowded out from the cab, came forward from his seat on a wagon and said quietly 'Did you mind to change those dampers at Pennyvenie?' Oh dear, no one had. I think I am correct in saying that no Waterside engine had had any ashpan before. No. 17 had, with dampers fore and aft, and she would steam only with the leading damper open. We blew up and resumed our journey. At Waterside furnace bank our big engine was not permitted to go over the weighs, so good old No. 4, no doubt with a chuckle at our misfortune, took over our rake for weighing.

But that was only an incident. No. 17 began a most successful career on the Pennyvenie Road. Her success was largely due to the skill and care of her driver, Alec Young. My uncle, a critical man, had nothing but praise for Alec's running and maintenance of his big engine. Actually there was no great change in the working. No. 17 could certainly take a bigger load than No. 14 or No. 16, but with loads of up to fifty wagons at times assistance in rear was still necessary, the 'Big Mine' engine doing the needful.

About this time a spot of bother had begun to develop at Pennyvenie Nos. 2 and 3. The line, after passing Craigmark, has a level course with easy curvature until, just approaching the pit, there is a sharp reverse curve over the glen of the little Sloanstone Burn. Then follows a steep upgrade past the pit bing. At the foot of this grade a subsidence had begun, and despite some filling in the track gradually sank until by the end of the First War the subsequent upgrade had steepened to something like 1 in 35. By that time rakes of empties were always *pushed* from Waterside to Pennyvenie, and to get them up the 1 in 35 the engine was always thrusting as hard as she was fit for round that reverse curve. Returning, the curve had to be negotiated with the engine's brakes hard on and the wagons bearing heavily upon her as they came down the grade. The track at this point was subjected to a great strain and one day something gave way.

It was a Tuesday morning, 10 September 1918. No. 17 had a moderate load of twenty-one wagons. Alec Young was driving, with Will Guthrie firing and Jimmy Geddes guard. A number of men were getting a lift to Waterside and presumably the footplate was full up, for two of the passengers perched themselves on the outside footplating beside the smokebox. One was that famous Dalmellington character Rab Wallace. The other was a man called Andrew Stewart, who had returned recently to his native valley from Stewarton. He was a mining contractor, and with his wife and five children had just moved to a house in Pennyvenie Terrace, adjacent to No. 4 Mine.

Nothing unusual appeared until No. 17 was almost round the reverse curve, when she suddenly left the road. With twenty-one wagons coming down hard it was impossible to stop. The derailed engine staggered blindly forward towards the crossing of the Chalmerston road, then she toppled sideways to the right and ground into a low cutting-side. Rab Wallace, with the luck which had carried him through many a scrape from the Boer War onwards, jumped or rolled clear. Andrew Stewart slid off as she tilted and was pinned by the cylinder against the cutting. He was dead when they dug him out.

I was on holiday when it happened and did not get up to the scene of the disaster until the Thursday evening. The engine had been removed, which must have been quite a task, and the road had been cleared for traffic, but smashed wagons were lying about at all angles. I noticed a Great Central wagon and thought it was a long way from Gorton. Only eight wagons at the end of the train remained intact.

This accident led to an important modification to No. 17.

(20a) *No. 24 leaving Minnivey for Cutler,* 17 *September* 1964
(20b) *No. 24 (with Giesl ejector) on empties to Minnivey,* 4 *March* 1965

(21a) *No. 20 on Coylton-Waterside train passing Hollybush station,* 1932

(21b) *Depth indicator, winding engine house, Houldsworth. Now in North Ayrshire Museum, Saltcoats*

My uncle had long advocated the removal of the flanges from the driving-wheel tyres. The management were doubtful, but after this accident they agreed to try it. The experiment proved quite successful.

No. 17 was the first DICo engine to be fitted with a rear bunker. I thought this quite adequate, and was much surprised to see her shortly after her arrival with the customary wagon attached as tender. This, of course, enabled a full day's supply of coal to be carried.

One day, probably in the 1920s, No. 17 was going up to Pennyvenie. Alec Young was driving, Kennedy Bryden was firing, and the guard was a cousin of Kenny's, Rab Bryden, locally known as 'Teuch'. They were shoving behind them their tender and a long rake of empties. The guard, as was customary, was in the leading wagon, and from the engine in the early morning light they could see the head of old Teuch above the wagon, his wee cutty-pipe sending the little puffs of smoke over his shoulder.

They topped the Laight Brae; the couplings of the rake tightened as they got on to the down grade. Then the coupling between the first wagon and the tender broke and away ran the rake on its own!

What was to be done? Could they catch them? They were game to try. Alec Young sent No. 17 rocking and rolling down the hill a lot faster than she had gone in her life. Kenny climbed round into the tender. Away ahead they could see the guard's head above the wagon. He was still puffing away at his pipe, serenely unconscious of the excitement behind him. They got near to the rake; Kenny fished for their intact tender coupling with his pole. He got it, they touched buffers, Kenny got the coupling on at the first shot. Gently they braked and got a steadying pull on them.

They stopped at Burnton Washer. Presently old Teuch came ambling back. He had on his face a look of deep disapproval. 'See here sir,' he said to Alec Young 'You were comin' doon that hill far too bloody hard!'

When the new line to Pennyvenie was opened in 1927 No.

17, now companioned by No. 22, transferred to the new route and continued her good work. I have a note of a day in 1937 when No. 17 pushed up the grade of 1 in 66, with its severe curvature, a rake of no fewer than fifty-three wagons. Forty-three wagons were empty, ten were loaded with pitwood.

The change to the new line made the working of 'The Cairriages' a little more complicated. On the morning of Monday 10 January 1936, Alec Young and No. 17 took a train of five carriages from the furnace bank to the crossing of the Burnfoothill road above Patna. There he embarked the Patna and Burnfoothill men. He then returned and picked up Waterside men at the furnace bank. To get thence to the new line, however, he had to reverse at the Cutler Tip and propel the carriages down to Cutler sidings. Half-way down were the facing points leading to the brickwork. Here the leading carriage became derailed. The second one followed. The first one fell on its side; the second trundled on until it hit a hut and a fence. The rest of the train was stopped without mishap. Two of the passengers were injured, fortunately not seriously, but in the darkness and confusion extrication was rather difficult.

Alec Young retired about 1938. Truly the Youngs were a family of engine-drivers. Three were in the service of the DICo—Alec, Rab, and the eldest, John whom they called 'Happy'. A fourth brother, Joe, was with the G & SW at Ayr shed. His colleagues used to call him 'Brigham'. Joe got the first of Whitelegg's 'Baltic' tanks when they came out in 1922, and he and John Hastings ran this engine, No. 540, on the Ayr-Glasgow expresses for some years.

No. 17 was given to Willie Clark, who carried on the good work throughout the Second World War. Like Kenny Bryden on No. 22 he died at a comparatively early age. No. 17 remained on the Pennyvenie. Her regular crew in 1965 were Mick Rooney, Joe Innes and George Sargent.

On Saturday 20 March 1965 a rail-tour of the NCB lines in the Waterside area was organised by the Branch Line Society. The itinerary comprised a journey from Waterside to Pennyvenic No. 4 and back followed by a trip to Houldsworth and back. Two British Railways' goods brake vans, newly painted, were provided and No. 17 received the place of honour. She was not, however, handled by her own crew. Being a Saturday job it was given to the crew whose turn it was to work that day—Jackie Heggie, Tom Hose and James Dunn. On a morning of bitter wind, with snow-wreaths showing ominously in various nooks on the hillsides, some thirty enthusiasts braved the elements to see what was left of the old DICo system. I returned from Houldsworth to Waterside on the footplate of No. 17, sorely puzzled to know how we got eight people into that confined space on that lovely August morning fifty-one and a half years before.

No. 18 (I)

0—4—0, with saddle tank, vertical sides, slightly rounded top, extending over smokebox and boiler barrel.

Built Andrew Barclay, Sons & Co., Ltd, Kilmarnock, 1913.

Makers' number: 1345.

Dimensions: cylinders (outside) 14 in by 22 in
wheels: 3 ft
wheelbase: 5 ft 6 in
heating surface: sq. ft: tubes 781, firebox 72, total 853
grate area: 11.7 sq. ft
working pressure: 140 lb p.s.i.
water capacity of tank: 700 gallons
length over buffers: 21 ft 3½ in
weight in working order: 28 tons

Dome on back ring of boiler. Ramsbottom safety valves on front ring. Boiler mountings cut down in order to pass through Quarry Brig. Steam brake. Cab roof cut away to clear tunnel roof.

Subsequent reconstruction: Cab roof extended to back of footplate and back plate fitted, but without windows. This was carried out some time in the 1920s.

Truly 1913 was a remarkable year in the annals of Waterside. *Two* new engines and both from Barclays! But No. 18 (I) was a very different engine from the great No. 17. The scrapping of Nos. 6 and 8 (I) had left the DICo rather short of engines capable of threading the constricted tunnel called the Quarry Brig. At the same time there was need of an engine for general shunting about the ironworks. Barclays' undertook to supply an engine suitable for both those duties. Moreover they would keep to dimensions which would clear the Quarry Brig without any dismantling of funnel. It took a bit of compression in the case of a 14-in engine, for the Quarry Brig, as has been stated, was only 9 ft 2 in from rail to crown of arch.

The result was a very neat little engine which was as efficient as she was neat. With the heating surface of a 16-in, and her small wheels, No. 18 (I) was a powerful little brute. They tell of one night when a G & SW goods engine was trying to shove up the wagons already in the Sillyhole Road in order to get another train of empties in. She retired defeated, whereupon No. 18 (I) came across, put her back to it, and set them up the required distance. When the G & SW men proceeded later on their journey to Dalmellington, they counted *eighty* wagons in the Sillyhole Road!

And she managed the Quarry Brig quite successfully, though it was a mighty tight fit. I was told that if you were to grasp the edge of the cab roof as you came through you would get your knuckles skinned. The Quarry Brig was also on a slight curve, and No. 18 (I) cut grooves in the stonework with the diagonal corners of her footplating.

I know singularly little of the men who drove No. 18 (I). I am told that Willie McGraw had her in her early days. There would be plenty for her to do during the years of the first war, but the closing down of the furnaces in March 1921 disrupted much of the work of the Waterside engines. No. 18 (I), thrown out of a regular job, became a spare, and not a very useful spare at that. The remaining jobs were mostly to distant pits, and No. 18 (I)'s wheels were too small for that. She *did* a bit of pit work—I have seen her at Pennyvenie—but she had long spells of idleness. About the beginning of World War II, the ubiquitous Jock Kaur was driving her.

After the coming of the NCB No. 18 (I) was deemed surplus at Waterside, and in November 1947 she was transferred to New Cumnock Collieries. Of her work there I have no record. She was renumbered East Ayr No. 7 at some date prior to January 1955, in which month another engine bearing the number 18 was sent to Waterside.

No. 19

0—4—0, with saddle tank, vertical sides, slightly rounded top, extending over smokebox and boiler barrel.

Built Andrew Barclay, Sons & Co., Kilmarnock, 1918. Makers' number: 1614.

Dimensions: cylinders (outside) 16 in by 24 in
wheels: 3 ft 8 in
wheelbase: 6 ft
heating surface: sq. ft: tubes 730, firebox 75, total 805
grate area: 12.5 sq. ft
working pressure: 160 lb p.s.i.
water capacity of tank: 850 gallons
length over buffers: 22 ft 2$\frac{3}{4}$ in
weight in working order: 33 tons

Dome in centre of boiler, protruding slightly above tank. Ramsbottom safety valves on top of dome. Steel firebox. Steam brake. Cab over footplate with rear supporting standards, but back of cab open above waist line.

Subsequent reconstruction: Steel firebox replaced by copper one. Back of cab closed in, with circular windows, c. 1922. New cab, with slightly different side-sheets, fitted after accident in 1929. Pop safety valves fitted recently.

October, 1918. *Two new engines* arrived at Waterside! Two in *one month*! It was a phenomenon. But no one at Waterside had time to bother about what it was. Nos. 19 and 20 were needed and needed quickly. They had probably been ordered a long time—maybe years—before.

There hadn't been a new engine since No. 18 (I) came in 1913. All through the busy war-time traffic the DICo engines had been kept going with the minimum of repair and a minimum of good treatment on the road. Early in 1918 my uncle gave me a list of engines which in his opinion were now fit only for scrap. It was a rather frightening list: Nos. 3, 9, 10 (I), 12 and 15—five engines out of nine. And he was not a man given to exaggeration.

No. 19 was, of course, a standard Barclay 16-in. In outward appearance she differed little from Nos. 14 and 16. There had been a slight increase in grate area and some rearrangement of tube heating surface. There were other small differences. The marks of war-time austerity were upon her, most prominent being her steel firebox. I think that it lasted rather longer than others of that material.

I have no record of No. 19's enginemen in her early days. She was most likely substituting for other engines absent on overhaul. About the middle 1920s John Ferguson got her.

John bore an illustrious surname, for he was a grandson of James (The Auld Deuce) who had driven No. 9 for so long. John Ferguson was a genial man, easy going, a favourite with all. In 1929 Tom Shaw was firing to him, with Jimmy Robertson as guard.

On Thursday 25 April 1929 John Ferguson was on the last rake of the afternoon from Pennyvenie. The carriages had preceded him, but a number of workmen had not finished in time to catch the carriages, so they got down with John Ferguson's rake. They left Pennyvenie with three workmen in the cab with the driver and guard. Several more were in the tender with the fireman.

The long, winding 1 in 66 descent from Craigmark levels out as it approaches Cutler Sidings. It is single line, but just after crossing the road leading to Cutler farm it divides in two. In 1929 the facing points were controlled by a simple, throw-over ball lever.

They were in rather a hurry that night, being short of

water, for which reason it was necessary to take the left-hand of the two roads, on which was the water-tank. John Ferguson was standing on the right of the footplate; the guard, Jimmy Robertson, stood on the left. Crowded up between them were the three workmen—a pithead worker Davie McGill, an electrician Peter Thomson, and a labourer Willie Ferguson, brother of the driver.

As they approached the sidings the driver called out that *the points were wrong*. In subsequent evidence no one seems to be certain what he meant by this. Were the points lying for the *right*-hand road, or were they, as was not unknown, stuck half-way, and the blades open for both roads?

The point lever was on the right-hand side of the rails. The guard was on the left-hand side of the footplate. He could not easily squeeze past the 'passengers', so he dropped off on the left-hand side and hoped to be able to run ahead and cross in front of No. 19 before she reached the points.

Willie Ferguson, the driver's brother, was nearer the right-hand side. He dropped off on that side and ran. Both he and the guard stated that they were too late, and that the engine reached the points before they could get to the lever. Willie Ferguson said that when he left the footplate his brother had the steam and hand brakes on and the sand open.

Whatever the circumstances, No. 19 left the road at the facing points. She swung one way, the tender and rake the other. She reared up and toppled backwards down the embankment.

The guard flung himself down the slope and escaped injury. The electrician, Peter Thomson, by some means managed to get out of the cab and jump clear. As No. 19 toppled over John Ferguson and Davie McGill fell to the lower side of the cab, which buckled, tore the stop-cock of the injector out of the boiler, and let the steam in on them.

It was a horrible business. Men stood helpless beside that cloud of roaring steam. It was not even known who was in the cab. Even when the steam had spent itself there was difficulty, for the faces were unrecognisable.

The tragedy shook Waterside. It was the only instance of a fatal accident to a Waterside driver. Both men had been well known and much esteemed. In later years, after my father and myself were left alone, John Ferguson's widow was our housekeeper. She was a faithful, kindly soul, but she never quite recovered from the shock of her husband's death.

There was an inquiry, a Fatal Accidents Inquiry, held on 22 May in Ayr Sheriff Court before Sheriff Haldane and a jury. Evidence was given in terms outlined above and a verdict of accidental death was returned. There was one rather illuminating little bit of information contributed by Police-Sergeant Donald Cameron of Dalmellington. He stated that after the accident he threw over the ball-lever, and the points stuck at 'half-cock'.

Of course there was a rumour. There generally *is,* after an accident. Rumour said that the men who ran for the points had not told the truth—that one or other *did* reach the spot and had the lever half over when the engine struck the blades. If so, one may ask, why conceal the fact? It was a brave attempt to set matters right and it failed through no fault of him who tried. Nevertheless, that man was, in theory, responsible for the two deaths. Such a man is not soon forgotten in a small working community.

No. 19 was left until the Sunday, when she was raised by two LMS cranes and taken to Waterside shops. She was not extensively damaged. The cab was renewed. Bobby Ferguson, engineer, patiently tapped out the dent in her tank, though you can still see traces in certain aspects of light. He also touched up the paintwork.

Tom Bruce got No. 19 after the accident, with Jimmy Rowan firing and Jimmy Robertson continuing as guard. Four and a half years later Jimmy Robertson was killed at almost the same spot as the accident of 1929.

In the dark of a winter morning they were starting for Pennyvenie, pushing the rake behind them. It was the guard's duty to ride in the leading wagon. Jimmy Robertson went along. They were moving slowly. He would put his hand on the buffer and swing up to grasp the top of the wagon.

It was just at the time that the electric lamps had been introduced in the pits. A number of these lamps had been left at the weighshouse to be sent up by the next rake. They called to Tom Bruce to stop and pick them up. Tom checked No. 19, the rake shook itself out, Jimmy Robertson was thrown off and run over.

I have never found the people of Ayrshire given to superstitious beliefs to any great extent. There were, however, some head-shakings over No. 19 after that event. However, the work had to go on, and No. 19 has certainly done her share of it. In later years, when those tragedies had been dimmed by time, two other adventures befell this engine, both of which, I am pleased to say, were of a happier nature.

The old shed at Waterside was chronically overcrowded. Two or more engines could find no resting-place and had to be left on the line which by-passed the shed and led ultimately to the Slag Hill. Access to the Slag Hill was over the Slag Brig. I can remember the old wooden structure, high above the road. Some years before the First World War it was replaced by a metal bridge.

After the closing-down of the furnaces, of course, no further slag was taken to the Hill, but a little way beyond the Brig a crusher was set up, and a considerable amount of slag was crushed and loaded into wagons for dispatch to various customers. The metal bridge was of light section and the Barclay 16-in and heavier engines were prohibited from crossing it.

On this particular night No. 19 was crowded out, and was sitting on the by-pass line. Her regulator was in its usual state, leaking steam gently. They kindled her up in the morning and no one bothered about her till No. 19 suddenly gave a cough and started away on her own!

She had quite a bit of ground to cover, right along in front of the engineer shop and round the sharp curve to the Slag Hill. Several people saw her moving, but probably paid little attention. Those around the shed who saw her were too far away to catch her.

John Bryden and George Dunn were on an engine taking water from the tank down beside the main line. They looked up and saw an engine crossing the Slag Brig, and a Barclay 16-in at that! Up they went, scrambling up the cutting-side, raced over the Brig, and there was No. 19, in among the wagons at the crusher. They boarded her and shut off steam.

So far so good. But she had to be got back over the Brig. It had stood up to one journey of this heavy engine. Would it bear a second? They were taking no chances. One remained on the far side of the Brig. He started her and then jumped off. The other stood on the near side and caught her as she came over.

Her other was a mild adventure—a journey to 'foreign parts'. The great new colliery at Killoch had gone into production and diesel shunting engines had been provided for work in the colliery sidings. A number of failures of those diesels had left them very short of power, so No. 19 was dispatched to fill the gap. Killoch was now connected with the outside world by a railway line from Drongan station, so No. 19 was taken all the way under her own steam. Driver Willie Bryden and a fitter went from Waterside, with a driver and fireman of British Railways, Ayr motive power depot, to show them how! Her stay at Killoch was not of long duration, and she was soon back at Waterside to continue the good work. Her crew in 1965 were Tom Ferguson driver (no relation of John), Gerry Mooney fireman and Willie Woods guard.

No. 20

0—4—0, with saddle tank, rounded to the contour of the boiler, and extending over smokebox and boiler barrel.

Built R. & W. Hawthorn, Leslie & Co., Ltd, Newcastle-upon-Tyne, 1918. Makers' number: 3351.

Only known dimensions: cylinders (outside) 14 in by 22 in
wheels: 3 ft 6 in
wheelbase: 6 ft
working pressure: 140 lb p.s.i.

Dome in centre of boiler, with small brass cover above saddle tank. Ramsbottom safety valves over firebox. Steel firebox. Steam brake. Cab over footplate with rear supporting standards, but back of cab open above waist line.

Subsequent reconstruction: Back of cab closed in, c. 1920. Steel firebox replaced by copper one, 1925.

This was the only engine supplied to the DICo by this firm. Why they got the order I do not know. Possibly governmental direction; possibly only the difficulty of supply in war-time.

No. 20, like No. 19, came in that final October of the First War. I remember walking down to Waterside on the dark night of 22 October 1918 and finding her in the shed, brand new. Hughie Hendrie showed me proudly over their new possession, though I had to make my inspection mainly by *feel.* I was surprised at the circular section of the regulator handle.

The most urgent requirement was a replacement for the veteran No. 10 on the Coylton Road. No. 20, being the lighter of the two new arrivals, got the job. It was very odd that the old Hawthorns of Leith should have been replaced, after forty-four years' service, by another Hawthorn, but of Newcastle.

No. 20 was fitted at Waterside with the connection to the pulsometer at Martnaham Loch. This, however, was fitted on the left-hand side, and she was therefore able to work in the orthodox 'funnel to the north' manner.

On Armistice Day, 11 November 1918, I cycled from Dalmellington to Ayr. My saddle was set too low, so I stopped at Patna signalbox to see if I could borrow a spanner from Willie Clark. When I was there No. 20 came up from Coylton and stopped for a time while the crew discussed the end of the war with the signalman. Her rather absurd little dome cover glinted merrily in the bright sunshine of that infinitely hopeful day.

Jimmy Geddes would be driver that day, Tom Bruce fireman, and John Weir guard. Poor Jimmy Geddes had not long to go on his new engine. He continued at work under conditions of physical infirmity which make me marvel at his courage. When he died about 1921 his place was taken by Adam Ferguson—'The Squirrel'.

There was by that time only one round trip in the day between Waterside and Coylton, and on return to Waterside in the early afternoon the Coylton engine had to do some further work. In her turn she had to bring down a rake from Burnton Washer, and on 5 February 1925 I travelled on her footplate on that job. The Squirrel was in charge, with Davie Ferguson fireman and Francie News guard. With a great deal of slipping we drew ten loaded wagons out of the Washer and weighed them. Then they gave her a fire—rather higgledy-piggledy—turned on the blower and got her up to 140 lb. In a heavy shower we tackled the Laight Brae. She was drawn up one notch and the regulator laid full open. The injector remained off until we reached the summit, at which point we had only 100 lb of steam. Fireman and guard dropped off and pinned down so many brakes that we had to steam down the 1 in 37! Then at the foot we had a lengthy stop to lift them, followed by the usual run at the bank. It was queer to think of those old boys doing all this without stopping. Of course you can't climb over modern wagons and set handbrakes like you did in the old days.

No. 20 was on the Coylton until the branch closed in 1935. She was not on this job so exclusively as No. 10 had been. I used to see No. 15 on it frequently, for what reason I do not know. Whatever engine was on that job got sore abuse. The permanent way in its latter days was beyond description. My uncle was down at a derailment one day. He saw an aged and rather frail surfaceman coming towards him. The surfaceman was carrying one sleeper under one arm and *two* under the other! They were only 'squarings' of pit props.

After the Coylton closed No. 20 was just one of the group working at Waterside. She took her turn of jobs to Pennyvenie, to Burnton Washer, and to the Houldsworth. She was never a very popular engine, being cursed with bad injectors.

About 1952, or earlier, she was transferred by the NCB to Mauchline Collieries.

No. 21 (I)

0—4—0, with saddle tank, vertical sides, slightly rounded top, extending over smokebox and boiler barrel.

Built Grant, Ritchie & Co., Ltd, Kilmarnock, 1920. Makers' number: stated to be 435.

Only known dimensions: cylinders (outside) $12\frac{1}{2}$ in by 20 in
wheels: 3 ft 8 in
working pressure: 140 lb p.s.i.
weight in working order: 28 tons

Dome in centre of boiler. Ramsbottom safety valves over firebox. Boiler mountings cut down in order to pass through Quarry Brig. Steam brake. No cab.

The preference for the Kilmarnock firm of Grant, Ritchie over Barclay is probably explained by the pressure of post-war work at the latter yard. Grant, Ritchie made a very neat job of this engine, despite the restricting dimensions. These explain the absence of a cab. No. 21 (I) was evidently intended to replace old No. 3.

As usual, my uncle Davie Larmer ran her in. After a few days they wanted to go to Dalmellington to turn. They then found that since the war the G & SW had gone all red tape. Forms had to be filled up, permission awaited, and an Ayr driver and fireman sent up to take this little engine those three open, level miles to Dalmellington and back. Willie Walker and his mate, looking rather foolish, presented themselves. 'I'm not layin' a hand on her,' says Walker. 'Drive her yoursel'. Lot o' stuff and nonsense.' Some days later Wallace Boyns, Chief Engineer, came down with a note that No. 21 (I) was to go to Coylton on some errand or other. 'My goodness,' says my uncle 'if we had to get a man from Ayr to take her to Dalmellington, we'll need a man from Carlisle at least to take her to Coylton!' However, they went down to the station and asked Jimmy Allan the signalman for a tablet. He gave them one and away they went. What Kilmarnock didn't know did them no harm.

As a matter of fact, No. 21 (I) started off with a quite long spell on the Coylton Road. She then replaced No. 3 on the Slag job. Of course, she had only a month or two on that when the furnaces closed down.

After that No. 21 (I) faded into obscurity. She probably did odd spells for engines which were in the shops, but usually I would see her sitting dumbly in the short left-hand road in the shed. Willie Bryden tells of a day or two on her after he had started in 1929. Jock Kaur was driving, Jimmy Black firing, and Willie running for them. On Willie's first trip through the Quarry Brig, Geordie McCulloch, Traffic Manager, was on the footplate and he told Willie he'd have to keep his head down going through. Willie obeyed, but in the middle of the tunnel he got a great bang on the head. But it wasn't the arch, only Geordie McCulloch's hard first.

But she was a poor little ghost of an engine. Few people at Waterside can now remember her.

It was about 1932 that she was sold to a firm of chemical manufacturers in Leith, J. & J. A. Cunningham—the only Waterside engine to be sold intact to any outside firm.

I never saw her after she left Waterside. Cunningham's works were taken over by Scottish Agricultural Industries, Ltd, together with this engine. Friends of mine saw her, latterly in very poor shape, on the premises of SAI. One, a very reliable observer, copied for me the makers' number, 435. He was as puzzled as I was. My uncle had not, unfortunately, a note of the number she carried at Waterside, but I myself remember the year 1920 on the plate. A 1920 production of this firm should have been numbered in the 700s at least. There was no question of her being an old engine rebuilt. She was new throughout in 1920. I regret that I can offer no explanation. SAI sold her for scrap in 1942.

No. 22

0—6—0, with side tanks and back bunker.

Built Andrew Barclay, Sons & Co., Ltd , Kilmarnock, 1923.
Makers' number: 1785.

Dimensions: cylinders (outside) 18 in by 24 in
wheels: 3 ft 9 in
wheelbase: 6 ft + 5 ft 6 in
heating surface: sq. ft: tubes 850, firebox 90, total 940
grate area: $18\frac{3}{4}$ sq. ft
working pressure: 160 lb p.s.i.
water capacity of tanks: 1,185 gallons
coal capacity of bunker: 35 cwt
length over buffers: 29 ft $8\frac{3}{4}$ in
weight in working order: 47 tons

Dome on centre of boiler. Ramsbottom safety valves on back ring. Flangeless tyres on driving wheels. Steam brake. Large circular spring buffers. Overall cab with rectangular windows back and front.

When the first DICo six-coupled engine had been put into traffic in 1913 we had no doubt that she would be followed by another. We had to wait ten years before this happened. In the interval there had been a world war.

My uncle, much as he liked No. 17, thought engines of this size rather unprofitable for the DICo. They could not take the big loads over the Laight Brae unaided. If they had to be assisted, then two 16-in engines could do the job as well and be available for a much greater variety of work. However, another six-coupler was ordered.

The DICo requested particularly that there be provided a greater capacity for carrying water than that of No. 17. Barclays complied with this, giving an increase of thirty-one per cent. The boiler appeared to be of similar dimensions to No. 17's, but there had been a modification of heating surface and grate area. Flangeless tyres were fitted to the driving wheels from the beginning.

In general there was a harshness of outline—the shape of the cab openings caught the eye—a harshness which had been absent from the nicely curving lines of No. 17. Engineers who had the repairing of both engines found a vast difference between the smooth finish of No. 17's motion and the jagged edges of the post-war product.

No. 22 was brought up to Waterside in the afternoon goods on 20 March 1923. Bob Wallace accompanied her. They took her on to Dalmellington and had her turned there and then. She returned with the goods to Waterside and was duly run in.

No. 22, of course, went to the Pennyvenie Road, working in conjunction with No. 17. Jock Kaur, lately on No. 16, got No. 22. A cheery soul Jock, but as a driver he had none of the finer touches. My uncle probably put it stronger than that. He had to repair her.

I had been neglecting the DICo sorely when on 15 September 1938 I spent an afternoon on the footplate of No. 22. The kindly welcome that I received from her crew made me almost ashamed. Old Jock was at the regulator, Billy McGill was fireman, and Willie Bryden guard. We left Cutler Sidings pushing behind us thirty-two empties and two of pitwood. With regulator just over half open and full back gear, No. 22 went up the 1 in 66 at about nine to ten miles per hour. Not very impressive maybe, but the friction of buffers and flanges on those sharp curves must be terrible. After some shunting at Burnton Washer we proceeded along the level towards Pennyvenie at 19 mph, with regulator seven-eighths open and one notch up from full back gear. Again not impressive, but 3 ft 9 in wheels are not for express work. We got our rake up the 1 in 35 to the pit and that was all that mattered.

After the war Jock Kaur moved down to Doonbank, a new housing area half-way between Waterside and Patna. This was not so handy for the early morning start of No. 22. Kennedy Bryden who drove little No. 23 had a later starting hour, so an exchange of jobs was arranged—Kenny got No. 22 and Jock Kaur No. 23. He was a nice lad, Kenny. His death, at a comparatively early age, was much regretted.

No. 22 got a new firebox fitted by Barclays in 1952. She is still at work on the Pennyvenie Road. Her crew in 1965 consists of James Black driver, George Heggie fireman and John McLean guard.

Of late months a considerable change has taken place in the outward appearance of No. 22. Her funnel being in need of replacement, a new one was ordered from Barclays. But the present standard funnel for this class of engine is a bit shorter than the old. It is lower than the dome, a circumstance which always mars an engine's appearance. It is also getting the blame for a deterioration in steaming quality.

No. 23

0—4—0, with saddle tank, vertical sides, slightly rounded top, extending over smokebox and boiler barrel.

Built Grant, Ritchie & Co., Ltd, Kilmarnock, 1911. Makers' number: 531.

Only known dimensions: cylinders (outside) 14 in by 22 in
wheels: 3 ft 8 in
working pressure: 140 lb p.s.i.

Dome on back ring of boiler, with Ramsbottom safety valves on top of dome. Funnel parallel, with very narrow beading. Steam brake. Cab with back standards, but completely open at back except for a hand-rail about 4 ft above floor level.

Subsequent reconstruction: At Waterside. Back of cab closed in, with circular windows. Reversing quadrant set forward to clear right-hand door opening to footplate. Barclays supplied new tyres. Pop safety valves fitted 1963.

Bairds & Dalmellington Ltd bought no new engine for the Waterside stock, but they gave them an old one which had belonged to one of the component companies.

The Grant, Ritchie engine began life as 'Wm. Baird & Co., Ltd, Eglinton Iron Works. No. 6'. Eglinton Iron Works were adjacent to the town of Kilwinning in central Ayrshire.

Eglinton Iron Works closed down about the same time as those at Waterside—about 1920-1. Certain coal pits remained in production for some years and gave employment to the firm's engines, but they also closed down and in 1937 Eglinton

No. 6 was reported to have lain idle for six years. In 1937 her fate was being debated. Her price as scrap was £150. After their engineering staff had inspected her B & D thought she would be more value to them alive than dead, so my uncle was dispatched to Kilwinning to get her ready for transfer to Waterside. He did so, and one day in April 1937 he was picked up at Byrehill Junction by the 9.35 a.m. freight from Glasgow.

The 9.35 was the return working for a 2P 4—4—0 which had gone into Glasgow with one of the morning business expresses. Jacob Wilson of Ayr shed was on it that morning and he was in a state of great excitement. Someone at Glasgow had told him that he had won the Irish Sweepstake. So he was driving furiously for home and by the time Eglinton No. 6 reached Ayr she had collected a fair allowance of hot boxes. Poor Jacob hadn't done much better. The rumour was inaccurate—it was the Ayr engine-shed sweepstake that he had won!

However, they got No. 6 cooled down at Waterside. She was overhauled and amended as described, and, repainted as 'Bairds & Dalmellington, Ltd No. 23', she took her place in the Waterside stable and soon proved a most useful and popular unit. Kennedy Bryden had her for a long time, then, as narrated, he swopped with Jock Kaur.

About the middle 1950s No. 23 was transferred to Mauchline Collieries, and we presumed she had vanished for ever from the Waterside scene. Not so. She returned in 1963, having received a good overhaul. On 14 February 1965 I saw her in Waterside shed. She was not in steam, and though clean enough bore on her tank sides no vestige of owner or number. I feared for her, but in May of the same year I was informed that she was out again and hard at work every day.

No. 1 (II)

0—4—0, with saddle tank, vertical sides, slightly rounded top, extending over smokebox and boiler barrel.

Built Andrew Barclay, Sons & Co., Ltd, Kilmarnock, 1947.

Makers' number: 2244.

Dimensions: cylinders (outside) 16 in by 24 in
wheels: 3 ft 7 in
wheelbase: 6 ft
heating surface: sq. ft: tubes 659, firebox 69, total 728
grate area: 12.5 sq. ft
working pressure: 160 lb p.s.i.
water capacity of tank: 1,030 gallons
length over buffers: 24 ft 10 in
weight in working order: 35 tons

Dome on back ring of boiler, protruding slightly above tank. Ramsbottom safety valves on top of dome. Steam brake. Overall cab. Circular windows in front. Three windows in back plate, thus: O o O

The coming of this engine was a notable event. But in the depth of yet another winter of austerity and gloom few people knew or cared. Even my uncle Davie Larmer, when reporting her arrival, said 'Oh, she's only another Barclay sixteen-inch'. Maybe so, but we forgot that more than twenty-nine years had passed since Waterside had got their last Barclay 16-in—No. 19. Also, twenty-four years had passed since the last *new* engine had come to Waterside. It was the longest such interval in Waterside's locomotive history.

No. 1 (II) was a fortnight old when I first saw her—on 2 January 1948. My uncle had been unwell and it was deemed best that he remain indoors—the first time I had ever known him restrained by weather. My cousin Jim took us across to the shed in the gathering darkness. No. 1 (II) was sitting in the short right-hand road, and we inspected her, mainly by the help of a portable electric lamp.

As might have been expected, the design of a Barclay 16-in had been changed in some respects over the years. Most prominent was the larger saddle-tank. Its height was markedly increased, and boiler mountings had been cut down slightly from the height of those on No. 19. The side sheets of the cab were now vertical, instead of having a curved cut-out, but this form had been fitted to No. 19 after her accident.

The new engine was painted black, with neat red and yellow lining, and the sides of the tank bore the unfamiliar legend: 'Ayr & Dumfries Area'. Although Bairds & Dalmellington had employed a black livery for such engines as they had repainted, black seemed a little strange for a *new* engine, and we were a bit puzzled by her number. Was this the start of a new series, or were NCB merely employing the numbers of engines which had been withdrawn? We were also puzzled about NCB policy. Only a month before it had been decreed that Waterside had too many engines, and No. 18 (I) had been sent to the New Cumnock district. Now we had been presented with a brand new engine, and we didn't know what to do with it. However, there was no use looking a gift horse in the mouth. No. 1 (II) was a good and capable engine. She was given to Tom Bruce, who drove her for a long time. I think Jock Douglas got her then. Ted Smith was driving her in 1963. She worked in a group with the others, taking her turn of the jobs.

No. 1 (II) no doubt braved many perils in the course of her journeyings, but her greatest adventure occurred in as sheltered a spot as the original engine shed at Waterside provided. This shed, dating from before 1857, had four roads, two in the centre which accommodated two 0—4—0s apiece, and a short road on either side, with room for one engine only.

It was 23 October 1951. Shunting was in process at Pennyvenie No. 4 (The Big Mine). Unobserved, three wagons loaded with dross got away on their own. More than a mile of steep descent past Pennyvenie Nos. 2 and 3 gave them a grand start, carrying them over the level half-mile to Burnton, after which they simply hurtled down the two miles of 1 in 66 to Cutler sidings.

David Johnston, farmer in Cutler, had just gone over the level crossing in his car, and had got out to close the gate when this thunderbolt went past. Along the level at the sidings they raced, and even the sharp upgrade to the engine shed slowed them not at all.

In the left-hand of the two 'long' roads in the shed were two engines. No. 1 (II) was at the head of the road, with No. 16 next to the door. Both had the handbrakes applied. On the other long road, Willie Hutchison was engaged in cleaning No. 14. As engines went to the shed they uncoupled their tenders and left them outside. Several of these tenders were lying in the approach roads.

Willie Hutchison, cleaning No. 14, heard the roar of rushing wagons. He looked up inquiringly, just in time to see a tender fly to pieces, while a torrent of coal and debris showered into the shed. A pair of wagon wheels were found in an inspection pit. The cleaner had barely time to dodge to the other side of No. 14 when the runaways, their momentum scarcely diminished by the first collision, crashed into No. 16. Handbrake and all, No. 16 was driven forward, to cannon in turn into No. 1 (II). After that there was no more room, so No. 1 (II) went out through the end wall of the shed, finishing up a few feet from a dwelling-house.

In 1964, with the amalgamation of the areas into one termed 'Ayrshire', No. 1 (II) was apparently found to be duplicating another No. 1 in the same area, so she received the most famous of Waterside numbers, 10, that of old Coylton Nanny.

The crew of No. 10 (II) in the summer of 1965 consisted of John Smith driver, John Seton fireman, and James Mooney guard.

No. 21 (II)

0—4—0, with saddle tank, vertical sides, slightly rounded top, extending over smokebox and boiler barrel.
Built Andrew Barclay, Sons & Co., Ltd, Kilmarnock, 1949.
Makers' number: 2284.

Dimensions and description are identical with those of No. 1 (II).

There was a bit of a mystery about No. 21 (II)'s early career. A friend of mine on a visit to Barclays on 21 November 1949 saw this engine. She was duly painted and numbered '21, Ayr & Dumfries Area'. He was informed that she was destined for 'Dunaskin' (the postal address of Waterside) and would be delivered shortly. In actual fact, No. 21 (II) did not reach Waterside until the summer of 1951. It was then reported that she had been working at Mauchline and Muirkirk. I have since ascertained that she came to Mauchline Collieries 'brand new', but her stay there was very short—three weeks at most, after which she appears to have vanished into the wilds of eastern Ayrshire.

As has been noted, there was little to distinguish No. 21 (II) from her companion of two years before, No. 1 (II). The only prominent item of difference was the length of the funnel. On No. 21 (II) this had been cut down still further to a very squat little affair. Nevertheless, it preserved Barclay's characteristic of neatness in outline.

There was not at first a great deal for the new engine to do. For a time she lay spare, being given to drivers whose regular engines were undergoing overhaul. She thus took her turn of the jobs, and proved as useful as the rest of the 16-in. Then after a time Harry Graham, son of Harry Graham who had fired to Yorston on The Hill, got her. Harry drove No. 21 (II) for some years. Then Tom Ferguson succeeded him. No. 21 (II) is still at work, her crew in 1965 being Jackie Heggie, Tom Hose, and James Dunn.

No. 8 (II)

0—6—0, with side tanks and back bunker.
Built Andrew Barclay, Sons & Co., Ltd, Kilmarnock, 1953.
Makers' number: 2335.
Dimensions: cylinders (outside) 18 in by 24 in
wheels: 3 ft 10 in
wheelbase: 6 ft + 5 ft 6 in
heating surface: sq. ft: tubes 808, firebox 98, total 906
grate area: $18\frac{3}{4}$ sq. ft
working pressure: 180 lb p.s.i.

water capacity of tanks: 1,185 gallons
length over buffers: 30 ft 6 in
weight in working order: 50 tons 10 cwt

Dome in centre of boiler. Pop safety valves on back ring of boiler. Flangeless tyres on driving wheels. Steam brake. Circular spring buffers. Tops of tanks sloped forward for some distance. Overall cab with rectangular windows back and front.

The plans of the NCB for an extensive exploitation of the coal reserves in the Pennyvenie area led naturally to the provision of adequate power to cope with the traffic which would ensue. It is therefore not surprising that it was decided to add to the stock of six-coupled engines at Waterside.

No. 8 was, I presume, a standard Barclay 18-in. Her kinship to No. 22 was unmistakable, but once more a long period—no less than thirty years—had elapsed since the last six-coupler had been delivered, and the design had suffered some changes. The flat-topped dome and the pop safety valves caught the eye. So did the sloping tops of the tanks. This, no doubt, helped the driver's view of wagons ahead of him, but to a Waterside driver, usually alone upon the footplate and trying to hang out of both doors at once, the addition of a periscope and radar would not have been amiss! These changes admitted, it must be acknowledged that the new arrival was a very neat and purpose-like machine.

Dimensionally, the most remarkable feature was the working pressure. No other engine at Waterside had carried a pressure of 180 lb. This, however, reckoned little. It is now the custom at Waterside to work all engines with cylinders 16-in or larger at a uniform 160 lb p.s.i., with 14-in engines at 140. No. 23 is the only engine in the latter category. The figure for weight in working order given for No. 8 (II) is somewhat difficult to understand. Despite the sloped-down tank tops, water capacity is recorded as identical with that of No. 22, yet No. 8 (II) is shown to be no less than three-and-a-half tons heavier than the former engine.

No. 8 (II) arrived, true to the Barclay tradition, with funnel to the south. Her custodian, queried, said that they could get her turned at Dalmellington. To him the news was broken gently that in the process of running down the equipment of the branch, Dalmellington table had been removed some years before! So No. 8 (II) had to return to Ayr by the train which brought her up and there to be faced in the direction most fitted to Waterside's peculiar needs.

After she had been run in she was given to Willie Clark. He did one run on her—up with The Cairriages to Pennyvenie and back with a rake of coal. On return he was informed that Geordie McCulloch, Traffic Foreman, had taken seriously ill. Willie Clark had to take his job. Willie Bryden, spare driver, took over No. 8 (II) and a long period was to elapse before Willie Clark was back on her footplate.

He had not been missing much. For No. 8 (II) was proving herself to be one of those unfortunates that simply can't steam. I have heard no explanation of this circumstance, but so she remained until her sensational appearance early in 1965 equipped with the Giesl ejector.

This fitment has certainly cured any tendency to bad steaming. The trouble is that the blast, even at its adjustment to minimum velocity, is still too strong. Various coals, including some of low grade, are being used for test, and where the coal is small a large proportion of it appears to be transferred unburned from firebox to smokebox. The fitting of the ejector is apparently experimental, but I am afraid that conditions of operating at Waterside will not yield much useful data.

No. 8 was this engine's number in the West Ayr Area list. When in 1964 there was an amalgamation to produce an Ayrshire Area some other No. 8 in the area evidently had the preference, so Waterside's No. 8 (II) was altered to be Ayrshire Area No. 24. Her crew in 1965 were Tom Bruce Jun. driver, James Ferguson fireman, and Hugh Hainey guard.

No. 18 (II)

0—6—0, with side tanks and rear bunker.

Built Andrew Barclay, Sons & Co., Ltd, Kilmarnock, 1930.
Makers' number: 1985.
Dimensions: cylinders (inside) 18 in by 26 in
wheels: 4 ft 3 in
wheelbase: 6 ft 9 in + 7 ft 3 in
heating surface: sq. ft: tubes 953, firebox 110, total 1,063
grate area: 23 sq. ft
working pressure: 160 lb p.s.i.
water capacity of tanks: 1,000 gallons
length over buffers: 30 ft 6 in
weight in working order: 50 tons 10 cwt
Dome in centre of boiler. Ramsbottom safety valves on back ring of boiler. Steam brake. Flangeless tyres on driving wheels. Overall cab with rectangular windows back and front. Spring buffers.

She came unheralded at ten o'clock of a dark January night in the year 1955. The journey from Coltness had been made under her own steam, and I gather it had been a rough trip.

No one at Waterside knew anything about her. They noted the inside cylinders, and were not amused. Poor No. 18 (II). She was no beauty—an awkward, sprawling, gawky-looking engine—with inside cylinders.

Gradually her history was pieced together. I can go further back than most, for my friend Jim Aird, in 1930 an apprentice at Barclays, told me of his contortions to get inside her tanks for the attaching of her makers' plates. She went new to Coltness, and became Coltness Iron Company, Ltd, No. 3. What she did at Coltness I do not know. No doubt the locomotive workings there were disrupted by the running down of the various activities of the company. On one occasion NCB Waterside had to have the use of a British Railways steam crane, as their own had capsized. The driver who accompanied the crane strolled over to the engine shed and saw therein No. 18 (II). 'Oh,' he said 'have you got *that* engine here? She lay at Coltness for years and years and did nothing.'

When you got over her somewhat awkward appearance there was quite a lot to marvel about on the new acquisition. Her wheelbase was longer than that of any previous engine which had come to Waterside. No Waterside engine had had a cylinder stroke of 26 in. No Waterside engine had had a heating surface of more than 1,000 sq. ft. Her grate area exceeded the previous largest by twenty-eight per cent. The firebox was said to be 7 ft long. Altogether quite an engine. But Waterside men were mistrustful. It was said that NCB had got a bargain. That remained to be seen.

I think Jimmy Rowan was the first to get her. They probably tried her on the Pennyvenie but preferred their own previous 0—6—0s. She graduated to the Houldsworth Road, and on it she did by far the greater part of her work.

She was not long in commission before it was discovered that the term 'awkward' might not be confined to her appearance. First and foremost, of course, was the oiling of inside motion. Waterside men were not used to that, and a recess in her side tanks did little to assist this operation. It is possible that Coltness men had not liked this either, for her crank pins were rather sorely worn. New big-end brasses were no help, for they would not fit the worn pins. The price of a new cranked axle proved prohibitive. Very tantalizing was a story from Coltness that a spare cranked axle for No. 18 (II) had been thrown out in a load of scrap.

No. 18 (II) had more than that wrong with her. Her motion was in a bad way all round. Cotters she shed in profusion; smaller fittings were dropped all over the place. You could hardly pass a surfaceman on the Houldsworth Road but he was holding up some object designated as 'A bit that has fell aff yer injin'!' Oh she was a handful. Men shook their heads over her. A grower of dahlias christened her 'The Coltness Gem'. She still retains the nickname to-day.

Jimmy Rowan didn't have her very long. Willie Bryden got her on his first regular driving turn. He had her for a long time. I gather that he got quite fond of this recalcitrant locomotive and coaxed the best out of her. He was all the time on the Houldsworth Road, his usual crew being Joe Innes fireman, and Gerry Mooney guard.

You were close to nature on the Houldsworth Road. The Downieston bull didn't get out of the way in time one day and they cut his tail clean off without inflicting any other injury. Houldsworth colliery was completely unfenced, and the sheep wandered unchecked among the wagons and the pithead gear. They slept in any building which had not a securely fastened door; they slept under wagons; if the fire had been cleaned there was competition for a bed among the ashes.

Lambs were a pest. The revolving wheels of a wagon seemed to fascinate them and they would race along beside a rake in dire peril of their lives. Shunting operations were frequently suspended while fireman and guard carried struggling lambs to a place of safety.

I had thought that the long wheelbase of No. 18 (II) would give trouble when working in sharply-curved or ill-laid yards, but this did not prove to be the case. Her two notable derailments were on relatively good pieces of line, and no defect of track or engine could be discovered to account for the mishap.

Willie Bryden had a derailment on his way to Houldsworth just north of the old road to The Hill. No. 18 (II) came to rest on an even keel and no great harm was done. The other derailment occurred on 6 March 1964, after Willie had left her. Ted Smith had her then. He was hauling a few wagons out of one of the Cutler sidings when No. 18 (II) left the road, wandered to the edge of a low embankment, and slid a little way down at an alarming angle. This was a job for a main-line crane.

This Cutler derailment seems to have been the last straw. Ted Smith got a bad fright, and the affair probably didn't lose anything in the telling. No. 18 (II) was hauled into the engine shed for examination. She got a clean bill of health, but she could not get a driver. Not a man at Waterside would take her after that. I do not think she has worked since. There (October 1965) she lies, in the top of the right-hand road, with her motion bone-dry, the dust thick upon her, and the rust on her tyres. Poor old Coltness Gem. The luck was never with her.

MODIFICATIONS REQUIRED TO ENABLE ENGINES TO PASS THROUGH QUARRY BRIG

P permitted NP not permitted

Engine No.		
1 (I)	P	No modification required
2	P	Funnel hinged to fold back
3	P	do.
4	NP	Too long
5 (I)	P	Funnel hinged to fold back
5 (II)	NP	Too big
6	P	(After removal of cab) Funnel hinged to fold sideways
7	P	No modification required
8 (I)	P	Funnel hinged to fold sideways
9	NP	Too high
10 (I)	NP	Too high and long
11	NP	Top of safety valves too high
12	P	Funnel detached and raised by block and tackle on wall above tunnel mouth
14	NP	Too big
15	NP	do.
16	NP	do.
17	NP	do.
18 (I)	P	No modification required
19	NP	Too big
20	NP	do.
21 (I)	P	No modification required
22	NP	Too big
23	NP	do.

Quarry Brig line abandoned by the time that subsequent engines arrived.

APPENDIX 1

LIST OF PITS & DRIFT MINES IN THE DOON VALLEY & VICINITY OPERATED BY THE DALMELLINGTON IRON COMPANY & ITS SUCCESSORS.

		Started	Stopped	Depth fathoms
BOWHILL				
No. 1	Ironstone	1872	1913	65
„ 2	„	1873	„	100
Mine	Coal	1936	1947	mine
POLNESSAN				
No. 1	Ironstone	1865	1879	55
„ 2	„	1866	1874	31
DOWNIESTON				
No. 1	Coal	1845	1854	
„ 2	„	1851	1854	20
„ 3	Ironstone	1854	1858	39
„ 4	„		1892	62
CARNOCHAN				
No. 1	Coal	1856	1868	49
„ 2	„	1861	1872	
DALHARCO				
No. 1	„	1854		
„ 2	„	1864	1894	92
HOULDSWORTH				
	„	1899	1965	206
JELLIESTON				
No. 1	„	1865		70
„ 2	„	1867	1902	110

			Started	Stopped	Depth fathoms
BURNFOOT					
	No. 1	Ironstone	1849	1852	12
	,, 2	,,	1849	1852	12
	,, 3	,,	1849	1855	16—20
	,, 4	,,	1850	1855	
	,, 5	,,	1850	1852	12
	,, 6	,,	1852	1855	28
	,, 7	.	1852	1855	29—33
	,, 8	,,	1852	1855	12
	,, 9	,,			59
	,, 10	,,	1852	1855	12
	,, 11	,,	1866	1893	96
DRUMGRANGE					
	No. 1	,,			
	,, 2	,,			46
	,, 3	,,	1857	1860	42
	,, 4	,,		1860	20
	,, 5	,,			28
		(Not worked. Two mines 70 ft from shaft)			
	,, 6	,,	1866	1873	30
	,, 7	,,	1866	1873	17
	,, 8	,,	1871	1883	40
	,, 9	,,	1878	1898	66
	,, 10	Coal	1894	1904	65
DUNASKIN					
	No. 1	Ironstone			
	,, 2	Fireclay	1866	1920	9
CORBIE CRAIGS					
	No. 1	Ironstone	1850	1860	40
	,, 2	,,	1859	1878	54
	,, 3	,,	1862	1877	30
	,, 4	,,	1866	1901	87
	,, 5	,,	1870	1883	50
	,, 6	,,	1876	1890	61
	,, 7	,,	1893	1901	68

		Started	Stopped	Depth fathoms
No. 8	Ironstone	1907	1919	124
LAIGHT	,,	c.1884	c.1901	mine
CRAIGMARK				
No. 1	Coal	1866	1883	39
,, 2 (I)	,,	1879	c.1901	9
,, 2 (II)	,,	1913	1920	mine
,, 3	,,	1913	1927	,,
,, 4	,,	1916	1923	,,
MINNIVEY				
No. 1	Coal & Ironst.	1848	1863	
,, 2	Coal	1852	1862	
,, 3	,,	1852	1862	
,, 4	,,	1956	——	mine
,, 5	,,	1956	——	,,
BOGTON	,,	1929	1947	,,
SILLYHOLE				
No. 1	,,	1845	1862	
,, 2	,,			
,, 3	,,			
,, 4	,,	1852	1862	52
,, 5	,,	1852	1862	49
,, 6	Coal & Ironst.	1855	1862	97
CHALMERSTON				
No. 1	Coal			
,, 2	,,		1883	22
,, 3	,,	1865	1883	12
,, 4	,,	1924	1959	mine
,, 5	,,	1924	1959	,,
,, 6	,,	1925	1935	pit
PENNYVENIE				
No. 1	,,	1868	1908	
,, 2	,,	1881	——	88
,, 3	,,	1881	c.1960	39
,, 4	,,	1908	1961	mine
,, 5	,,	1910	1955	,,

		Started	Stopped	Depth fathoms
No. 6	Coal	1926	1937	mine
„ 7	„	1946	——	pit
CLAWFIN				
No. 1	„	1905	1928	mine
„ 2	„	1922	1937	„
BENBAIN				
No. 1	„	1896	1901	„
„ 2	„	1900	1924	„
„ 3	„	1902	1924	„
„ 4	„	1930	1945	„
„ 5	„	1936	——	„
	(Renamed Beoch No. 4, 1938)			
BEOCH				
No. 1	„	1850	1891	„
	(Reopened as No. 2, 1924)			
„ 2A	„	1890	1912	„
„ 2	„	1924	1950	„
	(Still in use for pumping and ventilation)			
„ 3	„	1910	1937	„
„ 4A	„	1924	1925	„
„ 4	„	1936	——	„
	(Ex Benbain No. 5)			

The underground workings of Beoch Nos. 2, 3 and 4 are inter-connected, but at present (1966), the only adits open are those of Nos. 2 and 4. Lists of mines show Nos. 3 and 4 in use. This is not correct.

APPENDIX 2

The DICo in Cumberland

The middle 1860s showed a tendency for Scottish ironmasters, hitherto content to exploit their own adjacent ironfields, to venture furth of Scotland. The causes were probably two-fold, a prudent consideration of possible exhaustion of local supplies, and the necessity to use a proportion of haematite ore. New processes in course of development were demanding a considerable admixture of haematite with the native product. The nearest source was the field of West Cumberland.

The obvious course was to purchase ore from Cumberland mining firms, but this had little attraction for these men who 'did it themselves'. The firm of Bairds were early on the scene in Cumberland. The DICo were not far behind.

Cleator Moor

DICo activities centred in the district of Cleator Moor some five miles east of Whitehaven. Negotiations were begun with the Yates Holebeck Estate, and here in 1869 the first DICo pit was sunk. This, No. 1 shaft, was situated 60 yd north of Holebeck House, and some 250 yd south-east of Frizington station, on the Whitehaven, Cleator & Egremont Railway. The station was about a mile south of the village of Frizington and a similar distance east of the town of Cleator Moor.

Rail access was given by a siding with a trailing connection about 250 yd west of the station. From this siding a spur led in the opposite direction to pit No. 2, to the south of the railway and 400 yd west of the station. A later pit, No. 4, was served by an extension of this spur.

R

Holebeck

Four of the pits circled Holebeck House. Nos. 1, 3, 5 and 6 were there. No. 3 was very close to High House. No. 5, known as the Bog Pit, had its shaft beside the Cleator-Cockermouth main road.

We know little of the working of these first pits. Their early days do not seem to have been very successful and John Hunter, General Manager, reported adversely upon them. However, the DICo appear to have had faith, and £30,000 was expended upon the purchase of the mineral rights.

A portion at least of the iron ore produced in those pits went to the furnaces at Waterside. John Smith, who was a clerk at

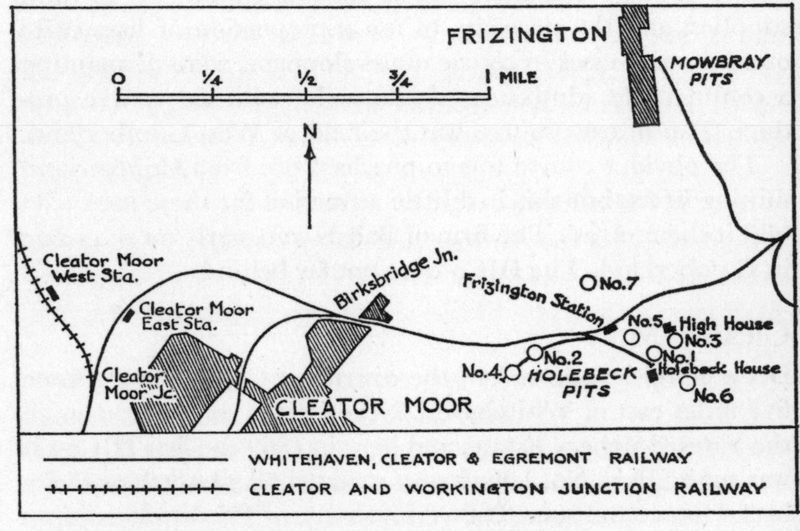

DICo pits in Cumberland

Waterside station in the seventies, recalled the arrival of iron ore in *Maryport and Carlisle Railway* wagons. This would point to a routing *via* Marron Junction and the Derwent branch of the M & C. He recalled particularly that in wintry weather the ore frequently arrived frozen solid in the wagons, causing great difficulty in unloading.

William McGill, who fired on the Dalmellington line in the

seventies, told me that the Belston Junction to Holehouse Junction line, completed about the beginning of 1873, was intended to provide a shorter route for the haulage of the DICo's 'Cleator Moor ore' to Waterside. I never heard of its being used for this purpose, however.

Holebeck pits Nos. 1 to 6 would appear to have been rather small establishments, working at no great depth, but in 1894 there was sunk Pit No. 7, on a considerably bigger scale. This shaft was some 250 yd north of Frizington station, the only DICo pit on that side of the railway. The Royalty owners were the Lowther Estates, Ltd, the Crossgill Estate, and the Holebeck Estate. As this pit opened up the older pits closed down, their dates of abandonment being given as 1897-8. By 1900 Holebeck No. 7 had a labour force of 101 men underground and 22 above. In that year the eight iron ore pits working in the parish of Arlecdon produced 140,442 tons of haematite, of which 'Holebeck's' contribution was 22,611 tons. In December Holebeck No. 7 is recorded as 'abandoned'.

The DICo Depart

The reason for this strange and sudden decision we do not know. It was the last effort of the DICo in this far-off land. Like the Arabs, they folded their tents and as silently stole away.

Other pits continued actively in the district. Apparently the local owner was not satisfied that all the goodness had been extracted from his land, for in 1902 we find 'Fletcher's High House Mining Company' operating a small pit entitled 'High House' somewhere in the area formerly worked by the DICo, and it may be significant that the manager of this High House pit was Joseph H. Woolcock, who had been manager of Holebeck No. 7.

In the course of his duties as general mining manager for the DICo my grandfather David Smith had to visit his Cumberland pits once a month. Unfortunately he left no notes of his observations there.

As the Holebeck pits were situated close to the main railway line, with only short sidings connecting therewith, there was no necessity to employ any engines to work DICo traffic, and I have no record of any so employed.

I have spoken of the apparent routing of the Holebeck ore in its transit to Waterside in the seventies. It is worth noting that in 1894 the company's address is given as 'Frizington, *via Carnforth*'. It is doubtful whether much, if any, of the Holebeck ore was then being sent to Waterside. With adequate supplies of Spanish ore available at comparatively cheap sea rates, it may have paid better to sell to iron and steel works in Cumberland or Lancashire.

Acknowledgments

This is not a treatise composed in some short period of intensive study. It is the product of sixty years of listening and learning and memorising and note-taking.

My basic knowledge was derived from my relatives. I can number at least seventeen who were in the service of the Dalmellington Iron Company. All in greater or less degree contributed to my knowledge, but one must be singled out for special mention, my uncle David Larmer.

At his trade of engineer my uncle was unsurpassed. Also, he was possessed of a marvellous memory. To his own store of facts he had added an equal store conveyed to him by his father. All this, with the utmost patience and diligence, he taught to me over the years. Without him, my history of the company would have been a colourless thing. Without him, my history of its locomotives could not have been written.

A certain amount of the history of the Dalmellington Iron Company *has* been written. In 1948 Mr J. L. Carvel produced a history of The Coltness Iron Company. As the Dalmellington Iron Company was promoted by the same family, the Houldsworths, there were lengthy references to the Dalmellington company in that book, and I acknowledge my debt to Mr Carvel for much of my information. My data upon the mining activities would have been somewhat scanty had it not been for the kindness of Mr F. Porteous, Chief Surveyor, NCB, Ayrshire Area. For my knowledge of the Cumberland workings, I am wholly indebted to Mr C. Humphreys of Whitehaven, and to the late Mr W. McGowan Gradon of Altrincham.

Another man with an excellent memory, Mr James McMillan, gave me most valuable information concerning various aspects of the work in and around the furnaces. Mr Robert Ferguson revived my memory of happenings in the engineer shop and contributed some fresh data. Four men of the locomotives, Mr John Campbell, Mr William Bryden, the late Mr Thomas Bruce and his son Tom have helped me very greatly to build up my knowledge of happenings in recent years. Mr Jack Templeton has supplied me with information concerning certain engines. Mr John Moore pursued investigations on my behalf and discussed with me numerous items concerning which we were in some doubt. Mrs Hogg, daughter of the late Mr James Frew, Chief Engineer, Dalmellington Iron Co., told me much of great interest concerning her father's good work and the events of their life in Waterside.

Messrs Andrew Barclay, Sons and Company, Limited, have been more than generous in supplying prints of, and information concerning, the engines built by them.

For the account of the loss of the company's steamer I have to acknowledge the courtesy of the staff of *The Ayr Advertiser,* who permitted me to take notes from their files. Mr A. W. H. Pearsall of the National Maritime Museum most kindly checked over my story, and helped me with further details.

The illustrative maps and drawings of engines are the product of much work on my behalf by three good friends, Miss Ruth Dundas, Mr David Newlands, and Dr E. M. Patterson. Dr Patterson's advice and help in the general planning of the book have been invaluable.

The resources of various libraries have been drawn upon for information—the branch library of Ayr County Libraries at Prestwick, the Carnegie Library, Ayr, the Mitchell Library and Stirling's Library, Glasgow. In all of these I have received much kindness and help. But I must mention especially the generous treatment accorded to me by the staffs of two of my sources of information. One is the Railway Records Office in Edinburgh, the other the Headquarters of Ayr County

Libraries in Ayr, in which I was formerly employed. To Mr Hogg and his staff in Edinburgh, and to Miss Cunningham and her staff in Ayr, I record my grateful thanks.

The illustrations: Author's collection, plates 1 (frontispiece), 2a, 2b, 2c, 4a, 4b, 5a, 6a, 6b, 8a, 8b, 18a. The late J. Henderson, Patna, plates 2d, 3a, 3d, 11 and 12. Bara, Ayr, plate 3b. The late J. Gavin, plate 3c. The late John Talman, plate 5b. The late W. Clement, plate 7a. J. N. Walker, Ayr, plate 7b. Andrew Barclay, Sons & Co., plates 9a, 9b, 10a, 10b, 14a, 18b. E. Goddard, plates 13a, 13b. The late W. Winning, plate 13c. The late Quintin Larmer, plates 14b, 15a, 15b. Derek Cross, plates 16a, 16b, 17a, 17b, 19a, 19b, 20a, 20b. J. B. Aird, plate 21a. Dr E. M. Patterson, plate 21b.

Author's Notes

'The Dalmellington Iron Company, Limited.' It is a lengthy title. It will be used many times in this book. Can it be abbreviated?

I recall the little cast-iron plates on the older wagons. They bore the letters DICO. The same letters appeared on the bricks manufactured by the company. I have adopted this contraction, but with the final 'o' in lower case, as it is not an initial letter.

The word 'locomotive' is likewise a long one. Doon Valley people generally referred to the DICo locomotives as the 'Pugs'. A 'pug' is a term frequently applied in Scotland to a tank engine. I found, however, that the enginemen were sparing in their use of this slightly derisory term. To them these were the 'Injins', and as 'engine' is a shorter word than 'locomotive', I have used it in preference.

Scottish railwaymen hardly ever refer to a route by the name of 'railway' or 'line'. It is invariably a 'road'. I have followed DICo practice in this, as in the 'Pennyvenie Road' or the 'Coylton Road'.

On the DICo system a train of wagons was always called a 'rake'. I have employed this term. Small wagons on narrow-gauge sections, referred to in other districts as 'tubs' or 'trams', are here always called 'hutches', and a narrow-gauge section was a 'hutch line'.

I have followed local practice regarding certain peculiarities of *number*. Thus the 'iron works' was always referred to in the plural, whereas the 'brickwork' was always in the singular. Then there is the strange Scottish custom of calling an inn 'The Inns'. I have used the plural form in two instances in the narrative.

Surnames of certain local people were always rendered in their Scottish form, which differed greatly from the English equivalent. Where I thought that the English spelling would produce a name unfamiliar to local readers, I have endeavoured to give the Scots version, using phonetic spelling.

Various relatives are mentioned in these pages. It might be helpful if I tabulated some names and particulars.

My paternal grandfather, DAVID SMITH (1830-1913). Began work as a shepherd and gamekeeper. Entered DICo service 1849. Studied mining. Manager pits Dalmellington area, 1857-1884; general mining manager, 1884-1901. Married MARY WIGHT.

My father, JAMES WIGHT SMITH (1871-1957). Headmaster, Waterside school, 1894-1898; headmaster, Dalmellington school, 1898-1926. Married MARGARET LARMER.

My maternal grandfather, DAVID LARMER (1835-1907). Traffic manager, DICo, 1857-1873; furnace manager, 1873-1901. Married MARGARET GAVIN.

My uncle, DAVID LARMER (1871-1949). Engineer, DICo, 1888-1948. Married AGNES MULRAE.

My uncle, WILLIAM SMITH (1868-1918). Assistant and successor to David Smith, 1892-1901; general mining manager, 1901-1918. Married MARY SMITH, daughter of David Smith aforesaid.

My mother's uncle, ALEXANDER GAVIN (1835-1920). Secretary, DICo, 1876-1906; general manager, and finally managing director, 1906-1919. Married MATILDA BULKELEY.

Index

Bold type indicates illustrations